BRIEGER

Just
Talk

Just Talk

Narratives of Psychotherapy

LILIAN R. FURST

THE UNIVERSITY PRESS OF KENTUCKY

Publication of this volume was made possible in part by a grant from the
National Endowment for the Humanities.

Scholarly publisher for the Commonwealth,
serving Bellarmine College, Berea College, Centre
College of Kentucky, Eastern Kentucky University,
The Filson Club Historical Society, Georgetown College,
Kentucky Historical Society, Kentucky State University,
Morehead State University, Murray State University,
Northern Kentucky University, Transylvania University,
University of Kentucky, University of Louisville,
and Western Kentucky University.
All rights reserved.

Editorial and Sales Offices: The University Press of Kentucky
663 South Limestone Street, Lexington, Kentucky 40508-4008

03 02 01 00 99   5 4 3 2 1

Library of Congress Cataloging-in-Publication Data

Furst, Lilian R.
    Just talk : narratives of psychotherapy / Lilian R. Furst.
        p.   cm.
    Includes bibliographical references and index.
    ISBN 0-8131-2113-2 (cloth : alk. paper)
    1. Literature, Modern—20th century—History and criticism.
    2. Psychotherapy in literature. 3. Psychological fiction—History
    and criticism. 4. Psychotherapy—Case studies. I. Title.
    PN56.P92F87   1999
    809'.93353—dc21   98-49584

This book is printed on acid-free recycled paper meeting
the requirements of the American National Standard
for Permanence of Paper for Printed Library Materials.

Manufactured in the United States of America

dass meine Krankengeschichten wie Novellen zu lesen sind

[that my case histories read like stories]

— Freud

Contents

Preface

This book originated in the discussions of the University of North Carolina's psychoanalytic theory reading group, of which I have been a member for over ten years. Although we began with and periodically returned to Freud, "psychoanalytic" was interpreted freely to include a great spectrum of approaches to psychotherapy. Our readings have been from the works of the therapists themselves as they explicated their belief systems and their methodologies, which at times entailed references to case histories. The most famous and extensive examples of this genre are Freud's cases, published in the first twenty years of this century, although some case histories had appeared in the late nineteenth century either as discrete presentations of unusual syndromes or as illustrative of a wider argument about the treatment of disorders on the borders of neurology and psychiatry as in Charcot's lectures on hysteria and Mitchell's on nervous diseases. Once my interest in the subject had been aroused, I also read various manuals of psychotherapy ranging from the reminiscently meditative *Listening with the Third Ear* by Theodor Reik, one of Freud's disciples, to the newer, briskly practical guides for budding practitioners such as Sheldon Roth's *Psychotherapy: The Art of Wooing Nature*, Anthony Storr's *Art of Psychotherapy*, and Lewis Wolberg's *Technique of Psychotherapy*.

But what of patients' perspective? How did they for their part experience psychotherapy? Early on when our reading group discussed Freud's "Fragment of an Analysis of a Case of Hysteria" (1905), popularly known as "Dora," a number of conjectures were put forward as to why she had abruptly walked out on Freud. Much information has become available, especially in the past twenty or so years, about the identity and lives of Freud's and Jung's patients, but this is very different from knowing their response to the course of psychotherapy. One of Freud's late patients, H.D. (Hilda Doolittle, 1886-1961), who underwent analysis for four months in 1933 and a further six weeks in 1934, published in 1944 her *Tribute to Freud*, based on notes taken at the time (in contravention of Freud's categorical instructions), and on almost daily letters to her part-

ner, Bryher. However, as the title implies, this report is primarily
hagiographic. Another of Freud's patients, the Wolf-Man, who was
prompted later in life to record his "Recollections of Sigmund Freud"[1]
and who was subsequently interviewed over several years by the Aus-
trian journalist Karin Obholzer, proved extraordinarily devious, contradictory, and secretive. Tilmann Moser's *Years of Apprenticeship on the Couch*
centers chiefly on his training analysis. The only sustained effort to give
access to patients' perspective is made in Rosemary Dinnage's *One to
One: Experiences of Psychotherapy* (1988) in which twenty taped monologues are transcribed. Dinnage concedes that her method was "quite
unscientific": she tracked down forty people who, she had heard, had
undergone various types of individual psychotherapy, and then selected
the twenty "most vivid and fluent" (11). But apart from a very brief introduction, an epigraph, and a three to four line description of the locale for
each person, Dinnage makes no comments on what the patients divulge.

Interesting and provocative though this collection is, it leaves open
the major questions about patients' angle on the processes of psychotherapy: What factors are important or even decisive for the formation
of a therapeutic alliance? Alternatively, what underlies failure to create
such a rapport? How does the patient's relationship to the therapist in
an idealizing or hostile transference affect the progress of the therapy?
How does the patient deal with resistances? What is meant by a successful (or an unsuccessful) outcome? And what determines it? Is it directly
dependent, as the theoreticians would have it, on the presence of a positive transference? What is the role of the patient's activity induced by
the therapist, either cooperatively or oppositionally? To what extent do
patients' perceptions of the optimal ways to conduct psychotherapy coincide with, or diverge from, those of therapists? In contrast to the manuals that seek to offer consistent guidelines for the treatment of patients,
my reading of fictions that encompass scenes of psychotherapy suggest
that in patients, especially the emotionally disturbed, many irrational,
subconscious, indeed unpredictable elements come into play in the elusive chemistry of healing.

The questions I am raising can be addressed only to twentieth-century writing because there are few, if any, accounts of psychotherapy
before. The reasons for this lacuna are not hard to find. First, mental
disorders were not generally treated by talk before Freud launched psychoanalysis; Janet's experiments with automatic writing in 1886 and automatic talk in 1891 are sporadic ventures, harbingers of patient talk,

tried but not systematically pursued. In the nineteenth century either patients were silenced or, at best, attempts were made to distract them from whatever was troubling them by means of various regimes, all of which precluded or even prohibited talking about symptoms. The historical section of this book, "From Eyes to Ears," outlines the radical change in psychiatry represented by the instatement of talk at the heart of psychotherapy.

Our normative acceptance of talk as playing an essential part in the healing of psychological ills is in fact quite recent. It has a precedent in the Catholic ritual of confession in secrecy to an unseen listener who has the power to bestow absolution for guilt through penance. But since such confession takes place within the framework of specific religious tenets, it differs fundamentally from the secular, deliberately nonjudgmental principles of twentieth-century psychotherapy. Also, because I am dealing with professionally administered psychotherapy, the long line of confessional writing is excluded. Such romantic heroes as Goethe's Werther (1774), Chateaubriand's René (1805), and Foscolo's Jacopo Ortis (1816) engage in a self-searching but also self-deceiving examination of their feelings and problems that resembles what patients might produce in therapy. While each of them finds within his circle one or two listeners who respond with corrective advice and suggestions, the situations in these narratives depart from psychotherapy in one crucial aspect: the interlocutor is a friend. This contravenes a basic axiom of psychotherapy as understood today, namely that the relationship must be to a professional trained to "be both so close and yet so distant,"[2] able simultaneously to empathize with patients' difficulties and to maintain a degree of detachment that friends cannot achieve and that is considered central to an effective therapeutic alliance.

The second reason for the absence of accounts by patients before the twentieth century stems from the shame then strongly attached to emotional (as against physical) disorders. So long as mental illness was regarded as a disgrace to be strenuously concealed, patients were understandably reluctant to write of their own experiences. The most renowned rendition of mental breakdown, Charlotte Perkins Gilman's *The Yellow Wallpaper* (1892) chronicles a descent into total disintegration, not the healing that is my primary topic.

Only in the latter half of the twentieth century has the patient's voice come to be heard alongside the therapist's. As psychotherapy has become a widespread mode of treatment, it has also increasingly found literary expression in both fictional and autobiographical form. Such records of depression as Styron's *Darkness Visible* (1990) and Manning's *Undercurrents* (1995), and of bipolar disorder as Jamison's *Unquiet Mind* (1995) and Sutherland's *Breakdown* (1976), have aroused the interest of a quite large readership. But these openly autobiographical accounts of mental disorders dwell far more extensively on the distressing symptoms of illness than on the therapies that lead to eventual recovery. Styron, for example, who writes vividly about the onset of his acute and severe depression, is dismissive of the Dr. Gold who first treats him and no more than mentions the art therapy that helped him after he was hospitalized. Sutherland, a professor of psychology, is similarly expansive on his illness and grudging about the therapies he tried. While Manning and Jamison are more positive about their therapists, they too concentrate on the devastation of sickness rather than on the process of recuperation. Likewise, Susanna Kaysen in *Girl Interrupted* (1993) describes graphically the years she spent in late adolescence in a psychiatric hospital in Boston among psychotic patients; although she receives psychotherapy, she pays scant heed to her therapists, and gives no explanation of how she managed to emerge from this phase. So these pathographies reveal little about the workings of psychotherapy.

A far more comprehensive and differentiated insight into the healing potential of talk is afforded by such narratives as Plath's *The Bell Jar*, Mortimer's *The Pumpkin Eater*, Cardinal's *Les Mots pour le dire* (*The Words to Say It*), Robertson Davies's *The Manticore*, or Greenberg's *I Never Promised You a Rose Garden*. Several of them are undoubtedly autobiographical in origin; Jeffrey Berman in *Talking Cure* has charted the precipitate of personal experience in the writings of Plath, Philip Roth, and Greenberg (among others), while Marilyn Yalom in *Maternity, Mortality, and the Literature of Madness* (49-57) has traced Cardinal's history. Similarly, Italo Svevo's interest in Freud has been well documented. Precisely because so much attention has been paid to the autobiographical strands, I want to steer the focus of my study in another direction, namely to *the literary portrayal of psychotherapy from the patient's perspective*. In our "advanced psychiatric society," to cite the title of a book by Castel, Castel, and Lovell, information about psychotherapy has become common knowledge through its diffusion in films and narratives as well as open discussion by the many individuals who are or have been "in therapy" of one kind or another. There is therefore no need (and no gain except for biographical purposes) to ferret out any substratum of authorial experience. Indeed, to insist on so doing amounts to a devaluation of the writer's imaginative powers. David Lodge did not necessarily have to go through a bad knee, aromatherapy, Chinese massage, or cognitive behavioral therapy in order to write his comic, satirical novel *Therapy*. It is the imaginative construct of the patient's projection that is paramount. So, for instance, when Cardinal repeatedly refers to her therapist as "le petit bonhomme" (the nice little fellow), the description implies not so much that he is five foot four rather than six foot two, but more that she registers him as benign and nonthreatening. If the perception of psychotherapy in these narratives is at times critical or reductive, it is because that is how the fictional protagonists occasionally experience the transactions between their therapists and themselves. The skepticism emanates from them (and/or possibly from the authors), not from me.

I take as a basic premise the quintessential and unavoidable subjectivity of any report of psychotherapy. There are no witnesses to the confidential transactions between therapist and patient, no possibility of so-called "reality checks." Nor are there any absolute truths, only the perceptions of the participants in the healing endeavor. By this I do not mean to deny the validity of more or less objective criteria for mental disorders such as the complex taxonomy in the American Psychiatric Association's *Diagnostic and Statistical Manual (DSM)*,[3] aimed to attain a diagnosis as a preliminary to the most appropriate mode of treatment. Therapists, too, in their clinical notes strive for a certain objectivity, not least through translation into technical language and by following the conventions of psychiatric case charting. Patients, however, hold their own psychic reality, which is bound to be subjective. Therefore all narratives of psychotherapy cannot be other than fictions in the wide sense of constructs filtered through the writer's consciousness and presented as the protagonist's view. Their fictional nature is heightened by the act of writing the self as an extension of talking the self. The propensity of even the actual case history to read like fiction is the theme of Freud's lament that forms the epigraph to this study. The recent migration of the case history from the medical into the literary sphere in such works as Irvin Yalom's *Love's Executioner* (1989) and Stanley Siegel and Ed Lowe's *The Patient Who Cured His Therapist* (1992) also points to its aptitude for fictionalization. What is more, those authors who are known to be clearly drawing on their own experience transform their selves into fictional alter egos, for example Plath's Esther Greenwood, Joanne Greenberg's Deborah Blau, and Roth's Alexander Portnoy. The distinction between real and fictitious patients is thereby erased; the actual patients in the final section of this study, too, cross the bisection of reality and fiction by being endowed with pseudonyms that have the effect of distancing them from the preexistent persona. In narratives of psychotherapy reality becomes fiction in the same way as the fiction had become a reality.

By what means and in what ways, then, has psychotherapy been portrayed in literary texts? Its verbal character opens it to ready conversion into narrative. Although it does occur in drama (e.g. Peter Shaffer's *Equus* [1973]), its predominant genre is narration where the patient's perspective can most directly be explored, frequently in the first-person format. Issues of both a psychological and a literary nature come into play in narratives of psychotherapy. The five operative psychological variables have been defined as patient variables, therapist variables, social and environmental variables, transference and countertransference variables, and resistance variables.[4] These translate in practice into the questions I outlined above. Equally important are the literary factors that determine the configuration of each text: what is the function of psychotherapy as a plot device? which are the preferred literary techniques: monologic, dialogic, or scenic? how are memories evoked? what is the tone adopted: serious, humorous, ironical, or satirical? what are the indicators of self-betrayal or self-deception? how does the protagonists' capacity for verbalization shape the narrative?

The answer to this last question determines the organization of this study insofar as patients turn out to fall into two main types: overtalkers and undertalkers. The overtalkers are the spontaneous, at times exuberant speakers whose voices are so domineering as to overwhelm that of the therapist. Examples of this type are the narrators in Marie Cardinal's *Les Mots pour le dire* (1975), Philip Roth's *Portnoy's Complaint* (1969), Svevo's *The Confessions of Zeno* (1923), and David Lodge's *Therapy* (1995). Among the undertalkers, reluctant or resistant to express or even to acknowledge their feelings, are Josephine in Jennifer Dawson's *The Ha-Ha* (1961), Mrs. Armitage in Penelope Mortimer's *The Pumpkin Eater* (1962), Esther Greenwood in Sylvia Plath's *The Bell Jar* (1963), and David in Robertson Davies's *The Manticore* (1972). In addition to these mainly solo voices and particularly revealing of the dynamics of psychotherapy are the duets, where therapist and patient provide separate but parallel renderings of the same therapy. Duets are most diverse in manner, ranging from the regularly alternating pattern of Irvin Yalom and Ginny

Elkin's *Every Day Gets a Little Closer* (1974), the looser choral structure of Fayek Nakhla and Grace Jackson's *Picking Up the Pieces* (1993), to Ludwig Binswanger's reading of his patient's words in "The Case of Ellen West" (1944-45), and the intertextual consonance between Dr. Frieda Fromm-Reichmann's papers in *Psychoanalysis and Psychotherapy* (1959) and Joanne Greenberg's novel *I Never Promised You a Rose Garden* (1964).

Curiously, there is no study of the literary representation of the "just talk" that is psychotherapy. Berman has commented that "literary critics have not adequately explored the role of transference and countertransference in fictional accounts of the talking cure,"[5] while the eminent historian of psychiatry, Henri Ellenberger, maintained that the role of patients in dynamic psychiatry had been all too neglected.[6] The purpose of this book is to examine how the delicate transaction between therapist and patient has been shown in literary guise and to ask what narratives of psychotherapy reveal about the healing process over and beyond what is taught in the textbooks of technical case management.

It is my pleasure to express my gratitude to the many colleagues and friends who have helped me along. First, of course, the faithfuls of the University of North Carolina's psychoanalytic theory reading group and its able convener, Susan B. Landstrom. Two of its members should be mentioned especially: Terri Lange, who read the manuscript as it was being written and whose enthusiasm and encouragement have been very important to me; and William Peck who drew my attention to *The Manticore* and to Tilmann Moser. Peter W. Graham and Esther Zago lent willing ears and gave me the benefit of their sound judgment. During summers at Stanford, the Humanities Center generously extended hospitality, and I had the privilege of sounding out my ideas with Susan Groag Bell, Joseph Frank, Edith Gelles, Irvin Yalom, and Marilyn Yalom. Warm thanks go to Thomas Nixon, reference librarian at the University of North Carolina's Davis library and to Sonia H. Moss, specialist in interlibrary borrowing at Stanford University's Cecil H. Green library for their valuable research into Ellen West. My successive research assistants, Melissa Moorehead, Kristin E. Daly, and S. Vida Grubisha have done more than be my good legs. Mark G. Perlroth, M.D., has given me books and articles as well as acting as my personal medical hotline. Last but perhaps most thanks to Stephen M. Ford, M.D., who has lent me various books and who has been such a superbly perceptive, understanding, and supportive listener to my talk.

1

Talking of Many Things

"The time has come," the Walrus said,
 "To talk of many things:
Of shoes—and ships—and sealing wax—
 Of cabbages—and kings—
And why the sea is boiling hot—
 And whether pigs have wings."
                    —Lewis Carroll, *Through the Looking-Glass*

"But what is going to happen doctor? Is it just going to be talk?"[1] According to the distinguished British psychiatrist Anthony Storr, this is the "very natural question" often put by puzzled patients at their initial interview with a therapist. Actually, the first of these questions, "what is going to happen?" is neither so naive nor so easy to answer, for exactly what does transpire in psychotherapy—and even more so, how—is a matter of debate. The second, however, "Is it just going to be talk?" meets with an affirmative reply from Storr as he explains: "You have had these problems for some time. If we are going to understand them together, it is necessary for us to go into them in a lot of detail. This is why we must meet on a number of occasions" (13). "Just talk," he adds, will in the course of the subsequent meetings, if they go well, acquire a new meaning for patients. For one thing, they will learn that their input is vital to the therapeutic endeavor. While the therapist will certainly interject questions or comments, later on offer interpretations and, most likely, reassurance, it is the patient who propels the journey that is psychotherapy. In this respect psychotherapy differs from other branches of medicine, where patients, having stated their symptoms and undergone sundry physical examinations and tests, then await from the physician diagnosis, prognosis, and prescriptions for treatment. Physicians will talk *to* patients, but they assume the dominant part in the exchange in contrast to psychotherapy that deliberately elicits patients' input and fosters their participation. Although the amount of prompting needed to get talk going will vary from patient to patient, the principle of patients as the active agents in the probing and exploration of their problems is central to psychotherapy. This was already acknowledged in the romantic period when Karl Wilhelm Ideler (1795-1860) posited that cure could be accomplished only by psychic self-activity, which the physician should stimulate and direct.[2]

This priority of the patient as the talker, with the doctor as the listener, underlies the perplexed questions of Storr's patients. They come, he muses, "expecting medicines or electricity or some other dramatic intervention" (13). Quite probably nowadays, depending on the complaint, medications will be tried alongside talk. But "dramatic intervention" is not the normative style of psychiatry, where the expectation is of gradual progress, dependent on perseverance and patience on the part of both doctor and patient. In this, too, psychiatry is distinct from medicine where spectacular high-tech procedures such as organ transplants, coronary bypasses, joint replacements, and laser surgery have come to attract much attention and to form patient expectations of a speedy cure. Psychiatry has on the whole been moving away from invasive interventions. Lobotomy, for instance, the destruction or removal of the prefrontal lobes of the cortex of the brain, introduced in 1935 by the Portuguese psychiatrist Antonio Egas Moniz as a means of controlling aggressive or violent behavior, has been abandoned because of its devastating impact on patients, who became virtual vegetables. Only in the face of extreme obsessive-compulsive disorder are partial lobotomies, specific to a certain (cinguloid) area of the brain, still occasionally performed. Psychosurgery has indeed become so suspect that in some states of the United States special boards have been set up to review all such proposed operations. Similarly, electroconvulsive therapy (ECT), introduced in 1938 and prevalent in the 1940s as a treatment for severe depression, is now used only rarely for obdurate cases that have proven unresponsive to drugs and psychotherapy. Modifications in its administration through anaesthesia and unilateral application to the nondominant side of the brain lessen the common adverse side effects of shock, fractures, and memory loss. Electronarcosis, which produces sleeplike states, and electrostimulation without convulsions are attenuated versions. This retreat from violent interventions has in part been precipitated by the rapidly growing armamentarium of psychotropic drugs since the 1950s. The widespread recourse to such drugs together with the emphasis on cost containment through the rise of managed care is reducing long-term talk as an expensive luxury in favor of shorter alternative treatments. Nevertheless, the mere prescription of drugs alone is recognized as inadequate in the long run; "just talk," that is, attention to the individual sufferer's voice in an essentially humanistic format, remains central to psychotherapy.

That some of Storr's patients do not understand what psychotherapy consists of is not surprising although the meaning of the actual term is not at all unclear: it denotes the psychological treatment of mental, emotional, or nervous disorders. *The Oxford English Dictionary* offers "action upon the mind, by hypnosis, suggestion, etc.," while Ehrenwald, in the preface to *The History of Psychotherapy,* defines it in a broad stroke as "mental healing" (5), and others align psychotherapy with "faith-cure."[3] The most precise "comprehensive working definition" is given by Wolberg at the beginning of his textbook, *The Technique of Psychotherapy:* "Psychotherapy is the treatment, by psychological means, of problems of an emotional nature in which a trained person deliberately establishes a professional relationship with the patient with the object of (1) removing, modifying, or retarding existing symptoms, (2) mediating disturbed patterns of behavior, and (3) promoting positive personality growth and development" (3). Wolberg amplifies each phrase in succession (3-5) before concluding the opening chapter, "What is Psychotherapy?" with thirty-nine further definitions (10-13). In light of the increasing scope and expanding methods of psychotherapy, he describes it as "a *body of procedures* that overlap techniques used in counseling, social casework, education, and rehabilitation" (6). The guiding principle of these procedures, underscored also in many of the alternative definitions cited, is the emphasis on verbal communication as the predominant vehicle for treatment, fundamental to most of the large spectrum of theoretical and practical approaches encompassed by the term. No fewer than twenty-six "Schools of Psychiatry" are listed in the table at the end of the *American Psychiatric Glossary* (143). While some therapists opt to adhere to a single overarching system, favoring one creed or another, others are flexibly eclectic, adapting their method to the needs of the particular patient. Whatever its specific form, the overall aim of psychotherapy is to enable patients to attain a deeper self-understanding of their behaviors, motives, personality, and relationships that will lead in turn to a better understanding of the impact of their habitual conduct on both themselves and others. The insight gained in psychotherapy is intended to act as a catalyst to change in the patient. By working through a conflict or probing a problem, one may achieve a successful resolution in lieu of the persistent, rigid repetition of destructive and self-destructive patterns. Through the medium of talk difficulties can be aired and confronted in a positive manner conducive, ideally, to modifications that will result in a less stressful life.

The complexity of psychotherapy is compounded by its distinctive position astride a number of professional disciplines. Frequently, though by no means invariably, psychotherapy is a facet of psychiatry. Yet psychiatry itself, more so than other medical fields, deals with aspects of human behavior that are not necessarily, or only marginally, pathological but that nevertheless create disruptions, disturbances, disability to varying degree. For this reason, "in its most comprehensive meaning psychiatry is a social function" that goes back to its original organization to meet "a specific social need,"[4] namely the segregation of those with florid disorders, dangerous to themselves or to others. Although psychiatry's social function has changed radically in the past century, it continues to be a preeminent facet of the discipline with the result that as a specialty it "is inevitably shaped by extramedical factors—with comparatively few defining technological boundaries" (248) compared to the purely somatic areas of medicine. As a consequence, the boundaries of psychiatry are fluid, and its work shades over into that of allied helping professions. This porosity is nowhere more apparent than in psychotherapy which is often in the hands of those with qualifications in psychology, social work, public health, education, or divinity, in addition to medically trained personnel. The words "therapy" and "therapist" can, therefore, cover a considerable range of practices and practitioners from the Board Certified M.D. to the "psychotherapist" who advertises a session, "Discovering Your Life Mission," which holds out to participants in "this experiential event" this promise: "discover your unique gifts and talents, identify elements of a fulfilling and satisfying life, and insight into your ultimate purpose in life"—all in one and a half hours![5]

Such dubious claims are by no means new to psychotherapy. The sources of dynamic psychiatry[6] are generally traced back to Franz Anton Mesmer (1734-1815), a German physician who believed in the potency of "an imponderable fluid permeating the entire universe, and infusing both matter and spirit with its vital force."[7] He believed that recovery from diseases and disturbances would follow the redistribution of this fluid within the body to achieve equilibrium. This healing process,

Mesmer maintained, could be activated with the aid of magnets to draw out the negative qualities of astral and terrestrial fluids. Mesmer presented his system of magnetism as primarily a physical realignment of bodily elements, but it also relied heavily on the exercise of interpersonal psychological influence; the mesmerist's spellbinding trance has strong links to primitive rites of exorcism. In propagating magnetism throughout Europe, Mesmer was hailed by some as a magician and reviled by others as a mere charlatan. However, his magnetism is a precursor of hypnosis which for a time in the later nineteenth century played an important role in the beginnings of psychotherapy.

The appearance of the word psychotherapy itself is a byproduct of efforts to apply it as a method of healing. The neologism "Psycho-therapeutics" was coined by the British psychiatrist Daniel Hack Tuke (1827-95), coeditor of the *Journal of Mental Science* and compiler of the *Dictionary of Psychological Medicine* (1892).[8] Tuke included a chapter on "Psychotherapeutics, Practical Application of the Influence of the Mind on the Body to Medical Practice" in his book *Illustrations of the Influence of the Mind upon the Body* (1872). In the 1880s hypnotism was revived in a medical context by a French country doctor, Ambroise-Auguste Liébeault (1823-1904), and by Hippolyte Bernheim (1840-1919) at the University of Nancy. Bernheim and his followers conceived psychotherapy as suggestion to the patient in the waking state (in contrast to the quasi-sleeping state of hypnosis). The vague notion of suggestion was superseded by the more decidedly scientific concept of psychotherapy in 1887 when the Dutch psychiatrist and poet Frederik van Eeden (1860-1932) founded a clinic in Amsterdam for hypnotic treatment together with his fellow physician, Albert Wilhelm van Renterghem. In his autobiography, *Happy Humanity* (1912), Van Eeden recounts how he had been sent to Paris by one of his professors to study the problem of nutrition in tuberculosis, but had instead become fascinated by "the wonders of hypnotism and suggestion" (33) at the clinic of the eminent neurologist Jean-Martin Charcot. He went back to Paris and also in 1891 to Nancy to learn more about what he regarded as "the true cure for humanity" (35). After observing the "*suggestive atmosphere*" produced by Liébeault among his patients, he decided to adopt his method "(called *Psychotherapy* by us for the first time)" (68). It is curious that Van Eden should insinuate his neologism in a parenthesis. But he is quite categorical in his conviction that "the cells of the body . . . are directed and assisted by what we call *psyche,* that part of the body which is not directly perceptible to the senses" (71). At the International Congress on Hypnotism in Paris in 1889 Van Eden gave a description of his "Clinic of Suggestive Psychotherapy" in which he insisted on the distinction between hypnosis and suggestion. In 1908 the magazine *Psychotherapy: A Course of Reading in Sound Psychology, Sound Medicine, and Sound Religion* was launched in the United States. When the term was used by psychiatrists at the Boston Psychopathic Hospital in the first two decades of the twentieth century, "they usually meant by it persuasive talk" ranging from "the simple 'Cheer up' or 'Forget it' kind to the more subtle sorts that worked by means of suggestion."[9] Apart from exhortations by physicians, talk, "a relatively new, untheorized form of treatment" (177), was common at this innovative institution between patients and their attendants at their own volition, although it was difficult for patients to comprehend and for psychiatrists to conceptualize how the power of talk might have a therapeutic function.

Long before the systematic exploration of the potential of psychotherapy by Bernheim, Liébeault, Van Eeden, and above all by Freud and his followers, a certain amount of informal talking and listening between patients and doctors about emotional problems was an integral part of the eighteenth- and nineteenth-century tradition of the physician as "confidential *friend.*"[10] Even after medicine became increasingly wedded to the sciences in the mid- to later nineteenth century, some doctors upheld the custom: for instance, Frederick Parkes Weber, who had a high-class practice as an internist in London in the 1890s, devoted much of his time to nervous complaints and lent a sympathetic ear for many a year to wealthy middle-aged women.[11] But such willingness to listen was regarded more as a benign gesture than as a medically legitimate treatment, for "the administration of psychotherapy was, at best, a haphazard business in Victorian and Edwardian medicine."[12] Indeed, very likely neither physician nor patient was aware that they were engaging in psychotherapy. It is important to note, too, how much greater emphasis was attached at that time to the doctor's empathetic listening than to the patient's talking. According to Paul Dubois (1848-1918), a Swiss disciple of Bernheim, the physician should listen to the patient's plaints with utmost patience, never appear hurried, and give the patient the impression of lively interest. But Dubois's notion of therapy also comprised lecturing the patient on the evils of selfishness and providing lessons on rational conduct that instill a strong moralistic tinge into the enterprise. The healing effect of what the British called "a good chat" was to emanate more from the persuasive words uttered by the family doctor than from any opportunity afforded to patients to voice their distress. The benevolent impact of exhortation by a trusted medical man took precedence over the relief attainable by the expression of feelings. At its origins psychotherapy was therefore understood "as the therapeutic use of the doctor-patient relationship allied in an intimate and informal context."[13] The sequel to such late-nineteenth- and early-twentieth-century encounters between doctor and patient and their transformation into a closer approximation of modern psychotherapy is documented in *The Doctor, the Patient and His Illness* by the Hungaro-British psychiatrist Michael Balint. In his 1957 version of the "good chat," which he calls "the long interview," patients were encouraged to air their anxieties rather than merely being the passive recipients of advice.

With the development of psychoanalysis at the turn of the century the balance between the respective roles of doctor and patient shifted, and so did the conceptualization of psychotherapy. Judgmental or moralizing pronouncements were absolutely anathema in classical Freudian analysis; the analyst, seated out of the analysand's sight at the head of the couch, was to maintain a high degree of reserve, while analysands were under the obligation to say whatever occurred to them. Through the 1920s, 1930s, and 1940s psychoanalysis was the dominant form of psychotherapy. Its central purpose is the interpretation of unconscious conflicts, and its major resource is the analysis of the relationship to the analyst, itself seen as a repetition of earlier disturbing situations.[14] Psychoanalysis was superseded by other modes of psychotherapy because of growing doubts about its therapeutic efficacy;[15] it continues to be available as one form of psychotherapy, though it has become marginal to medical practice, holding greater interest today for literary critics than for most psychiatrists. The goals of psychoanalysis and those of psychotherapy have been described as disparate: "Psychoanalysis aims at a systematic and total resolution of unconscious conflicts with structural alteration of defenses, and the character organization. Psychotherapy is less ambitious, reaching for the practical and less arduously achieved goals of resolving some conflicts, modifying others, and even retaining and strengthening certain neurotic defenses that permit individuals to contain their anxiety and to function."[16] Ironically, perhaps, precisely because the purpose of contemporary psychotherapy is here designated as "less ambitious" than that of psychoanalysis, it is more feasible and fruitful, not least on practical grounds by being within the reach of patients whose time and financial resources are limited. In place of the radically cathartic abreaction of the repressed memories and fantasies excavated in years of psychoanalysis, psychotherapy nowadays seeks above all to strengthen the ego so that the patient may function—and live— better. The focus is on the immediate difficulties more than on uncovering their genesis in past traumas.

This greater concentration on the present than on the past forms a significant distinction between psychoanalysis and current types of psychotherapy. In psychoanalysis the present enters into play mainly in the immediate analytic situation, the transference that the patient develops toward the analyst and the latter's corresponding countertransference. On the other hand, in many varieties[17] of psychotherapy currently practiced, the search for the sources of the disorder is secondary to early remediation or alleviation. Behavioral therapy, for instance, as its name implies, seeks by cognitive conditioning to effect modification of undesirable behaviors without, however, inquiring into underlying causes or etiology. It operates on the planes of the present and the future. More subtle and complicated are those modes of psychotherapy that devolve from the perception of interpersonal relationships as the fundamental arena of psychiatry. Interpersonal theory, developed in the United States by Henry Stack Sullivan (1892-1949), embodies two salient features of most current modes of psychotherapy in its orientation to the present and the future and its recognition of the importance of the "ability to relate appropriately to others rather than on the basis of some pressing, unconscious personal needs."[18]

Insofar as one of the foremost aims of psychotherapy is to nurture this capacity, it functions as "a dress rehearsal"[19] for real life relationships. In the safety of the therapeutic situation, where patients are assured of suffering no damaging rejection, they can experiment with new behaviors, and thereby strengthen their ego. For this reason the relationship between patient and therapist is "the core of the therapeutic process."[20] It is essentially "a collaborative undertaking" (4) in which the therapist must deliberately plan and foster in the patient "expectant trust" (30) as well as hope, liking, and faith. So three basic elements are identifiable as defining psychotherapy: "a healing agent," "a sufferer who seeks relief from the healer," and "a healing relationship."[21] Although the last of these three is at once the most crucial and the hardest to grasp, the primacy of the therapeutic relationship is ubiquitously emphasized. Storr, for instance, insists that it is vital "to convey to the patient, right from the start, that psychotherapy is a joint enterprise rather than a series of interviews in which the patient is given instructions or advice."[22] His use of the first-person plural pronoun, "we," in explaining the treatment to patients further underscores its cooperative nature.

As Storr's phrase "joint enterprise" suggests, the image of the shared journey offers an apposite summation of psychotherapy. In its implication of movement and progress it is more appropriate than either a "safe place"[23] or "that asylum of the close relationship known as psychotherapy."[24] Both of these are static terms that denote the locus of psychotherapy as a sheltered sanctuary where the work of therapy can be pursued rather than the dynamism inherent to it as a process of recovery and growth. In addition, "asylum" still carries negative undertones derived from the eighteenth- and nineteenth-century institution for the isolation of the mentally sick, whereas psychotherapy is directed to the very opposite: the restoration to full participation in normal life.

Awareness of the momentum of the special connection between therapist and patient has a lengthy history, though it was poorly understood. Like the beginnings of psychotherapy itself, it dates back to Mesmer: a concomitant of his magnetic technique was the discovery that "a peculiar 'rapport'"[25] was being established between magnetizer and subject. Since the results obtained by mesmerism were found to be based on the patient's imagination, the relationship too was thought to stem from the same source despite—or perhaps because of—the realization of the subject's increasing dependence on the magnetizer. Only much later, largely through Freud's insights, was the reality and the potency of the relationship openly acknowledged. Smith Ely Jelliffe, a New York psychiatrist, spoke in 1908 of the existence of a "special rapport" that "is the element in psychotherapy which cannot be taught."[26] Yet to teach the force and function of this element is precisely what Balint aimed to do in initiating a group of British family practitioners into the benefits of the "long interview" in which patients were given the opportunity—and the time—to expose their latent anxieties instead of repeatedly presenting at the office with minor, often unfounded physical complaints. Balint very well knew the value of "a good chat," derived from the persuasion that doctors could exercise by virtue of patients' trust in their professional judgment. The contention that "historically the term [psychotherapy] has meant the therapeutic manipulation of the doctor-patient relationship,"[27] while somewhat simplistic, nonetheless has a certain validity.

In this scenario, then, compatibility between patient and therapist is of utmost importance. This does not mean necessarily similarity of personality or coincidence of interests and belief systems. On the contrary, the very differences between patient and therapist may serve to promote the latter's detachment, although this in turn must be delicately balanced by imaginative empathy. The importance of the psychotherapist's attitude for successful therapy was intuitively appreciated by August Forel (1848-1931), professor of psychiatry at the University of Zurich and supervisor of the famous Bürgholzli mental hospital.[28] In psychoanalysis, too, despite the analyst's hidden position and programmatic reserve, personality has been deemed the "major tool."[29] This statement has to be taken to refer to "personality" in an impersonal sense, almost generically and symbolically, as it were, to denote the analyst as the possessor of secret knowledge and hence the wielder of secret power. More recently, in tandem with the focus on the present, greater attention has been paid to the intellectual and emotional traits essential to the good therapist's professional persona. Storr devotes an entire chapter (14) of *The Art of Psychotherapy* to "The Personality of the Psychotherapist," citing a humanistic interest in the world of the personal, the disinclination to be authoritarian, and self-control, including the potential for self-abnegation and passivity in granting the lead to the patient. Wolberg is even more specific, enumerating among "personality equipment" "sensitivity," "objectivity," "flexibility," "empathy," and the "relative absence of serious emotional problems" such as "tendencies to be domineering, pompous, and authoritarian," the "need to utilize the patient for the gratification of repressed or suppressed impulses," "inability to tolerate the expression of certain impulses," and "neurotic attitudes toward money" (441-44). However, in contrast to Storr, Wolberg regards "passivity" (443) as a negative attribute associated with "submissiveness." This disagreement about passivity, or rather about the proper degree of activity on the therapist's part, indicates the central paradox of psychotherapy, "a therapeutic Catch-22" that resides in the contradictory signal the therapist has to send: "Do what I suggest, but do it yourself!"[30] So a tricky course has to be steered between explicitly showing the way and encouraging patients to find and follow their own way. The therapist's task is less actually to help patients than to enable them in the long run to help themselves.

The maintenance of a firm relationship between patient and therapist also entails certain qualities on the patient's side, notably the capacity to enter into a sincere human connection and to sustain intelligible two-way communication. "Psychotherapy demands that at the very least one part of the personality, which we speak of as the 'adult' part, is strong enough to make a contract with the psychotherapist, based on aims and objectives, on a genuine wish to grow, and on the acknowledgement that such growth requires change which in turn may be painful."[31] In concrete terms this means that psychotherapy is more likely to be successful with patients whose disorders are mild to moderate than with the more severely disturbed who suffer delusions and hallucinations.

But classificatory demarcations as well as their terminology evolve and change; moreover, as the criteria for differential diagnosis are refined, atypical features may result in mixed syndromes. Until quite recently a basic distinction was upheld between neurosis and psychosis according to the scope of the mental disorder and the degree of its severity. "Psychosis" originated in Vienna in the 1840s, brought into currency by the physician-philosopher Ernst von Feuchtersleben (1806-49) in his *Lehrbuch der ärztlichen Seelenkunde* (1845; Principles of medical psychology), and began to appear in the English-speaking world in the 1870s and 1880s. It was used to distinguish functional nervous disorders from those of a more radical nature where there is "a primary disturbance of the libidinal relation to reality."[32] "Neurosis" and "psychosis" still feature as separate entities in the 1988 *American Psychiatric Glossary*, drawing on *Diagnostic and Statistical Manual (DSM) IIIR* (1987), where neurosis is said to signify a limited number of specific diagnostic categories, all of which are attributed to maladaptive ways of dealing with anxiety or internal conflict (69). Similarly, in the 1995 *History of Clinical Psychiatry* (ed. German E. Berrios and Roy Porter), the second part bears the title "The Functional Psychoses" while the third comprises "Neuroses and Personality Disorders." However, "neurosis" has been wholly banished from *DSM-IV* (1994) as undefinable.[33] "Psychotic" symptoms, on the other hand, are listed as "delusions, hallucinations, disorganized speech or grossly disorganized or catatonic behavior" (302), a state "in which a person's ability to think, respond emotionally and remember, communicate, interpret reality and behave appropriately is sufficiently impaired so as to interfere grossly with the capacity to meet the ordinary demands of life."[34] A distinction is made between "psychotic" and "nonpsychotic,"[35] yet it is subject to flux. Psychotic episodes may, for instance, occur briefly in major depressive, manic, or bipolar disorders as well as in full-blown schizophrenia. At what point can patients with a major depressive disorder but without delusions or hallucinations be said to have lost the ability to interpret reality because they are in the grip of their own negative view of the world? Affective disorders can shade into psychosis.

In light of this fluidity, the suitability of patients for psychotherapy has become less clear-cut than in Freud's day when neuroses were divorced from psychoses and neurotics formed the clientele for psychoanalysis. Now the choice of patients is governed by many variables. Wolberg, for example, lists no fewer than thirty-one factors as likely positive or negative prognostic signs in the patient (538-40). They comprise age, intelligence, motivation, insight, absence of severe childhood traumas or neurotic disturbances, good prior adjustment, adequate recreational pursuits, assertiveness and self-esteem, no previous emotional illness or psychotherapy, strong immediate environmental precipitating factors, social maturity, a temperate conscience, and the capability to endure reasonable anxiety and to handle reasonable stress. This profile of ideal patients is such as to make one wonder why they would need psychotherapy if they are already so well equipped emotionally.

Curiously, Wolberg does not mention the primary requisite for psychotherapy: the capacity for intelligible verbal formulation of emotions and thoughts. Perhaps he takes this for granted as obvious, but in "just talk" it is as vital as the much discussed capacity to form and sustain a relationship with the therapist. The inability to communicate is, indeed, one of the hallmarks of psychosis that tends to make it less amenable to psychotherapy. Nonetheless, attempts were made, notably by Sullivan and Frieda Fromm-Reichmann, to use talk with those suffering from schizophrenia. A good outcome is portrayed in Joanne Greenberg's *I Never Promised You a Rose Garden* (1964) as the brilliant and persistent Dr. Fried manages to draw her young patient, Deborah, out of the grip of her delusions and the esoteric language in which they are enacted. Since then, with new drugs, schizophrenia has become more controllable so that the prospects for effective psychotherapy have improved.

Another signal change in the demography of psychotherapy is the disappearance of any reference to the patient's social level, an aspect often mentioned in earlier times. In the eighteenth century, madness was seen as "a failing of the aristocracy or the poor; the middle class cannot accept it."[36] In the late nineteenth and early twentieth centuries social class played a far more prominent role in the selection of patients for psychotherapy than today as a reflection of the widespread prevalence of social stratification. The congruence of the patient's social level with that of the therapist was thought to favor negotiation between them,[37] whereas the class subordination of the master/servant hierarchy would be a drawback. Freud's patients, like those subjected to the rest cure devised by the American neurologist Silas Weir Mitchell (1829-1914), belonged almost solely to the comfortable upper middle class, able to afford the luxury of care and psychotherapy. It was also to the urban upper-middle class that psychoanalysis had the greatest appeal in the 1920s as private clinics began to advertise it as an addition to the repertoire of treatments. In Thomas Mann's *Zauberberg* (1925; *The Magic Mountain*), for example, patients have the option of psychoanalytic lectures and therapies with the black-coated Dr. Krokowski in his underground office as a supplement to the physical regime of the tuberculosis sanatorium. Private clinics catering to the affluent, such as the outpatient facility directed in Berlin by one of Freud's circle, Max Eittingon, and Schloss Tegel, a residential sanatorium in the city's outskirts run by Ernst Simmel, treated in the early 1920s a whole range of what were then called "psychoneuroses." This earlier exclusivity of psychotherapy has yielded to a confluence of factors: the replacement of psychoanalysis, so demanding of the patient's time and resources, with shorter and less intensive modes of therapy; the greater social flexibility that has overlaid the old class structure; and the spread of medical insurance to cover psychotherapy. What is more, "pluralistic tolerance of a considerable variety of assumptive systems affords a multitude of routes to mental health"[38] among which patients can choose. But this openness is currently changing as managed care circumscribes treatment options, not only by limiting the number of visits but above all by giving preference to brief, cost-effective modes of therapy. The radical abbreviation of psychotherapy as just talk is also connected to the growing use of psychotropic drugs whose rather speedy impact in a matter of weeks (provided there are no serious side effects) obviously endears them to insurance companies over the laborious months or years associated with conventional psychotherapy.

The dramatic transformation of patients suffering from a variety of emotional disturbances when they were put onto Prozac is described by the Rhode Island psychiatrist Peter Kramer in his best-selling book *Listening to Prozac* (1993). Even after their original complaint had been dispelled, these patients clamored to continue Prozac because it made them more energetic, competent, hopeful, and successful in their professional and personal lives. In the face of these "makeover"s[39] Kramer ponders the legitimacy of prescribing a potent drug not to treat illness but deliberately to implement a personality change, however positive. While his concern is with ethics, not cost, his experiences with Prozac lead him to a reconsideration of his own position and of the role of psychotherapy. The development of Kramer's thinking is paradigmatic of the revaluations and dilemmas raised by the latest generation of antidepressants, which have lesser side effects and correspondingly greater potential as a happiness panacea in a pill—which is how Kramer's patients envisage Prozac.

The issue is particularly challenging to Kramer because of his traditionalistic background and training in psychiatry, which he sketches in an earlier book, *Moments of Engagement* (1989). A history and literature concentrator at Harvard, he won a two-year graduate scholarship in modern literature to London, where he got "bogged down" (10) in trying to write a novel, and underwent classical psychoanalysis. In his "Freudian medical school" (69), he had "five years of clinical experience—all of it psychodynamic" (43). But his first residency placement was in an inpatient ward "headed by a hardened convert to neuropsychiatry" (43). In a section under the title "The Mind-Mind-Body-Problem Problem" (43-65), Kramer presents his encounter with a young patient who had been diagnosed as schizoid or borderline yet who responds well to drug treatment because he turns out to have a covert form of epilepsy. This marks the beginning of Kramer's own conversion into "a great afficionado of antidepressants" (54); so much so that he speculates whether the sorrows of Goethe's Werther, the prototype of the Romantic hero, were "electrophysiological aberrations," and the adolescent wanderings of another major literary figure of that period, Chateaubriand's René, the outcome of "endocrine and neurophysiological instability" (47). Yet he continues to feel uneasy about the "imperialism of the biological" (105), the emphasis on "the physiological underpinnings" (96), in short, the privileging of brain over mind in the rapidly evolving psychopharmacological branch of psychiatry that makes it possible—and simpler and cheaper—"to use medication to do what once only psychotherapy did" (97) as in his cure of one patient from homesickness by means of Prozac.

Kramer's writings are a clear exposition of the dualism still innate to psychiatry. As one thoughtful patient has mused, "whatever we call it—mind, character, soul—we like to think we possess something that is greater than the sum of our neurons and that 'animates' us. A lot of mind, though, is turning out to be brain. A memory is a particular pattern of cellular changes on particular spots in our heads. A mood is a compound of neurotransmitters. Too much acetylcholine, not enough serotonin, and you've got a depression."[40] With the proliferation of psychotropic drugs since the early 1950s[41] and recent advances in genetic research, psychiatry has undergone a revolution. In a curious retrograde loop that has gone unnoticed, late-twentieth-century neuropsychiatry with its chemical imbalances, its neurotransmitters and serotonin mechanisms is accomplishing what mid- and later-nineteenth-century researchers sought in vain in their pursuit of concrete brain lesions: to identify in physical, biochemical terms the sources of mental disorders. The vague diagnoses of the previous century such as hysteria or neurasthenia, superseded first by the Freudian concepts of neurosis and psychosomatic illness, are now being further revised in the wake of the growing understanding of chemical codes. The most recent theory in neuropsychiatry asserts that psychotherapy actually rearranges the structure of the patient's brain.[42]

Alongside the modulation within psychiatry, attitudes toward mental disorders have also been changing, although considerable prejudice still exists. The new biological models foster the perception of mental disorders as physically based diseases, parallel to bodily afflictions. Nonetheless, a peculiar polarity, a duality of recoil and attraction continues to characterize the stance toward psychiatry. Distaste surfaces in the refusal to give the same meaning to notions of illness in mental as in organic pathology. Foucault asserts that "our society does not wish to recognize itself in the ill individual whom it rejects or locks up; as it diagnoses the illness, it excludes the patient."[43] The locking up itself was kept secret in the upper classes as deranged family members were secluded under private care at home, as is Mrs. Rochester in Charlotte Brontë's *Jane Eyre* (1847) and the lord's son in Conan Doyle's *The Stark Munro Letters* (1895). Concealment was motivated by the notion that disgrace was intrinsic to a family record of mental illness, to which dark significations of demonic possession and hereditary degeneracy were imputed. In the lower classes, the patently insane were "branded as outsiders through their visibility,"[44] incarcerated in madhouses, and silenced. The persistent avoidance of psychiatric treatment as a stigma is a vestige of these earlier irrational beliefs and fears. So the tendency to speak generically and vaguely of "seeing a therapist" can be a verbal tactic to hide the fact that one is under psychiatric care.

Outweighing suspicion of psychiatry, however, is an increasing appetite for its services, amounting almost to dependency. Our culture has been deemed the "advanced psychiatric society,"[45] in which "millions of people each year receive psychotherapy in a multitude of forms."[46] A good half a century before the revolution wrought by the introduction of psychotropic drugs, psychiatry had undergone another momentous, though less immediately striking transformation as it began to deal at least as much with those whose problems are above all existential. The records of the Boston Psychopathic Hospital in the decade following its opening in 1912, examined by Elizabeth Lunbeck in *The Psychiatric Persuasion,* document this modification. If the weakness of her study is its limitation to a single institution, its strength lies in its specificity. By means of a meticulous inquiry into the kinds of cases treated Lunbeck shows "that the discipline that had in the nineteenth century been visible only at the margins—in the asylum—had by the second decade of the twentieth century established itself at the center of social and cultural life" (11). A number of the hospital's leading physicians, "eager to secure formal institutional and political power, . . . outlined an ambitious program that addressed a range of issues already defined as pressing— immigration, poverty, crime, delinquency, drunkenness" (20). Thus psychiatry switched "from a discipline primarily concerned with insanity to one equally concerned with normality, as focused on normal persons and their problems: sex, marriage, womanhood and manhood, work, ambition, worldly failure, habits, desires, inclinations" (3). In keeping with the change in the type of difficulties addressed, the projected outcome shifted from "cure" to "recovery" (175), more equivocal to be sure, but also implying a milder initial state and a gentler healing process. As "a discipline of the everyday" (23), psychiatry had by the 1920s moved from the margins into the center of social and cultural life. The psychiatrist, cast as "philosopher of the social life" (20), began to come into the cultural authority that the profession commands today through its perceived ability to correct maladjustments and to alleviate tensions and unhappiness. Lunbeck's argument is crucial in accounting for the spread in psychiatry's scope and prestige, but she overstates her thesis by skimming over the fact that more severe forms of mental illness also still remain within the specialty's province.

The "psychiatry of the everyday" (21) was in many respects already the core of Freudian psychoanalysis. In late-nineteenth-century Vienna Freud's principal aim was the attenuation of what he called neurotic symptoms, triggered by the stresses of life in a highly structured and sexually repressive society. The naturalization of this "psychiatry of the everyday" as a mode of professional help that does not necessarily imply a pathological state is endorsed by Storr who points to the trend away from the sick in the medical sense and toward the handling of problems in living. Psychotherapy is sought by those who are for some reason unhappy in hopes of clarification and subsequent improvement. What many patients "are seeking is self-knowledge, self-acceptance, and better ways of managing their lives. Psychotherapy, today, is more concerned with understanding persons as wholes and with changing attitudes";[47] it achieves such "imponderables" as "increased self-confidence, competence, and enjoyment" (149). Interestingly, these are the very qualities that Kramer's patients attain by taking Prozac. And they, too, are beset by everyday problems in living: depression following a reversal in business and the death of parents; obsessive-compulsive traits as an outcome of perfectionism; rejection-sensitivity; or ingrained social inhibitions. Whether the shortcut through chemical correctives is as lasting as the alteration in behavior effected by the slow process of "talking of many things" is a moot question.

In practice, of course, the choice is not either drugs or talk since the two are generally mutually supportive. Jamison, for example, puts "a strong emphasis upon the combined use of medications and psychotherapy,"[48] attributing her own recovery from bipolar disorder to "medicine for the brain and superb psychotherapy for the mind" (119). Trained in clinical psychology at a time when psychoanalytic theories were still predominant and only later introduced to a neurobiological approach at the University of California's Neuropsychiatric Institute in Los Angeles, she maintains that she has "never been able to fathom the often unnecessarily arbitrary distinctions between 'biological' psychiatry, which emphasizes medical causes and treatments of mental illness, and the 'dynamic' psychologies, which focus more on early developmental issues, personality structure, conflict and motivation, and unconscious thought" (59-60). However, the cost effectiveness of drugs for many patients has given rise to the need to justify "reason's debate with itself."[49] In his advocacy of "just talk," Storr, while admitting that it "is an act which is less simple than it appears,"[50] invokes a number of arguments in its favor: "Putting things into words has the effect of giving reality to unformulated mental contents" (25); "Putting things into words has another function. It is the means whereby we detach ourselves both from the world about us and from the inner world of our own actions and thoughts. It is by means of words that we objectify, that we are enabled to stand back from our experience and reflect upon it. Words about the self make possible a psychic distance from the self, and, without that distance, neither understanding nor control, nor willed, deliberate change is possible" (26). What in a British colloquialism was described as "getting things off one's chest" therefore allows not only an immediately cathartic release but also forms the starting point for a deeper remediation.

The gradual realization of the therapeutic value of just talk was a salient change in psychiatry as it assumed its modern form. In 1886 the French psychologist Pierre Janet (1859-1947) experimented in Le Havre with a patient named Léonie, getting her to engage in automatic writing as a way to uncover the cause and meaning of her fits of terror. Five years later in Paris he successfully tried automatic talking in the case of Madame D who was thereby able to recall unconscious memories while in a hypnotic state.[51] Such a method of self-disclosure was in absolute contravention to the accepted norms at the turn of the century. For instance, the most influential physician in the United States, William Osler (1849-1919), roundly asserted, "To talk of diseases is a sort of Arabian Nights' entertainment to which no discreet nurse will lend her talents."[52] Silas Weir Mitchell, the foremost American neurologist of the later nineteenth century, was equally outspoken in his opposition to any discussion of the patient's symptoms in the belief that they would disappear as the patient got "well" through physical measures.[53]

The reversal from silencing patients to inducing them to talk occurred with psychoanalysis, whose basic rule was that analysands had to express whatever came into their mind, no matter how absurd, immoral, or painful it might seem. In a departure from the usual view that Freud's discovery of the unconscious and the irrational parts of the mind is "the revolutionary contribution of psychoanalysis,"[54] Storr declares: "If I was asked which of Freud's many contributions to the art of psychotherapy was the most significant, I should say it was his replacement of hypnosis by free association."[55] Free associative talk as the fundamental tool of therapy distinguished psychoanalysis from earlier dynamic approaches that drew their observations from hypnotized patients, whereas Freud elicited the waking patient's active participation. Whatever the current revisionist momentum against Freud, notably the charge that his system lacks a sound scientific basis,[56] the introduction of psychoanalysis marks a momentous turning point in the treatment of emotional disturbances by advocating talk instead of silence as the pathway to remediation. The full significance of this inversion can be understood only in the context of an examination of anterior methods of dealing with mental disorders that reveal how startling a reversal the efflorescence of just talk represents in historical perspective.

In talking of many things in this chapter and particularly in considering the prehistory of psychotherapy in the following chapter, it becomes necessary at this point to address, however briefly, the problem of terminology. Behaviors that were up to the later middle of the nineteenth century subsumed under the blanket category of "madness" are specified in the newest *Diagnostic and Statistical Manual (DSM) IV* (1994) of the American Psychiatric Association under seventeen headings. "Madness" has been entirely banished from medical language; the latest occurrences cited in *The Oxford English Dictionary* date from 1879, 1884, and 1885, not by coincidence from about the time when the first edition of Emil Kraepelin's classificatory *Compendium of Psychiatry* appeared in 1883. "Madness" persists nowadays primarily as a literary concept: Foucault writes of "Madness and Civilization," while Marilyn Yalom examines "Maternity, Mortality, and the Literature of Madness." Styron subtitles his *Darkness Visible* "A Memoir of Madness" because he experiences his depression subjectively so intensely as to amount to the loss of self implicit in "madness." Jamison, too, appends the subtitle "A Memoir of Moods and Madness" to her *An Unquiet Mind,* and ponders "long and hard about the language of madness" (179) in the section "Speaking of Madness" (179-84). Paralleling "madness," "insanity" designates in criminal and civil law a mental incapacity that fundamentally modifies a person's status in regard to competence to stand trial, responsibility for one's actions, and appropriate sentencing.

As "madness" has waned, other words have gained in popularity. "Neurasthenia," described by the American "nerve doctor," George M. Beard, became highly fashionable in the 1870s as did "hysteria," studied by the French neurologist, Charcot. At the turn of the century, through Freud's writings, "neurosis" and "psychoneurosis" rose to prominence in psychiatric vocabulary. All these terms have now been discarded as excessively vague, and replaced by a more precise nosology. The changes have been gradual; neurasthenia, for instance, was still included in *DSM-II* (1968). Hysteria, after an exuberantly florid career, has been totally abandoned in *DSM-IV* in favor of such alternatives as "Histrionic Personality Disorder" (655-58), "Somatoform Disorders" (445-69), and "Factitious Disorders" (471-74). The evolution, in both conceptualization and terminology, of a large spectrum of psychiatric disorders has been meticulously documented in *A History of Clinical Psychiatry: The Origins and History of Psychiatric Disorders* (ed. German E. Berrios and Roy Porter). The continuance and rapidity of change are cogently illustrated by Appendix D of *DSM-IV* (773-79), in which the amendments since *DSM-IIIR* are listed with explanatory annotations. By a comparative analysis of the successive modifications from *DSM-I* (1952) through its revisions in 1968, 1980, 1987 to 1994, one could trace refinements in the nosology and the increasing differentiation in the perception of "mental disorders." That is the overall phrase currently in use; it is cautiously defined as "a manifestation of behavioral, psychological, and biological dysfunction in an individual" (*DSM-IV*, xxi), apparent in "distress, dyscontrol, disadvantage, disability, inflexibility, irrationality" (xxi). Despite caveats about its limitations, it is nonetheless posited as a portmanteau phrase for the areas with which psychiatry is concerned.

These denominational considerations may seem superfluous since I am not aiming to diagnose the disorders portrayed in narratives of psychotherapy. But they are necessary to avoid confusion. Although such concepts as "neurasthenia," "hysteria." and "psychoneurosis" are anachronistic, I shall continue to use them wherever they are period congruent. This guiding linguistic criterion of appositeness is intended to respect the integrity of the historical situation. If Charcot wrote about "hysteria," Freud about "psychoneurosis," and Jung about the "shadow," those are the words I shall invoke as appropriate. Similarly, although the accepted modes of treatment in certain disorders (e.g., schizophrenia) have changed radically since the introduction of new drugs, I shall discuss only the therapies portrayed in the narratives.

2

From Eyes to Ears

When more is meant than meets the eye
—Milton, *Il Pensieroso*

In October 1885 the twenty-nine-year-old Sigmund Freud embarked on a five-month visit to Paris to study under the greatest neurologist of the time, Jean-Martin Charcot (1825-93). Freud was one of many foreign students who went on such a pilgrimage to further the training he had already had in the new science of neurology at the Viennese Medical School. When he entered it in 1873, the dominant paradigm among the faculty, in keeping with the most advanced medical thinking of the period, was decidedly physicalist in its emphasis on the role of the central nervous system as the source of many disorders that would now be considered as emotional. Freud himself was at pains to insist that he had been properly "brought up" ("erzogen"), like other neuropathologists, in local diagnosis and electro prognosis.[1] In going to Paris he had every intention of engaging in brain research.

Charcot, ever since he had begun to concentrate on neurological studies in 1850, had insisted on the necessity of combining pathology with clinical research. His productivity was prodigious, especially in the decade between 1870 and 1880 when his focus was on cerebral localization,[2] that is, on determining exactly which parts of the brain or the nervous system were at the root of particular symptoms. In this pursuit of identifiable lesions Charcot was extending into neurology the approach that had led to so many fundamental discoveries in nineteenth-century medicine as specific disturbances in the function of discrete organs were found to correlate to recognizable syndromes. This understanding of disease specificity replaced the old belief that sickness resulted from an overall imbalance in the four "humors" (blood, phlegm, yellow bile, and black bile) of which the body was constituted. Using modern methods of research, Charcot made a salient contribution to neurology by isolating a new clinico-anatomical entity among the progressive muscular atrophies: amyotrophic lateral sclerosis, now known in the United States as Lou Gehring's Disease, was initially designated Charcot's Disease in tribute to the precision of his description. Charcot had attained enormous eminence, recognition, and authority in French social as well as medical circles by the time of Freud's visit.

Over twenty years previously, in 1862, at the age of thirty-seven, Charcot became chief of the medical service at a hospital for women with the curious name, La Salpêtrière. Founded in 1656, it was called after the arsenal for the storage of gunpowder (saltpetre) that had formerly occupied the same grounds. When Charcot took over the direction, its population had risen to some five thousand, comprising largely incurables and the insane. Under his reign, "this 'pandemonium of infirmities' was transformed from a custodial hospice into the world's greatest center for clinical neurologic research."[3] Charcot himself described it as a sort of living pathology museum ("une sorte de Musée pathologique vivant"[4]). It was indeed "a kind of scientific goldmine"[5] for the study of neurological disorders. During one of the periodic reorganizations at La Salpêtrière, when the renovation of a building required the redistribution of the patients, the epileptics and hysterics were separated from the psychotics. When the new unit was assigned to Charcot, he became intrigued by the tantalizing phenomenon of hysteria, an affliction thought to befall mainly women.

Charcot's perception of hysteria was conditioned by two major factors: his roots in neurology and pathology, and his personal predilection for visualization rather than verbalization. He aimed to show that hysteria was a disease of the nervous system on a par with other neurological disorders. By careful and sustained observation he was able to differentiate epileptic seizures from hysterical crises; sometimes at the outset he used the mixed classification "hysteroepilepsy," but he dropped the term as his categories came to be more clearly defined. He divided hysteria into a set of clinical typologies: the paralyses, the anaesthesias, the contractures, the spasms, the rhythmic choreas, and so forth. He also asserted that major hysteric attacks fell into four phases, but since he had patients repeat their crises for the benefit of other physicians and medical students, mimicry and suggestion could hardly fail to play a part in shaping the sequence of the expected phases. His ultimate goal was to find the underlying lesion, for he presupposed a hidden organicity although La Salpêtrière's microscopic laboratory was unable to discern anything. Charcot looked upon hysteria as an empirical reality that at the moment eluded physiological explanation. A malfunctioning of one hemisphere of the brain only was believed to underlie hemianaesthesia and periodic unilateral hallucinations, and so to provide evidence for the encephalitic origin of some types of hysteria. While admitting that hysteria was known solely by its manifestations, Charcot stuck to his somaticist suppositions, arguing that one form was unmistakably ovarian in source: "L'ovaire étant accepté comme point de départ de l'aura hystérique"[6] (The ovary being accepted as the originary source of the hysterical aura). He was therefore convinced that attacks could be stopped short by a systematic compression of the ovarian region, for which his students devised ovarian compressor belts in 1878 and 1881.[7]

But despite his pronounced neuropsychiatric bent, Charcot did not wholly dismiss the presence of the imagination in hysteria. In commenting on the sudden cure of a contracture of a limb in three cases, he does not hesitate to introduce the word: "Chez ces femmes, la guérison était survenue tout d'un coup, au milieu de circonstances bien propres à émouvoir l'imagination"[8] (In these women, the cure happened all of a sudden under circumstances very propitious to affect the imagination). However, imagination along with the entire field of psychology is appropriated into his theories by translation into physical concepts: "en matière de maladies nerveuses, la psychologie est là, et ce que j'appelle la psychologie, c'est la physiologie rationelle de l'écorce cérébrale"[9] (in nervous diseases, psychology is present, and what I call psychology is the rational physiology of the cerebral cortex). That statement made by Charcot in 1888 explicitly summarizes the later-nineteenth-century intent to subjugate the psychological to the physiological.

In consonance with this view of hysteria, the remedies applied at La Salpêtrière were predominantly physical. Apart from compression of the abdomen in cases thought to be of the ovarian type, conventional treatment relied on various kinds of friction and massage. Chemical substances such as ether, amyl nitrate, bromides, chloroform, and morphine were tried without success. With Charcot's approval, doctors experimented with their favored methods, including electricity and metallotherapy, which consisted of the application of copper, silver, or iron bars.[10] A report on metalloscopy to the Société de Biologie in 1877 concluded that a cerebral action was undoubtedly taking place.[11] Though ineffective in itself, it was metalloscopy that led to Charcot's interest in hypnosis, which was regarded as a form of animal magnetism, whose effect was thought to stem from the transfer of forces from person to person, as from metal to human being.

Very possibly hypnosis appealed to Charcot partly because it operated through the eyes. His extraordinary visual abilities were manifest in his medical practice through his penetrating powers of observation. In his hobby of sketching and his fondness for caricature too he reveals his innate capacity to pick out essential characteristics. In collaboration with Paul Richer, also a talented artist, he edited two volumes, *Les Démoniaques dans l'art* (1887) and *Les Difformes et les malades dans l'art* (1889). These collected artistic images of epileptics, ecstatics, and hysterics in such varied media as painting, mosaics, tapestries, icons, and bas-reliefs explored the relationship between the visible structures of physical appearance and neurological disorders.

The primacy of the visual is evident throughout Charcot's approach to his patients. The emphasis is invariably on what he can *see*. He casts himself as a witness ("témoin"[12]) facing a remarkable sight to be scrupulously observed and translated into a verbal record. So he repeatedly exhorts his students, "Voyez" (62, 125, 190; See), admonishing them to pay attention to what he has put before their eyes: "J'ai placé devant vos yeux" (149; I have placed before your eyes). The phrase recurs again and again throughout his lectures: "Je dois en terminant, Messieurs, faire passer devant vos yeux" (56; I must finally, gentlemen, make appear before your eyes); "Trois nouveaux sujets vont successivement passer sous vos yeux" (175; Three new subjects will in turn pass before your eyes); "le garçon que vous avez sous les yeux" (182; the man you have before your eyes). Charcot wants to show ("montrer," 182) in a visible manner, "vous faire constater *de visu*" (189; make you establish *by sight*) because he believes the visual sense to be the major means of access to disease. Only what he has seen with his own eyes has validity.

In his clinical demonstrations, Charcot always begins by noting exactly when he first saw ("j'ai vu") the patient. By this he means not what is understood nowadays by "seeing" a doctor, which consists of a mixture of physical examination with dialogue in history taking and discussion of the findings. For Charcot "j'ai vu" denotes literally the act of eyeing the patient. He gives the most detailed and precise notations of the physical appearance, aberrations, and peculiarities of each patient, often extending over several pages, and focused firmly on the visible features. Patients' personal and family situation as well as their mental state take a poor secondary place, and are presented in a relatively cursory fashion, compared to the density of specification of the physical characteristics. The words *observer* and *voir*, reiterated staples of Charcot's vocabulary, indicate the basis of his practice in a reading of the visible signs. From incongruities of external appearance he extrapolates, half intuitively half deductively, the nature of the illness.

To a man who was all eyes, photography was bound to have a tremendous appeal. Soon after its discovery in 1839, it was eagerly adopted by psychiatry in Western Europe for it seemed to offer "the ultimate means of creating an objective reproduction of reality."[13] Underlying nineteenth-century medical photography was the conviction that the photograph supplied a reliable source for observations, a view that was transferred without question onto psychiatric photography too. Because of the fleeting nature of facial expression, it was thought particularly important to fix it for study, and this photography could do even better than the physician's gaze.[14]

In 1856 photography entered programmatically into psychiatry through a paper, "On the Application of Photography to the Physiognomic and Mental Phenomena of Insanity," presented to the British Royal Society by Hugh W. Diamond (1809–86), who has been called "the founder of psychiatric photography."[15] Diamond, a doctor who had in the 1840s grown interested in the treatment of the insane, was resident superintendent of the female department of the Surrey County Lunatic Asylum from 1848 to 1858.[16] A presentation he made in 1852 to a London audience of a series on types of insanity marks the first systematic use of photography in psychiatry. In his 1856 paper Diamond asserted that "the Photographer catches in a moment the permanent cloud, or the passing storm or sunshine of the soul, and thus enables the metaphysician to witness and trace out the connection between the visible and the invisible in one important branch of his researches into the Philosophy of the human mind."[17] The emphasis is on the photographer's capacity to "witness" and to document "the visible" as the manifestation of "the invisible" impairment.

Charcot opened a photographic laboratory at La Salpêtrière in the mid-1880s and appointed Albert Londe, a chemist, as head of the photographic service, the first such full-time appointment at any hospital in Europe. Londe's charge was to document the progress and manifestations of disease by recording its stages on the patient's visible surface in both physiognomy and posture. The focus was on the hysteric's asymmetrical, unaesthetic face, and particularly on the eyes as the most evident expression of a disease believed to stem from a lesion in the neural network that controls the eye. The camera was perceived as a vital tool for cataloguing psychopathologies in the same way as histologic cross-sections formed the basis of pathological anatomy. The *Revue photographique des hôpitaux de Paris,* which flourished in the 1870s, was supplemented by the specialized *Iconographie de La Salpêtrière* in 1877-80; in 1888 the journal resumed publication as the *Nouvelle iconographie de La Salpêtrière.*

The concrete representation of physiognomy, posture, and paralysis was used as a means for visual proof of Charcot's nosological categories. But the photograph had the effect of reducing the patient to a totally mute, essentially passive entity. In photography control lay wholly in the eyes of the scientist-recorder and the physician-reader while the patient was objectified into a picture. Among the visual terms in Charcot's lectures "tableau" is another recurrent word, sometimes qualified by "clinique," at other times alone; it reveals how the observer's scrutinizing gaze captures the patient as a motionless, inert fixity, like a butterfly pinned onto a board. Through the reproduction of the image within the medical text, the patient is commodified. In these "now justly infamous"[18] photographs, the doctor's absolute control over the patient is an unvoiced but perceptible subtext.

To be only seen is tantamount to *not* being heard; hence there are "so many pictures of Victorian madwomen, and so few of their words."[19] This virtual silencing of the patient becomes most apparent in the famous clinical demonstrations Charcot conducted on Tuesdays. The patient is nothing but teaching material to be observed, described, and analyzed with utmost precision and often at considerable length, yet without the right to utterance except in response to the physician's questions. Even those questions are limited to a minimum by Charcot, the virtuoso at the art of reading signs with his eyes and drawing inferences from the visible. The paucity of dialogue with patients is striking. Formulated in curt phrases, the questions are without exception at the physician's instigation. Most important, they are closed, that is, designed to elicit a narrow answer in regard to a specific matter so that the patient is left absolutely no latitude to elaborate further.

Charcot's handling of the case of a thirty-eight-year-old railroad worker suffering from psychic shock following an accident is typical. Three printed pages (125-28) are required for Charcot's presentation, punctuated by the customary visual terms: "vous le voyez" (you see it), "nous avons vu" (we have seen), "pour vous montrer" (in order to show you). Only at the very end does this brief exchange take place:

M. Charcot (S'adressant au malade): Comment sont faites les petites attaques que vous resentez? Est-ce que vous avez des bruissements dans les oreilles, des battements dans les tempes? Vous avez le cou serré?
Le malade: Oui.
M. Charcot: Quel traitement suivez-vous?
Le malade: Le traitement par l'électrisation.
M. Charcot: Vous êtes en congé pour suivre ce traitement?
Le malade: Pour un mois.
M. Charcot: Depuis combien de temps? Le mois est-il commencé?
Le malade: Depuis huit jours.
M. Charcot: Allez-vous mieux?
Le malade: Je commence à sortir, cela me fait du bien.
M. Charcot: Vous travaillez la nuit?
Le malade: La moitié des nuits.
M. Charcot: Retirez-vous. (128)

[*M. Charcot (Addressing the patient):* What are your little attacks like? Do you have noises in your ears, beating on your temples? Is your throat constricted?
The patient: Yes.
M. Charcot: What treatment are you having?
The patient: Treatment by electric impulse.
M. Charcot: Are you on leave so as to receive this treatment?
The patient: For a month.
M. Charcot: Since when? Has the month begun?
The patient: For the past eight days.
M. Charcot: Are you better?
The patient: I am beginning to get better, it's doing me good.
M. Charcot: Do you work nights?
The patient: Half the nights.
M. Charcot: Leave.]

Charcot's silencing of his patients was determined by other factors too. His aim was scientific rather than medical: he was trying above all to understand disease processes and to locate physical causes. The therapeutic dimension was minimal, as is illustrated in the above case in the disproportion between the space devoted to description of the patient and the scant discussion of his treatment. The social level of the patient pool would also have discouraged talk. The patients were all working class, in many instances destitute and nonfunctional, either institutionalized in a public asylum, or walk-ins off the street. Nearly all had already been given high doses of sedatives to no avail. What is more, the conventions of doctor-patient relationships, particularly with the mentally disturbed, were at that time modeled on the *relation de tutelle*, the familial power of father over child.[20] Charcot's reserve and silence within his own family is of some relevance in this context as is his aversion to oratorical pomposity and platitudes. Not himself gifted verbally, he had recourse to other, mainly visual means to make his impact at his Friday morning lectures, which were attended by writers, journalists, actors, and socialites. Apart from drawing outlines of the anatomy of the nervous system on the blackboard with chalks of different colors, he was among the first to use projection equipment, which enabled him to present schematic figures and graphic resumes. His inborn acting talent stood him in good stead as he mimicked the gait, voice, and behavior of the patients being discussed that day before they were brought in. Charcot's audience, too, was expected to be all eyes.

In these clinical demonstrations, Charcot was following the custom of exhibiting the insane that goes back to the Middle Ages.[21] Looking at the mad was a popular entertainment in the eighteenth century when the Bethlehem Hospital (Bedlam) was thrown open to visitors every Sunday afternoon for a few pence; people paraded past the cells as if they were a circus sideshow. This practice, which brought in substantial revenue, was continued until 1815. Charcot's habit of displaying his patients differed, of course, from these primitive rituals because it had a serious, scientific, and didactic purpose. However, it was imbued with a theatricality that was obvious to many spectators, and that accounts in part for its attraction as a form of amusement. Charcot's own mimicry of symptoms set the stage for the often spectacular entrance of the patients who would be attired in such a way as to make their deficits easily visible. For example, those afflicted with tremors appeared wearing headdresses decorated with long plumes, whose feathery vibrations illustrated the different types of pathology.[22] Charcot's detractors had reason to mock the sometimes crude carnival of this medical spectacle.

A far graver issue is that of the patients' complicity, conscious or unconscious, in the performances being presented. The women have been described as "veritable actresses,"[23] who were repeating behaviors they had acquired. They could have learned them through the medical students who recruited those who wrote well to copy their notes on lectures and observations. Their histrionics were also abetted by Charcot's division of hysterical attacks into four component phases; patients' behavior could, therefore, be motivated by foreknowledge of the doctor's expectations, which it then in turn mirrored. The desire to please the doctor by responding in the anticipated manner fused with the power of suggestion to reproduce the predictable patterns announced by Charcot.

The implications of this bizarre situation have been discussed in relation to Charcot, but not to his patients. Clearly, the patients' complicity fostered Charcot's theory of the structured nature of the attacks, yet at the same time threw the validity of the entire concept into question. In his 1886 monograph *De la suggéstion et de ses applications à la thérapeutique* (*Suggestive Therapy and Its Therapeutic Applications*) Bernheim demolished Charcot's edifice on the grounds that it emanated from suggestion on the physician's part as well as from expectant attention on the patients' part.[24] From their perspective, the acting could be interpreted as a vehicle for self-expression. It was in fact the only means granted to them in Charcot's clinic since his method of examining patients almost exclusively by looking at them allowed for no verbal exchange. The priority of the eyes had as its concomitant an atrophy of speech. The inmates of La Salpêtrière at the end of the nineteenth century were still being as effectively silenced as their predecessors in the Bedlams of the seventeenth and eighteenth centuries. Despite earnest searches for a better understanding of the afflictions of those suffering from mental disorders, in this one salient respect, nothing had changed. They were still consistently denied a voice of their own, and radically disempowered in a continuance of the tradition throughout the ages of casting patients as the passive recipients of psychiatric care.

This is the environment into which Freud arrived in October 1885. There can be no doubt that Charcot made a strong and lasting impression on him: not only did he hang a portrait of the master on the wall of his office and name his eldest son, Jean Martin, born in 1889, after him, he also translated a volume of Charcot's lectures on nervous diseases into German in 1886. In the obituary that he wrote on Charcot's sudden death in 1893 he hails him as the greatest advocate and preeminent leader in neurology in all countries as well as one of France's leading men.[25] He shows a fine, broad understanding of Charcot's distinctiveness, above all as "ein Seher" (22; a visual person), able to construct new images of sickness through his capacity for observation. Freud gives a sincere and expert appreciation of Charcot's contribution to neurology.

Yet despite this homage, Freud moved further and further away from Charcot as his own system evolved on the basis of his experience with patients. To satisfy the interest in hypnotism aroused in Paris, he visited in 1889 the rival school in Nancy, headed by Bernheim, whose *De la suggestion et de ses applications à la thérapeutique* he translated into German in 1889 under the title *Die Suggestion und ihre Heilwirkung*. However, in the prevailing physicalist climate of Viennese medicine, both hypnosis and suggestion, partly because of the whiff of charlatanism earlier associated with Mesmer, remained dubious practices. Nor was their prestige as a potential form of medical treatment enhanced by the demonstrations in Vienna in 1880 by the Danish stage hypnotist, Carl Hansen. While his performances in the Ringtheater enjoyed such popularity that the entire city was described as gripped for several months by a "veritable attack of mesmeric-hypnotic fever,"[26] this representative of hypnotism in the guise of entertainment actually undermined the likelihood that it would be taken seriously as a scientific methodology. Hansen's appearances in Vienna were stopped by the police after consultation with the medical faculty—an indirect but telling expression of the disapproval surrounding hypnotism.[27]

Nevertheless, a kind of hypnosis was used in the early 1880s by Josef Breuer in the treatment of the patient known as Anna O. This upper-middle-class, educated young woman in her early twenties exhibited a concatenation of symptoms that she developed while nursing her moribund father. Apart from paralysis on the right side and intermittently on the left, a severe cough, anorexia, and an inability to swallow fluids despite intense thirst, she suffered a strange loss of her native language, although she could speak English. She would mutter phrases that Breuer encouraged her to continue in a hypnoid state. In response to these promptings, Anna O produced daydreams and fantasies, most of which took as their starting point the situation of a young woman at her father's sickbed. When she had narrated a series of such fantasies, "so war sie wie befreit und ins normale seelische Leben zurückgeführt"[28] (she was as if liberated and brought back to a normal psychic life). As her symptoms receded, this highly intelligent patient herself came up with the designation, "*talking cure*," to which she also referred jokingly, and still in English, as "*chimney sweeping*."[29]

Freud tells of the case of Anna O in the first of the five lectures he gave about psychoanalysis at Clark University in Worcester, Massachusetts, in September 1909, and adopts her designation for the therapy he had subsequently devised. His rationale for this mode of therapy was formulated retrospectively some ten years after the treatment of Anna O in the paper coauthored by Breuer and Freud, "Uber den psychischen Mechanismus hysterischer Phänomene: Vorläufige Mitteilung" ("On the Psychical Mechanism of Hysterical Phenomena: A Preliminary Communication"), which first appeared in the *Neurologisches Zentralblatt* (Neurological journal) of 1893 and was subsequently incorporated into the *Studien über Hysterie* (*Studies on Hysteria*) as its opening section.[30] Its central thesis is that the memory of the trauma underlying the conversion reaction can be brought permanently to light and the triggering affect discharged through the process of its being put into words: "**Wir fanden nämlich, anfangs zu unserer grössten Überraschung, dass die einzelnen hysterischen Symptome sogleich und ohne Wiederkehr verschwanden, wenn es gelungen war, die Erinnerung an den veranlassenden Vorgang zu voller Helligkeit zu erwecken, damit auch den begleitenden Affekt wachzurufen, und wenn dann der Kranke den Vorgang in möglichst ausführlicher Weise schilderte und dem Affekt Worte gab.**"[31] ("For we found, at first to our greatest surprise, that the **individual hysterical symptoms disappeared immediately and permanently, when the memory of the causative event had been successfully brought back fully to light so that its accompanying affect was also aroused, and when the patient had described the event in the greatest possible detail and had thus given word to the affect**"). This recognition that the act of "Aussprechen"[32] (literally: "speaking out") can in itself exert a therapeutic effect is the basis not only of classical psychoanalysis but also of its modified successors in their reliance on just talk.

In adopting just talk Freud implemented a radical shift of focus from the physical to the psychological as the source of nervous disorders. He broke away decisively from the nineteenth-century neurologists' search for an identifiable pathological lesion, ferreting out instead the demons hidden in the unconscious mind. This perception differs fundamentally from the old psychiatry, where demons possessed the sufferer without hope of release; Freud, on the contrary, was strongly convinced that inner demons could be vanquished if they were raised into the patient's

conscious understanding through open confrontation by means of verbalization. So these largely self-created demons were amenable to exorcism by self-activity, guided by the therapist. Freud propounded this
psychological view quite early in his career in a lecture to the Viennese
Association for Psychiatry and Neurology on 2 May 1896 in which he
categorically rejects "'feinere anatomische Veränderungen'"[33] ("'subtle
anatomical changes'") as the etiology of hysteria. That the phrase is placed
in quotation marks denotes that he is citing current opinion, represented
by Charcot, that such subtle anatomical changes into the pathological
did exist, but were as yet beyond the reach of the technology of the time.
Freud's comprehensive conceptualization of psychosomatic disorders
leads him to oppose the custom of local treatment on the grounds that,
in his experience, pain removed by the application of iodine, for instance,
recurs some months later as a nervous ("nervös"[34]) complaint. He is even
mildly critical of Charcot for setting up "eine einfache Formel"[35] ("a simple
formula") for the causation of hysteria, whereas his own investigations
always uncover a complex interplay of many factors from diverse areas of
the patient's life. In contrast to Charcot too, and in further rebuttal of
physicalist concepts of mental disorders, Freud "banished the depiction
of the insane as well as the study of the external phenomena of madness
from psychoanalysis."[36] The abandonment of Charcot's visual categories
and the wariness of illustrations is a concomitant of his increasing concentration on inner psychic dramas.

Freud's role—and his evolution—in transferring neuroses from a
putative physiological to a supposed psychological basis is nowhere better illustrated than in the series of case histories recorded in the *Studies
on Hysteria* which appeared in 1895 as a joint publication with Breuer.
Its second and central section covers five case histories: that of Anna O
by Breuer and four by Freud. In all five the patients are women, and four
of them come from the comfortable middle class. This early work has
been relatively neglected in favor of Freud's later, more extensive case
histories.[37]

Yet the *Studies on Hysteria* are extremely important for the history of
psychotherapy as just talk by actually showing Freud's gradual move away
from physical to psychological treatments as well as the development of
his own method. In the initial stages of some of the cases Freud still
resorts to the conventional therapies of the period. This is most evident
in the opening one, that of Emmy von N . . . , a wealthy forty-year-old
widow who had come to Vienna with her two teenage daughters to seek

relief from multifarious symptoms. To combat the sensations of cold and of pain in her right leg, Freud orders hot baths and twice daily massage, which he himself carries out (102). He experiments with other forms of touch, such as stroking her over the eyes to drive away disagreeable images (105), and also over her stomach under hypnosis to assuage discomfort in that region. Throughout the various treatments, and especially under hypnosis, he observes meticulously the vicissitudes in the patient's expression, using his eyes, like Charcot, to ascertain what disturbs her, and conversely what makes her face smoother and more relaxed. So while he is at one level acting like a traditional nerve doctor of that period, he is also astutely reading the signs emitted by the body, and above all registering mental states concealed beneath the surface.

By the final case in the *Studies on Hysteria*, that of Elisabeth R . . . , a twenty-four-year-old who had begun to have pain in her legs that impeded her mobility over two years previously while looking after her moribund father, Freud has no great hopes for the effectiveness of local treatments. The similarity of this case to that of Anna O may have helped to alert him to the essentially psychogenic nature of this patient's disability. An organic affliction comes into play in the location of the disorder since she had had a transient episode of a "leichte rheumatische Erkrankung" (a mild rheumatic illness)[38] in her right leg that determines the site of the complaint. Freud exercises proper precaution in ruling out a physical causation. As with Emmy, he begins with four weeks of physical therapy, acknowledging now, however, that this is no more than a "Scheinbehandlung" (appearance of treatment)[39] in which he no longer has much faith.

In place of the physical treatments favored by Charcot, Freud applies psychological methods of his own devising so that a fascinating picture of his growth as a therapist can be deduced from a reading of the *Studies on Hysteria*. With Emmy von N . . . he immediately declares his intention of using hypnosis: "Es war mein erster Versuch in der Handhabung dieser therapeutischen Methode, ich war noch weit davon entfernt, dieselbe zu beherrschen, und habe in der Tat die Analyse der Krankheitssymptome weder weit genug getrieben noch sie genügend planmässig verfolgt" ("It was my first attempt at applying this therapeutic method, I was still far from having mastered it, and in fact I neither sufficiently pursued the analysis of the symptoms nor followed through systematically enough").[40] This candid concession of his shortcomings and uncertainty at the outset forms the starting point of his quest for a more efficacious mode of therapy, which he actually comes to learn from this patient. Apart from urging her to speak under hypnosis, he interrupts her with questions in an aggressive manner reminiscent of Charcot. It is more or less by coincidence that Emmy begins to talk freely, during the massages, producing each time the memories and new impressions that had occurred to her since the previous conversation. Freud is quick to realize that her talk "ist nicht so absichtslos, wie es den Anschein hat" ("is not as unintentional as it appeared").[41] It was, he remarks, as if she had adopted his strategy, and was using the apparently casual ("ungezwungen") conversation, induced by chance, to supplement the hypnosis.

This experience with Emmy leads to a fundamental modification in Freud's thinking. In his concluding assessment of the case, he admits to harboring "zum ersten Male gewichtige Zweifel an der Richtigkeit des Satzes Bernheims, *tout est dans la suggestion*" ("for the first time weighty doubts about the correctness of Bernheim's sentence, *all is in suggestion*").[42] Although Emmy responds to hypnosis, Freud has begun to shift away from it because he sees greater potential in unforced talk. He comes to grasp too that his cardinal error ("Fehlgriff")[43] lies not in his occasional misunderstanding of what she says but in his interrupting questions, in short in not letting her do the telling at her own pace and will. His patient is teaching him a crucial lesson when she makes an open protest: "Nun sagte sie recht mürrisch, ich solle nicht immer fragen, woher das und jenes komme, sondern sie erzählen lassen, was sie mir zu sagen habe" ("She said quite crossly, I was not to keep on asking her where this or that came from, but to let her tell me what she had to say").[44] So it is a rebuke from a patient that sets him on the royal road to the spontaneous talk absent in hypnosis and quintessential to psychoanalysis.

The second of Freud's four patients in the *Studies on Hysteria*, Lucy R . . . , actually propels him further in his new approach by not responding to his efforts to hypnotize her. This failure prompts a lengthy insert[45] on his technique, and especially on his increasing skepticism about hypnosis. Freud is circumspect in his criticism, emphasizing that at Bernheim's clinic, the "art" ("Kunst")[46] of hypnosis had appeared legitimate and open to acquisition, but his experience had not borne this out. He does not conceal the possibility of severe limitations ("enge Schranken"[47]) in his own abilities in this respect. Be that as it may, he finds himself forced to experiment with other means to gain access to matter beyond normal consciousness. In place of hypnosis, Freud now asks his patients to practice "'Konzentration,'"[48] which is fostered by their lying down and shutting their eyes while he lays on his hands. Passing hands over and above the patient's body in order to bring on a trance conducive to healing was a principal tactic of Mesmer and his imitators, the so-called "magnetizers." Freud's adoption of this technique devolves not from the belief in the transfer of psychic force that inspired magnetism but from the supposition that patients "knew" ("wussten")[49] everything that had pathogenic significance and merely needed to be induced to impart it. This insight is the basis for the improvisational talk that became the cornerstone of psychoanalysis. Another major step forward in the formation of Freud's theory is taken in his recognition that the "forgetting" is intentional and desired, but only partially successful.

In the latter two cases of the *Studies on Hysteria* Freud's method is becoming clearer to him and more individualistic. Hypnosis is dropped. In its place as a stimulant to talk, Freud repeatedly applies pressure to Elisabeth's head with his hands, inculcating in her that this will trigger a mental image as a starting point to her memories. He makes no secret of the fact that he hits on the idea of this technique in order to extricate himself from a position of duress ("In solcher Notlage geriet ich auf den Einfall"[50]) occasioned by her resistance. Again and again in the *Studies on Hysteria* necessity is the mother of invention. This new method always works through its suggestive force, but often Freud has to persevere so as to overcome Elisabeth's contrariness ("Widerspenstigkeit"[51]). As with Emmy, he still asks questions, not as insistently, however; instead, he listens intently to what the patient has to tell: "Ich liess mir zunächst erzählen" ("I first let myself be told"[52]), he states in a direct verbal echo from the earlier case of Emmy ("erzählen lassen"[53]). The pseudopassive grammatical structure reveals the deference to the patient's words that he has now learned. With Elisabeth, Freud thus progresses toward the free association central to classical psychoanalysis. By this last case he has gained confidence in both his understanding of the processes of somatization and the efficacy of the talking cure.

If "what makes the patient ill is silence,"[54] the silence of repression, then language represents the medium for healing, that is, for retrieving unconscious ideations back into consciousness as a means of confronting and defusing them. Each of the patients is helped, if not in every instance entirely cured, by putting her misery into words; the process of objectification involved in expressing feelings in speech creates a certain emotional distance which facilitates self-understanding. Emmy becomes so engrossed in her own discourse that she resents Freud's interruptions of her stream of thought; this (literally) outspoken rebellion in an otherwise generally compliant patient shows how important the act of talking was to her. Lucy responds readily to Freud's invitation to tell ("erzählen"),[55] at first stirred by questions and later of her own volition. Her willing acknowledgment that she had been cherishing false hopes is reported in indirect speech,[56] with Freud assuming the position of reporter. The recurrent terms all turn on the telling: "Erzählung" ("narrative"),[57] "berichten" ("to report"),[58] "Beichte" ("confession").[59] The identical vocabulary of confessional talk pervades the story of Elisabeth. Her resistance makes her therapy more laborious, yet ultimately she is cured; Freud last glimpses her dancing at a private ball, and soon after he hears of her marriage.

When the attentive, forbearing ear displaces the scrutinizing, judgmental eye, a revolution of a dimension perhaps greater than any ever before took place in the history of psychotherapy. Encouraging patients to talk openly and listening to what they say—with an ear alert also to what they do not say—denoted a complete break with the long established tradition of silencing them and hoping to mitigate their distress by physical remedies or some sort of distraction. Whatever the controversies about the validity of Freud's actual theories, the method he devised is in many respects still at the core of individual psychotherapy as it is practiced today. For it is Freud who changed the role of patients through their talk, by having them tell their tale in their own way. Even if the degree of patients' empowerment remains an open question, at least they became active participants in their therapy instead of the merely passive recipients they had previously been forced to be.

This claim—that Freud stands at the fountainhead of psychotherapy as a talking cure—does not mean that his methods have persisted in the way in which he outlined them in his many writings on psychoanalysis. The extent to which Freud himself did exactly as he said is open to question. And classical psychoanalysis has certainly been modified by the trend for the analyst to maintain a less reserved and neutral posture. Even more important, just as Freud departed from his early mentor, Charcot, so several of his initial followers broke away from Freud to develop their own theories and methodologies. Alfred Adler (1870-1938), for instance, formally left the Viennese Psychoanalytic Society in 1911 along with six others to establish the Society for Individual Psychology which sponsored its own journal (the *Internationale Zeitschrift für*

Individualpsychologie). Adler focused on the dynamics of interpersonal relationships between the individual and the community as well as in small groups, with special insistence on aggressive drives.[60] Adler's work was a central impetus for several outstanding later therapists, including Henry Stack Sullivan, Karen Horney, and Erich Fromm.

The foremost alternative to Freud's system was that put forward by the Swiss Carl Gustav Jung (1875-1961). For a time following his visit to Vienna in 1907 Jung was closely associated with Freud: he accompanied him to Clark University in 1909, and from 1909 to 1913 he took an eminent part in the psychoanalytic movement as president of the International Psychoanalytic Association and managing editor of its journal. However, in 1913 he severed his relationship with Freud, and three years later founded the "Psychological Club" in Zurich. While Jung concurred with Freud in certain areas such as the importance of dreams and the conviction that patients often harbored a pathogenic secret, he did not accept other aspects of Freudian theory, notably the consequentiality of the Oedipus complex. Instead of seeking the roots of neurosis in remote childhood, Jung believed in paying primary attention to patients' present predicament. His analytic therapy was therefore essentially pragmatic, aiming above all to bring patients to an awareness of their practical real life situation. Rejecting Freudian psychoanalysis as reductive, Jung envisaged psychotherapy as a synthetic hermeneutic process of reeducation. Patients faced the therapist, perhaps as a symbolic part of the endeavor to induce them to face themselves by accomplishing what Jung called "individuation." Yet in contrast to Freud's secularism, Jung's system is suffused too with a mystical strain. The son of a pastor, brought up in a decidedly religious environment, he was intensely interested not only in myths but also in spiritism as a manifestation of unknown psychic forces. Later in life Jung became increasingly attracted to Eastern wisdom and to the investigation of the psychology of religion.

Long before these defections and despite his success in deciphering the roots of his patients' symptoms, Freud ends the *Studies on Hysteria* with an apologia for the fact that these case histories "sozusagen des ernsten Gepräges der Wissenschaftlichkeit entbehren" ("lack, so to speak, the serious imprint of scientific scholarship").[61] Freud's obvious embarrassment can best be understood in light of the continuing rivalry in the late nineteenth century between neurology and psychiatry, and the superior prestige of neurology as the more scientific. The search for localized lesions, such as Charcot pursued, seemed more promising to an age excited by discoveries in pathological anatomy, bacteriology, and pharmacology than the less tangible theories of psychology. Freud's own early work was in neuropathology; the histological research he conducted between 1883 and 1886 resulted in a paper on the roots and connections of the acoustic nerve, "Uber den Ursprung des Nervus acusticus," which appeared in the *Monatsschrift für Ohrenheilkunde* (Journal for ear diseases) in 1886.[62] In 1885 he was appointed an honorary instructor in neuropathology, and in 1891 he published a critical study of the theory of aphasia as well as a book on cerebral palsy in children written in collaboration with Oscar Rie. Freud "received nothing but praise as long as he was a neurologist."[63]

Freud was fully aware that his growing allegiance to psychological theories of nervous disorders was moving him away from the wholly respectable discipline of neurology into fields then regarded as questionable.[64] On 2 February 1888 he wrote to Fliess: "Die Gehirnanatomie ruht, aber die Hysterie schreitet vor und ist in der ersten Bearbeitung fertig" ("The brain anatomy is where it was, but the hysteria is progressing and the first draft is finished").[65] In the same year in another letter to Fliess, he describes his "Beschäftigung" ("occupation") as "Ein- und Ausreden" ("talking people in and out of things").[66] Because of the seeming *irregularity* of his method of treatment, he expiates on the *regularity* of his medical training, on his familiarity with the accepted modalities despite the unconventionality of his approach. His setbacks and hesitations prompt a curious mixture of self-incrimination and self-justification. Foremost among the latter is the reminder that he is a properly trained neurologist, cognizant of the standard modes of treatment even though he is breaking away from them. He validates the talking cure by arguing that it is proving more therapeutic in the kinds of disorder with which he is dealing than the customary neurological remedies. Yet he knows all too well that in advocating that patients should be encouraged to delve into their anxieties and to speak out about them he is going directly counter to the venerated medical norms of the time that prohibited discussion of the illness and advocated silence and distraction.

Even more provocative than the unscientific aura of psychology was Freud's conviction that neuroses represented a displaced surfacing of repressed sexual desires, a perception that was bound to arouse offense and scandal among the outwardly proper late-nineteenth-century bourgeoisie.[67] While "in Victorian medical debates, questions raised by disease eventually entered into the realm of morality,"[68] Freud pushed these issues into the taboo area of sexuality. Although there had been a steady increase in publications on the subject since Richard Krafft-Ebing's *Psychopathie Sexualis* (1882), interest in sex, as Krafft-Ebing's title implies, was widely seen as an aberration or a perversion, especially in women. Freud, on the contrary, envisages it as the norm. In *Die Traumdeutung* (1900; *The Interpretation of Dreams*) Freud relates the case of a lady in psychoanalysis whose dreams contained "überreichlich sexuelles Gedankenmaterial, dessen Kenntnisnahme sie anfangs ebensosehr überraschte wie erschreckte" (295; a very large number of sexual thoughts, the first realization of which both surprised and alarmed her[69]).

Freud's unease about his findings from these early cases is less surprising when seen from a historical perspective. For his recognition of the role of sexuality in the etiology of psychosomatic traumas had implications that challenged the entire structure of the medical opinion of his day. He transposed the idea of cause and effect, newly rooted in the sphere of general medicine as certain factors were identified as the direct occasioners of specific diseases, into the realm of mental health in an inverted form. By positing the sexual imagination rather than the ovaries as the source of nervous disorders in women, Freud reversed the established relation of the physical to the psychological. In according primacy to the latter, he saw bodily symptoms as secondary to emotional disorders, an externalized, somatized expression of an inner disarray that the patient felt unable to handle. As a result of this insight, he turned psychotherapeutic medicine as previously practiced upside down. The contrast with Charcot is very striking. The theater (literally) of Charcot's examination of patients was visible and often public too; he looked at "*l'espace du corps*" (the space of the body), filling in the picture with a plenitude of minute detail but at the same time leaving the psychological space as "le grand absent"[70] (the great absence). With Freud, on the other hand, the consultation becomes so private as to be almost secretive, and its arena is the invisible forum of the mind, with minimal attention to the body. The opposing attitudes lead to wholly antithetical styles of practice: Charcot is almost all eyes, Freud almost all ears in "a new kind of listening"[71] with what Reik calls "the third ear" brought into play. The beholding physician at the Salpêtrière casts patients as subservient objects of care when the perceptible manifestations of their disturbances are exposed to visual scrutiny and openly discussed in their presence. The listening psychoanalyst turns the speaking analysands into the active explorers of the underlying origins of their traumas. The focus has shifted not only from the visual to the verbal but also from the complaint to the complainer, and from the doctor to the patient.

Freud's anxiety about the unscientific semblance of his work is expressed once more in his regret, even dismay, about another aspect of his writing: "dass die Krankengeschichten, die ich schreibe, wie Novellen zu lesen sind" ("that the case histories I write read like stories").[72] This literary coloration is partly an outcome of his intensive probing into his patients' past as the source of their traumas. He often introduces metaphors from archaeology, of excavating layer after layer of experience to come upon the foundations. In his concentration on extensive biographical and psychological evidence Freud again stands out against Charcot and other nineteenth-century nerve doctors who give only brief background information. The change in the outer form of the case history stems from a fundamental divergence in the implicit belief systems: Charcot addresses the symptoms as physical manifestations in the present with scant attention to their formation, whereas Freud throws the spotlight on the past as the crucial key to the current impasse on the psychological plane. So Freud inevitably finds himself writing "stories" that transgress the norms of the medical case history. In place of the usual minimalized accounts, the schematic translations of disease (and the attendant reduction of the sufferer) into impersonal charts, graphs, and statistical tables, Freud gives highly personalized, essentially humanistic representations of individuals in their social environment. Oliver Sacks praises Freud's "matchless case-histories" for showing "with absolute clarity, that the ongoing nature of neurotic illness and its treatment cannot be displayed *except* by biography."[73]

Freud's case histories are literary too in their entire disposition insofar as they are organized along the lines of a familiar narrative genre, that of the detective thriller, except that the mysteries to be solved are not crimes but the "riddles of a disordered mind."[74] The cases are all told, like fictions of detection, in an "Umkehrung der Reihenfolge" ("reverse chronological order")[75] as the underlying causes of the overt symptoms are uncovered layer by layer, reaching down into ever more hidden strata. Also like the narrator of a mystery tale, Freud is, of course, in possession of retrospective knowledge of the outcome, but he conceals it in the course of writing, thereby heightening suspense and curiosity, again as in a literary artifact. He records step by step the processes of discovery, not merely the answers to the puzzles. So readers are given a sense of the unpredictability of his venture through their immediate participation in his struggles, tensions, and surprises.

In designating Freud as "a sayer,"[76] Reik patently endows the term with a positive connotation. Paradoxically, however, Freud regarded the literariness of his work as a defect, a lack of the streamlined, impersonal sparseness of the scientific style. His recourse to images not only of excavations but also of pain as his guiding compass is indicative of an expansive literary imagination. Yet, as Michel Certeau points out, "he knows that when he crosses beyond the terrain of the profession which authorizes him, he falls into the novel. But his discovery precisely exiles him from the land of the *sérieux*. Cleverly, he maneuvers between the 'nothing' of writing and 'authority' that the institution furnishes the text."[77]

Because Freud himself envisaged the literary nature of his case histories as a possible drawback, its merits have not been sufficiently appreciated. Freud was awarded the Goethe Prize for his writing, and his work has a lasting readability not least as a result of the crystalline clarity of his German, a quality unfortunately forfeited in translation. Although Freud often uses lengthy sentences, they are governed by a grammatical structuration of remarkable stringency. The deliberately sought linguistic lucidity is a metonymic extension of the precision characteristic of his expository argumentation. Perhaps because of his awareness of his deviation from the medical norms of his day, he strives all the harder, in partial compensation, for the limpidity necessary to scientific discourse. His pursuit of the most accurate verbal formulation represents a similar synthesis of the scientific with the literary. He exploits the flexibility of German in its verbal agglomerations, often satirized as uncouth, to great advantage for accuracy and concision, especially in his neologisms. "Weggesprochen" ("talked away"), used of Elisabeth von R . . .'s pain, is one striking example of an original fusion of particle with verb to form a word that exactly fits his need. A parallel instance, also concerned with speech and silence, occurs in the phrase, "[Ich] lernte es allmählich den Kranken an der Miene abzusehen, ob sie mir nicht ein wesentliches Stück der Beichte verschwiegen hätten" ("[I] gradually learned to see off patients' expression whether they had not remained silent on an important part of the confession").[78] "Abzusehen" denotes at once an observational and an interpretative notation. A third usage of the same type is the word "herausbeförderte,"[79] applied to the new strata that come to light in Elisabeth's case; meaning "to facilitate out," it perfectly captures Freud's discreet, remedial instrumentality in his patients' recuperation of buried thoughts.

The literariness of Freud's writing has a further important aftereffect: it is conducive to the migration of the case history from its original medical context into the realm of fiction. The verbal nature of psychoanalysis and of its successors in contemporary psychotherapy as a talking cure predisposes it to ready transfer into fictive story-telling. Just talk is the narration of a life by a speaker whose reliability is bound to be rendered questionable by subjectivity, however assiduous the aspiration to honesty. A narrator's inclination to self-deception or merely an unwillingness to face an unwelcome truth both complicates the construction of the tale and heightens its interest from the narratological perspective. So the preoccupation in twentieth-century narrative with point of view and its relation to degrees of reliability or unreliability creates a strong connection between narration and confessional talk. Narratives of psychotherapy are particularly apt for exploration of this issue in differing situations and from different angles. Yet diverse though they are, all these narratives are indebted to Freud's insights into the mechanisms of repression and the potential for reversing them by talk, to his understanding of the conflicts between self-knowledge and self-protection, between the desire for a healing openness and the resistance to avowal, as well as of the often contentious pressures of transference and countertransference between patient and therapist. These elements lend themselves to a spectrum of literary portrayals ranging from the serious through the ironic and the tragicomic to the verge of the grotesque.

PART I

OVERTALKERS

Overtalkers are those figures in any type of psychotherapy who require little or no prompting to just talk. On the contrary, they are voluble, at times to the point of compulsiveness, in their outpouring of their current thoughts, their retrieved memories, in short, the complaints, physical and/or psychological, that have impelled them to try the talking cure. Yet on occasion the overtalking may be an unconscious tactic to crowd out alternative perceptions of the speakers' behavior as well as to uphold a self-deceptive posture. In saying too much, the overtalkers may simultaneously and paradoxically be saying too little.

As overtalkers, these patients overshadow the therapist, whose presence is quite secondary to that of the dominant, often domineering speaker who holds and fills the stage. However, the therapist's reticence is also due to the fact that most of the overtalkers are engaged in classical psychoanalysis, in which the therapist is constrained to being the discreet catalyst of the patient's talk with only minimal intervention in tentative offers of interpretation.

Since the overtalkers tend naturally to self-absorption, their narratives are cast in the first person. This subjective stance leads to another striking feature of this type of narrative of psychotherapy: the almost total absence of other perspectives. The recurrent literary format is the monologue, punctuated by scenic flashbacks to crucial remembered moments in the speaker's past. This then is the primary route taken by the medical case history in its migration into fiction, into a telling by the patient. The therapist's account of unceasing listening is replaced by the talker's endless monologue.

Four instances of such overtalking will be discussed here: Marie Cardinal's *Les Mots pour le dire* (1975; *The Words to Say It*), a serious record of a seven-year Freudian analysis shaped into the form of a novel; Philip Roth's *Portnoy's Complaint* (1969), also a life-story presented in the guise of a Freudian analysis, though in a distinctively grotesque manner; Italo Svevo's *La Coscienza di Zeno* (1923; *The Confessions of Zeno*), which uses an analysis broken off at the patient's behest as a frame for a satirical vision of psychoanalysis; and David Lodge's *Therapy* (1995), a comic rendering of a series of therapies, including psychotherapy, tried by a successful television scriptwriter in a midlife crisis.

3

"Digesting" Psychoanalysis

Marie Cardinal's *Les Mots pour le dire*

And many a word at random spoken
May soothe or wound a heart that's broken
—Walter Scott

"The technical tools of analytic therapy such as free association, dream interpretation, resistance and transference interpretations produce a mass of data about the patient's life history, the healthy and the pathological sides of his nature, which, due to its bulk, is unwieldy and, if written up in undigested form, unreadable."[1] Anna Freud here reiterates, with an emphasis on readability, her father's caveat about attempts to write up an analysis: "It is well known that no means has been found of in any way introducing into the reproduction of an analysis the sense of conviction which results from the analysis itself. Exhaustive verbatim reports of the proceedings during the hours of analysis would certainly be of no help at all."[2] As if to illustrate this assertion Freud adds a lengthy footnote in this same case of the Wolf Man (228-31) to "discourage" readers "from asking for the publication of analyses which have stretched over several years" (231). Freud and the orthodox among his followers also believed that representations in the form of tapes or transcripts could not stand as surrogates for psychoanalysis because of the loss of immediacy. As Anna Freud insists, "to handle this raw material in a manner which produces, on the one hand, the vivid image of an individual person and, on the other hand, a detailed picture of a specific psychological disorder is no mean task and, as a literary achievement, far beyond the powers of most scientific authors."[3]

In composing *Les Mots pour le dire* Cardinal is, therefore, flying in the face of all these objections. As a novelist she sets out to do what is deemed to be "beyond the powers of most scientific authors," namely to give a lively sense of a seven-year psychoanalysis. Even before the closure of that analysis she promises herself "d'écrire un jour l'histoire de mon analyse, d'en faire un roman" (293; to write the story of my analysis, to turn it into a novel). Significantly, at this embryonic stage she can conceive the enterprise only as "des milliers de pages répétées pour exprimer interminablement le rien, le vide, le vague, le lent" (293; millions of repetitive pages to express interminably the nothingness, the emptiness, the vagueness, the slowness), that is, precisely what Anna Freud had predicted. And then into this immense monotony a few sparkling lines break in, seconds of luminous insight, followed by thousands more pages of the flat, the shapeless, the material in a state of gestation. She concludes, with Freud and his daughter, that "l'analyse cela ne peut pas s'écrire" (293; analysis cannot be written). In light of the patent impossibility—and undesirability—of aiming for any sort of mimetic reproduction, how does Cardinal "digest" the experience into a three hundred and forty-five page novel? What literary strategies does she choose to convert the years on the couch, first three times a week, then twice, and finally toward the end just once, into a gripping, shapely narrative?

Cardinal was already a successful novelist before embarking on this endeavor. Her first novel, *Ecoutez la mer* (1962; Listen to the Sea) was awarded the Prix International du Premier Roman (International Prize for a First Novel), and between 1964 and 1972 she published three further works. But it is *Les Mots pour le dire* that has brought her greatest fame, winning the Prix Littré in 1976, and selling 320,000 copies in a mere two years. It appeared in English in 1983 under the title *The Words to Say It,* however as an abridged adaptation.[4] Cardinal has continued to publish quite prolifically ever since, although she is still known foremost as the author of *Les Mots*. Its striking and rather unusually phrased title arouses curiosity as to what "it" is, as well as immediately positing "words" and "saying" as the pivotal theme. Through the words articulated in analysis Cardinal not only achieves liberation from her past and her suffering, but also in the discovery of the joy of words finds her vocation as a writer.

In her first-person narration Cardinal makes absolutely no attempt to conceal the novel's autobiographical source. This differs from the more usual situation in first-person narratives, which generally present themselves in the form of a self-narrated story that imitates its nonfictional counterpart, historical autobiography.[5] Often, where the personal origins are readily apparent, as in Joyce's *Portrait of the Artist*, Plath's *The Bell Jar*, or Thomas Mann's *Tonio Kröger*, they are veiled by the creation of a fictive persona. Cardinal shuns any such subterfuge; in planning her novel she envisages writing about "une femme qui me ressemblerait comme une soeur" (293; a woman who would resemble me like a sister). The French formulation carries a clear intertextual echo of Musset's reiterated line in *La Nuit de décembre*, "Qui me ressemblait comme un frère" (who resembled me like a brother). The reference to a famous nineteenth-century poem partially inserts Cardinal's work into a literary tradition without, however, reducing its subjectivity since Musset's poem is about an encounter with a double. In *Les Mots* the recovered woman and writer revisits her earlier self in an intimate identification that recaptures in full measure the initial despair, the slow, persevering, frequently painful process of therapy to the eventual healing.

Who, then, was the person who entered analysis, and for what reason? A married thirty-year-old woman with three children, who had taught philosophy for seven years, but had become increasingly incapacitated by an unknown illness accompanied by terror. Her presenting symptom is an incessant menstrual flow of three years' duration that no gynecological treatment had been able to stop. This mysterious affliction has turned into an obsession, "le centre et la cause de ma maladie" (11; the center and the cause of my illness), which manifests itself in sweats, palpitations, and panic attacks. She had been hospitalized in a private clinic from which she absconded with a friend's connivance. Psychoanalysis is a last resort for a woman so utterly demoralized that she fears insanity and feels she can no longer live. Overcome with shame and anxieties, she wonders whether she will ever be able to find the words to connect even to the analyst. It seems incongruous to place the self-enclosed, cramped woman of the opening among the overtalkers.

Yet although she has no recollection of how she managed to get to the analyst's office at the outset, she immediately feels "bien là, dans ce petit espace, à parler de moi" (34; comfortable, in this small space, speaking about myself). This small space becomes, in Leston Haven's terminology, "A Safe Place," at once a refuge from the world at large and an island of seclusion where she can begin to seek out her self. Significantly, the doctor's house, where his office is located, is situated in a "ruelle en impasse" (7; a little street in the form of a close), an enclave of tranquility in the middle of the city. The novel opens on the words, "La ruelle en impasse," and the word "impasse," constantly reiterated, becomes, in a metonymic and metaphoric extension, a cipher for her therapy. For a "close" is not only a sheltered spot; it is also one from which escape is hard so that the narrator is here forced to confront her problems. Although it is a physical symptom that has triggered her descent into an almost psychotic state, the doctor dismisses her complaint as psychosomatic, and orders her to speak of other matters ("Parlez-moi d'autre chose," 42). Such a belief in the priority of psychological over physical causation is in keeping with the analyst's Freudian orientation. While the analysand experiences the command as a slap in the face, she does comply. That the flow of blood stops abruptly and forever after just the first session is the least credible facet of *Les Mots*.

The analyst's injunction to speak of other things is the only instance when he openly asserts his power. He remains a shadowy presence, "masqué jusqu'au bout" (343; masked to the very end), described only as "ce petit bonhomme" (35; this little fellow), and never named.[6] The recurrent adjective applied to him ("petit"—small) signals that his slight stature makes him nonthreatening, just as the particle "bon" (good) suggests benevolence. Cardinal's presentation of the analyst bears out Reik's comment that "in the eyes of the patient the analyst is part of this realm between fantasy and reality. It is psychologically comprehensible that most patients do not know what their analyst looks like."[7] But he does exert some further control at the beginning by making her accept adult responsibility for her therapy in the form of payment, which obliges her to resume work. Her consent to this condition marks a first step toward taking charge of her life; in this way he actually empowers her. Moreover, by accepting her for analysis he demonstrates his faith in his ability to help her as well as in her capacity to work herself out of her demoralization. She is deeply grateful that he treats and addresses her as a normal person. So his impact is encouraging and supportive; he speaks softly and calmly, though dryly, without either pity or paternalism.

Nowhere throughout the rest of this narrative does the therapist speak as much as in the opening chapter. Mostly he is imperturbable, impenetrable, "raide, correct, muet, presque cruel, parfois ironique dans son comportement" (189; stiff, correct, silent, almost cruel, sometimes ironic in his bearing). Always, however, he is an extremely attentive listener who remembers all she says so that she never feels that she is talking into a void. In time she grows curious how he manages his feats of memory without a tape or as much as a pencil. On her side, the relation-ship is subject to considerable fluctuation: she alternates between trust and frustration, between regard and exasperation, between an image of him as a magician and as a charlatan, between a positive and a negative transference. Only her voice links them: "il n'y avait que ma voix entre nous, rien d'autre" (173-74). Occasionally he prompts her, rarely he ven-tures a comment; in the tempestuous process of her analysis, he tolerates phases of silence when her defense mechanisms are mobilized into re-sistance. Their sessions are enframed in a precise etiquette of entrance through one door and exit through another to preserve patients' privacy. The formal farewell "Au revoir, madame" with its response "Au revoir, docteur" functions like a choral refrain. These rituals serve to demarcate the safe place of the close, the arena of therapy, from the world outside, frightening and hostile to her. Within the verbal rite of just talk the analyst acts as a stabilizing facilitator. She recognizes that his unfailing commitment is "le point de départ de tout" (13; the point of departure for everything). More important, she learns to renounce concealment: "je finissais toujours par enlever le masque et dire l'exacte vérité" (174; I always ended by lifting the mask and saying the exact truth). So the same image is applied to patient and doctor: the former drops the mask, while the latter retains it in a professionally proper reserve. Nonetheless, his role as the agent of her rebirth is acknowledged in the dedication of *Les Mots* "Au docteur qui m'a aidé à naître" (To the doctor who helped me to be born). Although readers are limited by the first-person narra-tion to her view of him, we suspect that he is more compassionate than she credits except in retrospect. It has been suggested that the analyst made use of her "dependency needs in the establishment of a strong transference toward him" and that "it is very likely that she was able to resolve some of her unfulfilled filial longings in the context of the transferential relationship."[8] While there are no overt signs of such a relationship within the narrative itself, the dedication validates this hy-pothesis.

The material excavated in the analysis could have come straight from a Freudian case history. The narrator turns out to have been cast as the scapegoat of a family dysfunctional in many ways. Her elder sister, who died at eleven months, is idealized and perpetuated through regular vis-its to her grave. Her brother, five years her senior, is the favored child. Notwithstanding their Catholicism, her parents divorce, and her father's death from tuberculosis activates an exaggerated fear of germs in her

mother. It is ultimately her mother's pathological traits that are uncovered as the direct and indirect mainspring of the analysand's distress.
She learns that her mother, finding herself pregnant at the time of the
divorce, had attempted to abort her. Her mother's confession, which she
experiences as "autant de lames estropiantes" (164; so many crippling
knife blades) shows the power of words to hurt as they inflict a "vilaine
blessure inguérissable" (164; dreadful, incurable wound). An unwanted
child, she is the object of harsh discipline and deprived of real love except at times of sickness, when her mother does pay her constant attention. So flight into illness will become for her a means to avoid the
otherwise incessant criticism and to gain care. Her innate desire to please
her mother and to win her approval is repeatedly thwarted so that she
comes to see herself as a total failure. Her submissiveness and passivity
are manifestations of her fear of her mother, of a hatred she dare not
avow, and a tyranny she cannot cast off. She is haunted by "LA CHOSE"
(the thing), a sense of shame, guilt, and terror that casts a grim shadow
over her entire existence and eventually preempts any spontaneous feeling. In the course of analysis she is made to understand that it is her
mother, not she, who is "pas normale" (221 and 228; not normal). In the
long run, the mother is "rongée par l'analyse comme par un acide" (198;
corroded by analysis as by an acid). Her mother's final physical and moral
degradation by alcoholism results in the daughter's assumption of control, but only after her mother's death is there a deeper release, and even
a kind of healing reconciliation. This plot of a reversal of power is com-
pleted by the coincidence between mother and daughter of a central life
event at the same age: at twenty-seven her mother had tried to abort her,
and at twenty-seven the daughter had begun to bleed. So the psychoanalysis, by exposing the hidden layers of the past, has a therapeutic
effect in the present and for the future.

How is this complex material compressed into a novel of moderate
length, and above all, how is the process of psychoanalysis conveyed?
More than in any other narrative of psychotherapy, the analysis itself is
kept in the foreground in *Les Mots*. Apart from references to the "impasse" at the beginning of many chapters, the word "divan" (couch) becomes in its constant reiteration the symbol of the ongoing therapy. The
rituals of arrival and departure and the presence of "le petit bonhomme"
are frequently mentioned too as reminders that the story being told is
that of a therapeutic analysis. The continuous sound of the analysand's
voice is the novel's sustaining center. The absolute necessity of "parler,

parler, parler, parler" (84; talk, talk, talk, talk) is the doctor's major in-junction: "Parlez, dites tout ce qui se passe par la tête" (85; Talk, say everything going through your mind). It is the only remedy he offers her; in her despair she grasps at it, responding with "ce flot de mots, ce maelström de mots, cette masse de mots, cet ouragan de mots!" (85; this flood of words, this maelstrom of words, this mass of words, this hurri-cane of words!). For a while the narrator has difficulty in believing that "ma simple parole allait chasser définitivement mon désarroi, ce mal si profond, ce désordre dévastateur, cette peur permanente" (211; my words alone would definitely drive away my disarray, this deep sickness, this devastating disorder, this permanent fear). But as the months and years pass, and she begins to feel and to function better, she does become convinced of the efficacy of just talk as the core of therapy. Conversely, she comes to realize too the cumulatively destructive effect of the failure of communication between her father and her mother as well as be-tween her mother and herself.

The present time of the analysis, which forms the frame of the nar-ration, is complemented by a series of flashbacks to different phases in the analysand's life at the associative prompting of her memory. Far from being a sequential account, *Les Mots* is characterized by temporal dis-jointedness as it switches, sometimes abruptly, from the present to vari-ous points in the past and back again. By this means the erratic workings of recall are captured; conscious memories lead to fragments of early childhood, or dreams open up vistas onto the unconscious. Words, phrases, images, or objects set off a chain of associations that lead to the recuperation of determining experiences. This fluidity of the temporal disposition is the closest narratological approximation to mimicry of the psychoanalytic process. But obviously a considerable measure of artistic selectivity also comes into play. The phases of stagnation and relative silence are passed over quickly while the high points are elaborated in expansive detail.

This brings up a technique of utmost importance in the translation of an analysis into a novel, namely the reenactment of memories as live scenes. The virtually uninterrupted drone of a random subjective stream of consciousness, an analysand's normative production, is in *Les Mots* transformed into vivid episodes, "les mises en scène de mon passé" (128; the scenic performance of my past). Instead of the unreadability that Anna Freud saw as inevitable in the record of an analysis "in undigested form," the digested version, offered by Cardinal, is eminently readable because of the artistic control she exercises by manipulating the material through a rapid fast forward over the unproductive segments in favor of a live, performative presentation of the crucial encounters. *Les Mots* makes its impression precisely through the dramatic force of these remembered moments reenacted before readers' eyes: the Louis Armstrong concert, where the rhythmic beat of the music sets off a parallel, frightening beating of her heart (52-55); the rejection of the child's gift of pretty stones to her mother, who scolds her gruffly for bringing such dirty things into the house (88-89); the "séance d'initiation" (142) where the mother makes an inept attempt to explain menstruation, which she represents as something shameful to be concealed, and where she also endeavors to inculcate into her daughter the stringent moral codes of that time, place, and class, thereby arousing fear and anxiety (135-42); the contest of wills between her mother and herself in her infancy about finishing a plate of soup (212-15); the showdown with her husband who is so tired of her endless complaints that he contemplates divorce, but compromises by taking a position in a distant country (260-62). As this list shows, these intercalated episodes are inserted in a nonchronological order, in the same haphazard manner in which they might reenter conscious memory. The perspective remains that of the first-person narrator, but the opening up from monologue into dialogue injects variety and immediacy.

In all these scenes, the narrator recognizes herself as "à la fois spectatrice et actrice" (242-43; at once spectator and actress). This phrase aptly summarizes the patient's position in therapy where past experience has both to be relived and understood from a new vantage point in order to trigger the unlearning of old behaviors and their replacement with other, sounder ones. She clearly plays the dual role of actress and spectator in relation to the dreams and nightmares she recalls. They function as a screen onto which she projects images almost exclusively of fear. To remember the dream scenes and to hear one's voice telling them "cela équivaut à vivre deux moments complètement différents et pourtant il s'agit de la même histoire" (297; that is like living two completely different moments, and yet they belong to the same story). The dreams, which had been absent during the time of her illness, that is, of her repression, begin to surface during the analysis. Often the recurrent nightmares take her back to early childhood, sometimes to adolescence, and once even to babyhood. She dreams of being eaten by the animals at the zoo when she was six or seven and of being engulfed by snow during a winter outing. Since she was with her father on both these occasions, the dreams make her aware of her sense of her father's lack of power in the family. An important stage in the analysis is marked by a dream that points to the conflict with her mother and her longing to escape her restrictive dominance. Two other dreams of escape are linked to her increasing consciousness of sexuality as a threat. The most haunting dream-like memory, which produces the repeated hallucination of an eye watching her with disapproval, is traced back to a very early episode when her father sees her urinating in the woods and she rushes to hit him; scolded by her nanny and her father, she is made to feel shame both at having exposed her backside and at having then attacked the beholder. In dealing with the hallucination, which makes her fear insanity, the narrator cries out, "Docteur, aidez-moi!" (183; Doctor, help me!). Otherwise, however, the doctor is not shown as having any part in the interpretation of the dreams. The understanding of the dreams seems to be attributed to the analysand herself because the verbs are in the active mood: "Ainsi ai-je découvert" (78; Thus I discovered); "j'ai découvert" (80; I discovered); "j'ai pris conscience" (207; I became aware). Her assertion that "en général, grâce à l'analyse je comprenais mes rêves" (275; generally, thanks to analysis I understood my dreams) has equivocal implications; it suggests that maybe it was the analyst's input, though unrecorded, that enabled her to grasp the dreams' meanings, even if she appears to claim all the credit herself.

The analysand has a dual role in another respect too: as narrator, she commands retrospective knowledge of the outcome of her analysis, yet she writes in the present, that is, she knows but pretends not to know. Sometimes she does anticipate, for instance by disclosing early on that her mother's death will terminate the analysis, or by expressing her admiration for the analyst's ability to find exactly the right words for his interventions later in the analysis. So the attentive reader is made aware of her foreknowledge. More commonly, however, she uses strings of rhetorical questions to intimate the agitation and confusion besetting her during the analysis. The recourse to flashbacks, quintessential to the representation of the recollective nature of psychoanalysis, entails a multiplicity of time levels. Paradoxically, this narrative strategy both heightens the reality effect by reproducing the excavation of memory central to psychoanalysis *and* raises readers' consciousness of the artifice involved in the telling of the story. The analysand doubles both as spectator and actor, and as narrator and subject. This doubling is reiterated in the audience, the reader of the novel itself corresponding to the analyst within

the novel. The artfulness required to transfer the intimacy of analysis
into the public form of the novel becomes apparent here as readers are
cast as at once eavesdroppers of a private search and legitimate recipients of a published text.

The artfulness is evident again in the structure of this text, divided
into eighteen chapters, each with a dominant theme. The first consists
of exposition of the situation; the second is devoted to the history of the
presenting physical symptom; in the third the memories begin to flow,
focusing in the fourth chapter on the father, in the fifth on the mother,
and in the sixth on their home in Algeria. The middle third of the narrative starts with the revelation in the seventh chapter of the mother's
"saloperie" (infamy) in trying to abort her. This induces a terrifying hallucination in chapter eight, which marks the turning point in the analysis as the narrator, with gathering trust in the process, opens up deeper
layers of her unconscious. Chapters nine and ten show downs and ups,
resistance and progress leading up to the confrontation of the relationship with the mother in the eleventh chapter. With chapter twelve the
last third of the novel and a new phase of the analysis is initiated, one
that deals no longer with the past but rather with the narrator's discovery of her present self. So chapter thirteen is about her writing and her
marriage, and fourteen about the pleasures of the body, of laughter, and
of art. The analysis begins to draw to an end in chapter fifteen, and is
accomplished in chapter sixteen by the mother's death. The last session
with the analyst in chapter seventeen is recorded in a mere half-page,
signifying perhaps that the purpose of the flood of words has been
achieved. The final chapter is just one line: a few days later it was May
1968, the period of the great social and political turmoil in France.
The artistic design of *Les Mots* imposes on the free ranging
associationism of psychoanalysis a control necessary for its "digestion"
into a readable format.

That element of artistic design is discernible too in the story's internal pattern, particularly in the symmetries and reversals between mother
and daughter. There is a chiasmus within the parallels as the daughter
comes to rewrite her mother's life into a more positive version. Like her
mother, she has three children, but hers are healthy and happy. She also
succeeds not only in avoiding the divorce that ended her parents' marriage, but in rekindling her husband's affection and respect through her
writing and her strengthened personality. While her mother is never
capable of rebellion, of remarrying, of resuming her sexuality, the daughter,

through the analysis, finds her own identity and direction. Separating herself from the value system into which she was socialized in her youth, she becomes a freer, more forceful and self-confident individual. The engulfing guilt she had been made to feel in her early years is traced to the mother, who is unmasked as the evil genius in the family. The last part of the analysis is devoted to examining her now openly admitted hatred ("haine," 328) of her mother. Yet there is a final, slightly sentimental reconciliation when she visits her mother's grave, just as the latter had regularly visited her infant's burial place; now, at long last, she has the words to speak to her mother, and the readiness to avow her frustrated love for her. At points such as this, the scenario seems a little too neat, the "digestion" of the analysis into a well constructed novel somewhat too transparently contrived.

The novel's cohesiveness is further ensured by the recurrence of certain interwoven motifs. A whole cluster is grouped round the mother: propriety, bourgeois values, fear of microbes, keeping up appearances, which, of course, entails repression. Often the motifs appear in the abundant imagery: opening doors, accessing locks with the right key, getting rid of heavy baggage, debriding and cleaning wounds, taming the wild horses drawing the narrator's carriage, removing the debris and roots of rotten old trees. All these are striking emblems of the analytic process as well as testimony to Cardinal's power as a writer. The same imagery pervades her dreams, particularly the archetypal, repeated scenario of terror at coming upon something hideous behind a locked door, denoting her fear of fully facing her past. But dreams are not quite as common in *Les Mots* as might be expected in a classical analysis, perhaps because Cardinal's imagination is more verbal than visual. The most potent reiterated metaphor is that of birth and rebirth as the narrator experiences the liberating dawn of a fresh understanding of her self that paves the way for a revaluation of the past and the unfolding of her new personality.

Just talk before the analyst releases the springs of self-expression so that the verbalization practiced by Cardinal in analysis is then channeled into her profession as a writer. The title, *Les Mots pour le dire* (*The Words to Say It*) can therefore be read in a binary sense to refer at once to the words spoken in the analyst's presence and to those that make up this novel. In translating her psychoanalysis into a literary work, Cardinal has transformed herself too: from an overtalker who spills out words in torrents ("déverser . . . en torrents" [49]), contained only by the analytic hour, into an artist who exercises consummate control over her words. She has indeed been praised for her skill in making "chaos coherent"[9] and for "restructuring the thrice weekly sessions into an ordered work of literature."[10] But Cardinal has succeeded in doing more than merely creating order out of chaos. For she has devised a particular order that draws on literary conventions, for instance in the division into chapters, the familiar structure of reversal, and the importance of key images and motifs, while at the same time conveying the strangeness of spontaneously confiding one's most intimate, buried, secret thoughts and fears as they come to mind to a barely known professional listener. She shows what Anna Freud called the "tools of analytic therapy such as free association, dream interpretation, resistance and transference" at work in her case to bring into the open the healthy and the pathological sides of her nature. Beyond these technical aspects she infuses into *Les Mots* what Freud called that "sense of conviction which results from the analysis itself." He maintained that no means had been found to introduce this "into the reproduction of an analysis." Cardinal achieves the rare feat of giving readers a credible insight, almost a vicarious experience of her analysis not by simple "reproduction" of millions of words but by a discerning choice of the appropriate means from the literary repertoire. Ultimately, it is her brilliant success as a writer in *Les Mots* that makes us believe in the fruitful outcome of her analysis.

4

"Ritualized Bellyaching"

Philip Roth's *Portnoy's Complaint*

Qui s'excuse, s'accuse.
[He who excuses himself accuses himself.]

—Proverb

"I hear myself indulging in the kind of ritualized bellyaching that is just what gives psychoanalytic patients such a bad name with the general public," Portnoy laments to his analyst (105). The sentence suggests a certain ambivalence toward the therapy on which he has embarked; psychoanalysis seems to him to have acquired a tarnished reputation because it has come to signify self-indulgent complaining. This fundamental reservation sharply differentiates *Portnoy's Complaint* from *Les Mots pour le dire,* where the healing potential of analysis is unequivocally affirmed and demonstrated.

Still, there are many parallels between the two works. Like Cardinal, Roth depicts a psychoanalysis in a first-person narrative. The speaker is a thirty-three-year-old Jewish New York lawyer, Alexander Portnoy, who holds the somewhat nebulous position of assistant commissioner of human rights. The narrators in the two novels are, therefore, about the same age, and both have reached a point in their lives when they seem successful enough outwardly, yet inwardly they face a crisis which they hope to overcome through psychoanalysis. The content of *Portnoy's Complaint* is, again like that of *Les Mots,* a patently Freudian family drama, but its literary expression is far more radical. Also, Roth's novel is more fictionalized; for instance, names are given to both the speaking patient and the listening analyst, Dr. O. Spielvogel. Where these two representations of psychoanalysis are most at variance, however, is in their tone:

in place of the reverential seriousness of *Les Mots, Portnoy's Complaint* sports a grotesque black humor, manifest in its designation of psychoanalysis as "ritualized bellyaching." This metaphor of maldigestion indicates that instead of assimilating psychoanalysis to fairly traditional narrational strategies, as in *Les Mots, Portnoy's Complaint* spews and splutters it out with a dynamic, venomous energy that is quite breathtaking.

What is the nature of Portnoy's titular "complaint"? He himself asks early on, "Doctor, what do you call this sickness I have?" (40). Portnoy has a less pronounced physical presenting symptom than Cardinal's protagonist, although he does suffer from impotence with Jewish women, and he exhibits a tendency to hypochondria that escalates at times to panic. His malaise appears to be an agitated type of depression with low self-esteem, a pervasive sense of guilt, a bad conscience, and an endless string of "grievances" and "hatreds" (105). Because of his chronic self-doubts and deep-seated uncertainties about his identity, Portnoy feels compelled to "*excuse* myself" (115), and constantly to be justifying his actions and especially his desires. His fixation on sexuality as his central problem is closely connected to his resentment against his parents, particularly his mother, who is presented as inordinately domineering, while his father is passive and downtrodden. Portnoy is torn between the role expected of him and his own inclinations because he is still unable to free himself from the apron-strings of parental standards: "I'm still telephoning my parents to say I'm not coming home! Fighting off my family still!" (258). So he encounters "shame and shame and shame and shame—every place I turn something else to be ashamed of" (55) for at some level he has remained "the little over-earnest innocent endlessly in search of the key to that unfathomable mystery, his mother's approbation" (53). Since he cannot gain that approbation by complying with her wishes, he is beset by tormenting fears and fantasies of impending disaster.

Despite the divergence in environment, the fundamental situation in *Portnoy's Complaint* is not unlike that in *Les Mots*. Even more than Cardinal's narrator, Portnoy has a confused, dichotomized self-image: is he really good or bad? and by whose criteria is he to be judged? He begs the doctor, "make me *whole*! Enough being a nice Jewish boy, publicly pleasing my parents while privately pulling my putz!" (40). The mode in which he formulates his dilemma points to the histrionic traits in his personality. His complaint, voiced significantly at some points in a tirade addressed directly to his mother, often reaches hysterical pitch: "Because to be *bad*, Mother, that is the real struggle; to be bad—and to enjoy it! That is what makes men of us boys, Mother. But what my conscience, so-called, has done to my sexuality, my spontaneity, my courage! Never mind some of the things I try so hard to get away with—because the fact remains, I *don't*. I am marked like a road map from head to toe with my repressions. You can travel the length and breadth of my body over superhighways of shame and inhibition and fear" (138-39). Well into adulthood, established in his profession, Portnoy is trapped in the emotional insecurity of the little boy anxious to win love by bringing home good grades. But unlike the essentially pliable female narrator of *Les Mots,* Portnoy is also from the outset full of anger and resentment, voiced in a peculiar mixture of rage and elegy.

Contradictions, in fact, characterize him, as is evident already in his attitude to psychoanalysis. Despite his skittish comment on "ritualized bellyaching," he reveals himself to be steeped in Freudian concepts. He boasts of having read Freud's essay on Leonardo (116) and of having bought the *Collected Papers.* His vocabulary is saturated with psychoanalytic terms: "screen memory" (108), "superego" (181), the "Oedipal drama" (301), his parents wearing "their unconscious on their sleeves" (108). Mostly Portnoy endorses Freud as the valid framework of his self-conceptualization, with only an occasional derogatory questioning of this surrogate parent figure: "Who needs dreams, I ask you? Who needs Freud?" (203). That he uses a volume of Freud to put himself to sleep at night (208) is also a somewhat backhanded compliment. His cult of Freud has to be seen, however, as part of his overall bookishness, his tendency to intellectualization; he likes to contextualize his own life experience in literary precedents through liberal references to his reading of Shakespeare, Dostoevsky, Tolstoy, Coleridge, Keats, Yeats, and Kafka. His secular knowledge shows that, like Freud, he has moved beyond the narrow limits of the Jewish ghetto, though still tied to that orbit by his love/hate relationship to his parents. But he wants to believe that he is in possession of full self-knowledge, asserting that his psyche is "about as difficult to understand as a gradeschool primer!" (203). By exhibiting his familiarity with Freud, speaking of a fantasy "right out of the casebook" (95) or "a case like mine" (300), he strives for empowerment by, curiously, trying to set himself up as his own analyst. This maneuver necessarily backfires by disclosing only the extent of his narcissistic self-entanglement.

The primary agent of his disempowerment is, in Portnoy's eyes, his mother. The opening section is titled "The Most Unforgettable Charac-

ter I've Ever Met" (1-17), and the very first word of his monologue is
"she" (1). His is a "history of disenchantment" (8) as the child becomes
aware of the "mix-up of sexes in our house!" (45). Being a boy, he naturally identifies more with his father, though he soon comes to realize
how "oppressed" and "powerless" he is (43). The father's pathetic weakness is offset by the mother's swaggering pride, absolute self-assurance,
and need to control her husband's and her son's every mouthful and
every act. The image of this family is very negative as the autocratic
Sophie systematically emasculates her exhausted husband. His chronic
constipation is as much a symptom and a symbol of his disablement as
her name is an ironic undercutting, indeed a caricature of the wisdom it
is supposed to denote. What is more, this smothering Jewish mother,
however bizarre her idiosyncracies, is seen as a type. She has a parallel in
the novel in Mrs. Nimkin, whose "FUCKING SELFISHNESS AND
STUPIDITY" (109) is perceived by Portnoy as the cause of her son's
suicide. Ronald Nimkin therefore acts as a foil to young Alexander
Portnoy by illustrating the sheer desperation such a mother can engen-
der. By contrast, Portnoy is able to project himself not merely as a heroic
rebel but also as a valiant survivor in a struggle that is at once comic and
potentially tragic. Describing himself as "the son in the Jewish joke," he
adds ruefully, "—*only it ain't no joke!*" (39-40).

While there may not be a joke at the core of *Portnoy's Complaint,*
there is certainly a signal irony, the irony of the son's likeness to his
mother. Despite Portnoy's illusion that he commands total self-knowledge, this aspect of his personality remains largely repressed. Just as his
mother experiences her life to be "high drama" (103), so he admits, albeit in parentheses, "(For I have a taste for melodrama too)" (14). Similarly, she sees herself in her youth as "some sort of daredevil who goes
exuberantly out into life in search of the new and the thrilling, only to be
slapped down for her pioneering spirit" (104), yet she recoils from the
alien, Christian world represented by the transgression of once eating
lobster on a date, even though she maintains she took it for chicken. As
is so common in *Portnoy's Complaint,* a metaphor of food here doubles as
an emblem of sexuality. The son's sense of guilt at sleeping with non-
Jewish women parallels the mother's "sin" with the forbidden shellfish.
Both are simultaneously drawn to and repelled by what is, in their world,
illicit. The repetitiveness of generational continuities reaches back to
Sophie's own childhood: she recalls that "when she was a little girl her
family was always telling her to do this and do that, and how unhappy

and resentful it would sometimes cause her to feel" (127). Like the abused child who becomes an abuser, Sophie inflicts on her son the same kind of bullying she had suffered, and what is more, he reiterates the pattern in his self-flagellation. His exaggerated fears, his perception of dangers lurking everywhere are a direct echo of her stance. And just as "our books were written by Sophie Portnoy" (104), so this one is by Alexander Portnoy. His inordinate monologue duplicates hers, which had resounded throughout his childhood; his evident tendency to overtalking and exaggeration is a reprise of hers. The irony of his lacking the essential knowledge of his similarity to his mother explains the puzzling end to *Portnoy's Complaint* when the analyst, in his only directly voiced intervention, says, "Now vee may perhaps to begin" (300). This "PUNCH LINE" (300) of course drastically undercuts Portnoy; if, after his copious outpourings, the analysis is only about to begin, it must mean that he has much yet to learn and to face about himself. He needs, as he argues, to separate from the smothering mother, but he needs too—what is contradictory and therefore even more difficult—to accept his likeness to her, and with it, his Jewishness.

This central thematic paradox of Portnoy's rejection of *and* resemblance to his mother reappears in the novel's many dualisms. Like *Les Mots, Portnoy's Complaint* is a first-person narrative that presents a life through the filter of the teller's perspective: "what I was up against" (35) is the kernel of his complaint in the sense of a plaint, a lamentation. But even the plaint he intones is dyadic in its timbre. For while Portnoy's outcry rises to heights of hysteria with his mounting despair, it is constantly being redressed by the comic gusto implicit in the entire monologue. It is as if Portnoy were unabashedly verbally "whaking off" (18) in an "ejaculative performance"[1] that has the force of a sexual discharge. Apparently uncontrolled in an associative string, Portnoy's verbalization squirts out in all directions. He uses torrents of words as "bullets" (250) to take pot shots that hit everything in range, yet he is also masturbatory insofar as he turns his anger inward onto himself. Thus, loathing of others is inextricably linked to self-loathing.

But this boisterous monologue is preceded and contained by a brief foreword whose discourse is of an entirely different kind. Masquerading as an encyclopedia entry under the heading "*Portnoy's Complaint,*" it purports to offer a scholarly definition of a syndrome described by a Dr. O. Spielvogel in an article titled "The Puzzled Penis" which appeared in the journal *Internationale Zeitschrift für Psychoanalyse,* volume 24. In a

mimicry of psychoanalytic jargon it summarizes the main motifs of the
narrative to come in detached, cognitive terms. This satirical overture is
laden with contradictions. In its objective dryness it is the opposite to
Portnoy's subjective emotionality. It also simultaneously elevates and
deflates him by installing him in an international journal as a notewor-
thy case and reducing him to a set of rather unflattering symptoms. Thus
at one level the prologue validates Portnoy's story by its semblance of
erudition, yet at another it robs him of his uniqueness by turning him
into an example of a pathological case. By originating from the analyst it
gives both the first and the last word to the doctor, thereby, as it were,
enclosing Portnoy and setting limits to his otherwise boundless verbal
exuberance. Finally, and very importantly, this foreword prefigures the
seriocomic tone of the entire work.

The doctor, through the opening notation of his article and his closing
phrase, therefore enframes Portnoy's monologue. Since this garrulous
patient monopolizes the sessions, Dr. Spielvogel remains wholly mute
until the "punch line." Portnoy's breathless stream of talk allows him not
a moment for the interpretative interventions occasionally ascribed to
the analyst in *Les Mots* and customary in classical psychoanalysis. So
Roth shows an analysand of such extreme loquaciousness as completely
to silence the doctor; this represents not only a decidedly whimsical reversal of the nineteenth-century situation where the patient was the one
to be silenced, but also possibly a self-defeating travesty of psychoanalysis engineered by a patient who allows his analyst no opportunity to
provide any feedback whatsoever. Portnoy's analysis becomes yet another self-production rather than a therapy. Notwithstanding his enforced taciturnity, however, the doctor is a pronounced presence
throughout *Portnoy's Complaint.* Portnoy's frequent invocation of his
understanding and pleas for confirmation function as incessant reminders of the therapeutic context of his verbosity. In this respect Roth's novel
resembles Cardinal's in putting the doctor-patient relationship in the
foreground as a way to represent the ongoing analytic process. Admittedly, Portnoy is far less deferential than the young French woman is to
her "petit bonhomme." Generally addressed just as "Doctor," and often
simply as "you," Spielvogel is Portnoy's projected listener. Because of his
appropriation of psychoanalytic lore, Portnoy tends to be overfamiliar
toward his analyst as if he already could figure out his unspoken reactions: "this of course you will understand, this of course is your bread
and butter" (134); "(this'll amuse you)" (223); "wouldn't you say?" (262).

In the thick Germanic accent ascribed to him in his only utterance at the end, Spielvogel is, with the ambivalence characteristic of *Portnoy's Complaint*, sited in a venerable Austro-Germanic tradition, and at the same time made to sound ludicrous. The "O" of his first name could be interpreted as referring to Portnoy's plaintive appeal to him. His last name, Spielvogel, literally "playbird," suggests perhaps a creature "to be stroked, serenaded, seduced,"[2] but it also carries a sexual connotation in the German slang "vogeln," a term for intercourse. Judging by his dependence on Spielvogel's approval and authorization it would seem that Portnoy has a largely positive transference to him.

Spielvogel has a double in the novel in a figure who is mentioned only in passing: Dr. Morris Frankel, the analyst seen by Portnoy's girlfriend, "The Monkey." His name, though rather less Germanic than "Spielvogel," sounds Jewish, while the nickname given to him by Portnoy, "Harpo," is, through its lack of respect, in sharp contrast to the adjective with which he is introduced: "illustrious" (176). This secondary analysis in *Portnoy's Complaint* appears to be wholly unproductive: the Monkey has "thrashed around on Harpo's couch" (and, incidentally, claims to have spent $50,000) without learning what she wants to know (176). That she is "waiting for him to tell her what she must do to become somebody's wife and somebody's mother" (176) reveals how primitive and misguided her expectations of therapy are. Portnoy in fact doubts whether "therapy" is the right term in this instance. Harpo is portrayed with resentment because he never says "*Anything*!" (176). The Monkey's only assurance that he is actually alive comes from the fact that he has an answering service. He does emit a few sounds that are open to diverse interpretations; his cough is taken for "confirmation" (176), whereas his occasional grunts, belches, and farts are regarded by Portnoy as indications of "a negative transference reaction on his part" (177). Dr. Frankel's allegedly obnoxious behavior serves perhaps to enhance the prestige of Spielvogel, who certainly has greater significance for Portnoy than Harpo does for the Monkey. On the other hand, how is an analyst to treat a patient whose main aim in therapy is to acquire the skill to find a husband and who believes that it is her analyst's function to "tell her" how to do so? If Portnoy's analysis verges on a travesty, the Monkey's is a parody.

The duality of analysts and patients in *Portnoy's Complaint* is complemented by the duplication of the audience. As in *Les Mots*, we as readers are eavesdropping listeners to Portnoy's confessions. His common recourse to "you" denotes us, the interlocutors extraneous to the text as well as Spielvogel, the recipient within the text. Our overhearing parallels the voyeuristic experiment with Lina, the prostitute hired in Italy to participate in a sex threesome. When the Monkey chooses to "watch" (156) the sex act between Portnoy and Lina, she figurates our position in relation to the transaction between Portnoy and Spielvogel. Just as she looks, we listen with the analyst, and face the same task as he does in constructing the verbal thicket of the analysand's outpouring.

For as in *Les Mots, Portnoy's Complaint* moves on two levels, or indeed three if the foreground situation of the present analysis is included. At one remove from this encompassing context is the linear, chronological account of Portnoy's life from childhood through adolescence to adulthood, his relationship to the Monkey, their travels to Rome and Athens, and finally his visit to Israel. This Bildungsroman aspect of the novel is interrupted by reminiscent excrescences that represent regressions prompted by the free associationism of psychoanalysis. These interspersed flashbacks are nonchronological, as Portnoy's mind darts back to various ages and crucial moments of his past. For instance, from the point in his ninth year when he has to have medical attention for a testicle that is not descending, he suddenly reverts some twenty-five years from the present to the "spring of the year Four," when he is "so small" (48) and sees his mother putting on her stockings and wants "to growl with pleasure" (49). Memories come easily to Portnoy, who revels in the opening that analysis gives him to recall the awfulness of most of the experiences that shaped him into the neurotic that he now is. His bar mitzvah jostles with a more recent celebration when he takes the Monkey to a reception at the New York mayor's residence. At age seventeen, an invitation from his college girlfriend to her home in Iowa leads to the shock of his first direct encounter with mores wholly other than those in his family. The retrospect on the softball games he used to play at ages nine, ten, and eleven, when he had "good sense" makes him wonder, "How have I come to be such an enemy and flayer of myself? And so alone!" (280). In this temporal multiplicity the organization of *Portnoy's Complaint* is determined by the analysand's stream of consciousness. The pattern of sporadic intromissions in flashbacks, followed by abrupt resumptions of the story either of his life or his analysis, causes Portnoy— and the reader—to ask in bewilderment, "Where am I?" (236). So this narrative strategy has the effect, as in *Les Mots,* of mimicking the associative processes of psychoanalysis.

But, also as in *Les Mots,* this apparent randomness has an underlying literary structure. Besides the main themes of mother and sexuality, which are ubiquitously explicit or implicit, related motifs such as Ronald Nimkin's suicide and the drama of cousin Heshie, who was killed in the war but who had proposed to marry a gentile, surface as examples of developmental routes alternative to Portnoy's (both, incidentally, end even worse than he). However, the novel's major ordering principle is that of a series of crass contrasts: within the family, between his mother and his father, and between Alex, the rebel, not yet married and settled in his early thirties, and his sister, Hannah, compliant and conventional with a nice Jewish husband and two children. In the wider world beyond the family, Jews are throughout pitted against *Goyim* (non-Jews), or even against other ethnic groups such as the Chinese, and overall, immigrants or aliens against established Americans. These antithetical opposites are summarized in Portnoy's verbal witticism when he sees himself and the Monkey as "the perfect couple: she puts the id back in Yid, I put the *oy* into *goy*" (236). The cultural, religious, and educational incommensurability of this purportedly "perfect couple" underscores the absurdity of Portnoy's claim. Yet the phrase is brilliantly apposite as the shorthand for the tensions that govern *Portnoy's Complaint:* the modern psychoanalytic "id" in conflict with the traditional Jewishness of "Yid," and the woefulness of "*oy*" with the normality imputed to "*goy*."

Contrariety, and confusion, are illustrated too in the pervasive theme of food. Sophie is described as God's "mouthpiece on earth in matters pertaining to food" (100). Because of the Jewish dietary rules, food becomes a metaphor for leading a law-abiding or -breaking life. But not only sinfulness and righteousness are at stake, so also are health and sickness, since forbidden foods are seen as a threat to well-being, even to survival. The rebellious Portnoy quickly comes to condemn "all those prohibitive dietary rules and regulations" as being conceived with nothing "else but to give us little Jewish children practice in being repressed" (89). By envisaging the observance of the dietary laws as "duty, discipline, obedience . . . self-control, sobriety" (89), Portnoy injects a moral dimension into the issue of eating. Within this framework then, it is natural to conflate eating with sex as sanctioned or prohibited modes of behavior. The connection is spelled out in the parallel between the putative actions of Portnoy's father and his own: "did he fuck between those luscious legs the gentile cashier from the office, or have I eaten my sister's chocolate pudding?" (96-97). Even more explicitly, Portnoy's mother warns him against a "BLONDIE" with the phrase "A BRILLIANT INNOCENT BABY BOY LIKE YOU, SHE'LL EAT YOU UP ALIVE!" (212). But while his mother is feeding him "koshered and bloodless" steak and "*matzoh brei*" (89; porridge of unleavened bread), Portnoy's inner desire is to transgress in the bloody meat of the "blondies."

These basic contradictions are, however, undercut by the insinuation of ambivalences. As Portnoy roams through his memories, it is by no means always possible to distinguish realities from fantasies. "What exactly transpired?" (210), the question that Portnoy poses, is also asked by readers. It defies answer because the first-person narration limits our viewpoint to that of the narrating protagonist. Some elements can be fairly readily identified as fantasy; for example, Portnoy's wish, "Oh, to be a center fielder, a center fielder—and nothing more!" (80), is a transparent adolescent longing for sporting prowess as well as for a life thought to be simple and full of glory. Mostly the scenes that Portnoy imagines, especially the dreadful diseases and afflictions that could befall him as a result of his unruly (that is, breaking the family rules) behavior, can be read as manifestations of the fears that his mother has inculcated into him. Yet overblown and farfetched though these fears patently are, for Portnoy they assume a genuinely terrifying psychic reality as he elaborates on each ghastly scenario through his overtalking. He talks himself into the possibility of the venereal diseases, blindness, and paralysis that could assail him. As a result of his vivid verbalization, the fantasy becomes to him a reality into which his eloquence draws him deeper and deeper. If psychoanalysis meant to Freud "talking people in and out of things," as he wrote in his letter to Fliess in 1888,[3] *Portnoy's Complaint* depicts an analysand talking himself, out of sheer anxiety, into disaster scenarios without granting his analyst space to talk him out of them. While seeming to rest on neat contrasts, the novel suggests too the variable interpretability, uncertainty, indeed ambiguity of human conduct. Is Sophie Portnoy actually as her son portrays her? Or is she inflated into the monstrous primarily in his mind? In this first-person monologue of psychoanalysis there is no reality other than the internal one that drives Portnoy onto the couch. In defense of his "ritualized bellyaching" he asks rhetorically, "Could I really have detested this childhood and resented those parents of mine to the same degree then as I seem to now, looking backward upon what I was from the vantage point of what I am—and am not? Is this truth I'm delivering up, or is it just plain *kvetching*? Or is *kvetching* for people like me a *form* of truth?" (105). In this hesitant acknowledgment of the relativity of his truths, Portnoy probably comes closer to truth than at any other point.

The fluctuation between reality and fantasy is partnered by another duality in the switches from the normative onward rush of monologue to the dialogue that occurs at the most dramatic high points. Roth, like Cardinal, enhances the liveliness and immediacy of his novel through these intercalations which are a central narrational strategy for converting a psychoanalysis from an indigestible record into a literary artifact. Yet, as in *Les Mots*, the scenes maintain Portnoy's subjective perspective, retrieved from his memory and presented through his eyes. Frequently the confrontations with or between his parents are shown scenically as are his futile altercations with the Monkey, who resembles his parents in remaining obstinately impervious to his arguments. While the dialogic scenes add variety and vividness to *Portnoy's Complaint*, they do not modify Portnoy's fundamental self-image as "a brainy, balding, beaky Jew, with a strong social conscience" (172). In other words, he produces no positive daydreaming wishes of self-aggrandizement after his adolescent reverie of being center fielder; he has no respite from the struggle against what he sees as the forces of stupidity, prejudice, and dogmatism surrounding him. Just as the fantasies are negative ones of possible disaster, so the scenes are always occasions of dissidence.

The only realm where Portnoy is allowed unquestioned—and unbroken—sovereignty is in the verbal, and this is also where the novel's real distinction lies. With utmost virtuosity Roth creates a dynamic, breezy, colloquial, strikingly original mode of expression as the analysand's form of speech. Deemed "the rhetoric of neurosis,"[4] it is as pronouncedly manic in its immense comic verve as neurotic in its self-incrimination. Portnoy's verbal fireworks are the ideal vehicle for his agitated anger: the barrage of questions, exclamations, suspension points are the literary equivalent to his whacking off. In a reproduction of the associative, digressive pattern of psychoanalysis, he runs on and on explosively, passionately, trying to burst the seams of language, a metaphor for his attempt to break out of the confinement of his "complaint." If his discourse has to some extent become a period piece in its cultural references to the 1960s (Gary Cooper, Alan Ladd, Margaret O'Brien, Oxydol, Errol Flynn), it nevertheless retains its sharply satirical thrust. Roth uses to good effect the resources of the printed medium to capture the inflections of Portnoy's utterance, notably in the italics and lengthy passages in capitals where the analysand waxes most emphatic. Very cleverly he has Portnoy let out some of his central self-revelations in throwaway comments placed in parentheses: "(For I have the taste for melodrama too—I am not in this family for nothing)" (14); "(so Portnoy legend has it)" (64); "(moral: nothing is never ironic, there's always a laugh lurking somewhere)" (103-4); "(I heard myself pleading, last year, this year, every year of my life)" (118); "(you want to know everything, okay, I'm telling everything)" (149); "For 'a fully normal attitude to love' (deserving of semantic scrutiny, that 'fully normal,' but to go on)" (209); "(origins, of course, holding far more fascination for the nice left-wing Jewish boy than for the proletarian girl herself")" (234); "(essentially titless women seem to be my destiny, by the way,—now, why *is* that? is there an essay somewhere I can read on that? is it of import? or shall I go on?)" (244). Such asides, while still predominantly comic, are a fine means to convey how crucial avowals in psychoanalysis may emerge obliquely, almost involuntarily. It is in parentheses that Portnoy makes statements that hint that he has a better insight into his predicament than he is generally willing to admit.

Another key concession occurs in this characteristically—and perhaps deliberately—casual manner when he grants, "everything is purple (including my prose)" (165). Here the dominant black comedy of overstatement yields suddenly to a disarming self-debunking. The ironic rhythm of *Portnoy's Complaint* is a seesaw between the need for self-inflation (and self-justification) and the incursion of self-deflation (and self-condemnation). In remembering, for example, how his mother "taught me to piss standing up" (148), Portnoy asserts that she was making his future, and so he blames her for his continuing inability to urinate in the presence of another man: "A man's character is being forged, a destiny is being shaped, . . . oh, maybe not" (149). In accusing her, he is excusing himself, yet brusquely he retreats, acknowledging that the excuse is just that, an excuse for behavior for which he is as responsible as his mother. Inscribed in the hurricane-like onslaught of Portnoy's monologue are stylistic subtleties that mirror the way in which he himself plays hide and seek with himself even more than with his analyst.

Verbal acrobatics are a hallmark of *Portnoy's Complaint*. Though the speaker may not be likeable in his circular lamentations and evasive inculpation of his parents, his rhetorical performance is so dazzling as to astound and intrigue readers. Its ingenuity is a perpetual testimony to Roth's inventiveness. A prime example is the recurrence of *oy* in various guises: a Yiddish exclamation of sorrow, sometimes of *Weltschmerz*, it is part of the "argot" (263) that pervades the novel, endowing it with local color. It is the crux of the punning contrast between "*oy*" and "*goy*" (236) in which anxiety is attributed primarily to Jews. It crops up again in the outcry "*Oy*, civilization and its discontents!" (206), a clear though reductive reference to Freud. It is the prominent element in the analysand's last name as he repeatedly considers ways to amend it. Unlike "Feibish," his sister's married name, "Portnoy" is not immediately recognizable as Jewish, thereby facilitating his forays into the world beyond that where he was raised. So he fantasizes: "'Portnoy, yes, it's an old French name, a corruption of *porte noir*, meaning black door or gate. Apparently in the Middle Ages in France the door to our family manor was painted . . .' et cetera and so forth. No, no, they will hear the *oy* at the end, and the jig will be up" (167-68). The *oy* is the give-away. Experimenting with an alternative picked from the phone book, a "totally *goy*" name—"I am Alton Peterson, I am Alton Peterson—Alton Christian Peterson? Or is that going a little too far? Alton C. Peterson?" (185)—he becomes so preoccupied with it that he falls while skating and breaks a tooth and a leg. The disguise is thus proven a poor fit. Ultimately, in Israel he dubs himself "Portnoise! Portnose! Portnoy-oy-oy-oy-oy!" (304) in what seems like a rueful, still self-despising gesture. At this point he also mentions his first name, Alexander, whose distinctly heroic overtones, emphasized earlier in the ironic designation, "Alexander the Great!" (70), are strangely conjoined to the woebegone *oy* of his last name. His contradictory, problematical name is set off against the plainness of Mary Jane Reed, nicknamed the Monkey because only "Monkey business" (232) can bring them together. But Portnoy's scorn for the nicknames of the friends of another girlfriend who had been to Vassar, "Poody and Pip and Pebble, Shrimp and Brute and Tug, Squeek, Bumpo, Baba," dismissed as sounding like "Donald Duck's nephews" (263), manifests a certain cynical superiority to that arch-*goyish* world too.

Portnoy's most vigorous and often virulent linguistic bravado is directed against his parents. "These two are the outstanding producers and packagers of guilt in our time! They render it from me like fat from a chicken!" (39); "my mother is on the phone for days at a stretch and has to be fed intravenously, her mouth is going at such a rate about her Alex" (120). "What was it with these Jewish parents—because I am not in this boat alone, oh no, I am on the biggest troop ship afloat . . . only look in through the portholes and see us there, stacked to the bulkheads in our bunks, moaning and groaning with such pity for ourselves, the sad and watery-eyed sons of Jewish parents, sick to the gills from rolling through these heavy seas of guilt—so I sometimes envisage us, me and my fellow wailers, melancholics, and wise guys, still in steerage" (132). "He has *a mother who works*. Mine, remember, patrols the six rooms of our apartment the way a guerilla army moves across its own countryside—there's not a single closet or drawer of mine whose contents she hasn't a photographic sense of" (194). "*She never raised her voice in an argument*. Can you imagine the impression made on me at seventeen, fresh from my engagement with The Jack and Sophie Portnoy Debating Society? Who had ever heard of such an approach to controversy?" (244). Not until his visit to Kay Campbell's family in Iowa does he realize that "conversation isn't just crossfire where you shoot and get shot at. Where you've got to duck for your life and aim to kill! Words aren't only bombs and bullets— no, they're little gifts, containing *meanings*!" (250).

Portnoy's words, however, *are* bombs and bullets; in this respect, too, he is like his mother. Only the doctor's gentle phrase at the end cuts off the assault when Portnoy, worn out at last, can produce no more than a "pure howl" in his sustained "Aaaaaaaaaaaaaaaaaaaaaaaaaaaaaaaaaa aaaaaaaaaaaaaaaaaaaaaaaaaaaaaaaaaaaaaaaaaaaaaaaaaaaaaaaaaaaaaa aaaaaaaaaaaaaaaaaaaaaaaaaaaaaaaaaaaaaaaaaaaaaaaaaaaaaaaaaaaaaa aaaaaaaaaaaaaaaaaaaaaaaaaaaaaaaaaaaaaaaaaaaaaaaaaaaaaaaaaaaaaa aaaaaaaaaaaaaaaaaaaaaaaaaaaaaaaaaaaaaaaaaaaaaaaaaaaaaaaaaaaaaa aaaaaaaaaaaaaaaaaaaaaaaaaaaaaaaaaaahhhh!!!!!" (309). Finally, finally, this chronic overtalker has to cede, and only then, it is suggested, can the real analysis begin. This surprising, brilliant closing abruptly throws Portnoy's entire monologue into question. If the analysis with Dr. Spielvogel is now about to begin, what is the status of Portnoy's preceding talk, talk, talk? The irony at the heart of the narration in Portnoy's unwitting likeness to his mother comes into the forefront here again in another parallel between Sophie and her son. Just as she verges on a caricature of motherhood, so his obsessive overtalking is a grotesque representation of psychoanalysis. Both are extravagant, ludicrous, tragicomical, overdrawn, yet just sufficiently credible to be compelling.

5

Resisting Psychoanalysis

Italo Svevo's *The Confessions of Zeno*

> I never resist temptation, because I have found that things
> that are bad for me do not tempt me.
> —George Bernard Shaw

"I remember very little about that re-education. I submitted to it, and every time I left his room, shook myself like a dog coming out of the water. Like the dog, I remained wet, but was never drenched" (358). These are the graphic words in which the narrator-protagonist of *The Confessions of Zeno* describes his response to the "re-education" supposed to be achieved through his analysis by Dr. S. The comparison of the analysand to a dog undergoing training is a view of psychoanalysis not only reductive but quite mistaken since analysis seeks first and foremost to make patients recognize the sources of their discomfort as coming from within, not to impose re-education from without. Zeno quickly admits, "I have finished with psychoanalysis. After practising it assiduously for six whole months, I find I am worse than before" (350).

This skepticism about the therapeutic efficacy of psychoanalysis is expressed in Northern Italy just after the outbreak of World War I. *The Confessions of Zeno* was published under the name Italo Svevo, which means the Italian German, the pseudonym of Ettore Schmitz (1861-1928), who came from a prosperous business family in Trieste and was destined to follow in his father's footsteps. Sent to learn English at the local Berlitz school in preparation for a sales trip, Svevo had as his teacher James Joyce, who encouraged his ambitions to become a writer. His fluency in German and his situation in Trieste, then a part of the Habsburg Empire ruled from Vienna, gave him ready access to Freud's writings, which he read from about 1908 onward, though in a haphazard manner. Svevo was instrumental in introducing Freud into Italy, yet he always considered his theories more valuable for novelists than for patients.[1] He never fully either accepted or rejected Freud, maintaining a characteristically doubting ambivalence; when he sent Freud a copy of his novel, he was disappointed to receive no response. The plot of *The Confessions of Zeno* is overtly dependent on the practice of analysis, though in a questioning, ultimately subversive way. By maintaining that he got "wet" but "never drenched," Zeno implies that the analytic experience only touched the surface of his being without going deep enough to affect the core of his personality.

In pivoting on a resistance to analysis, *The Confessions of Zeno* departs from *Les Mots* and *Portnoy's Complaint*, although there are also some similarities. The major literary feature that it shares with the two later works is the first-person format. While Zeno is also quite an overtalker, his account of his life overlaps with the story of his analysis only in part. Dr. S., because he has to be away from Trieste for some time, persuades his patient "to write his autobiography" in hopes that this "would be a good preparation for his treatment" by helping "in the effort to recollect his past" (25). The doctor evidently fears this may prove difficult for Zeno because he is "old" (25), in contradistinction to the generally younger candidates for psychoanalysis. Whether Zeno's age proves a factor in his resistance remains moot. At first obedient to the doctor's wishes, Zeno writes about his life in chronological order, as a picaresque sequence, beginning with an attempt to evoke memories of his childhood, going on to his struggles to conquer his addiction to cigarettes, the scene of his father's death, the story of his marriage, his attachment to both his wife and his mistress, and his business partnership with his brother-in-law. As he gets caught up in the events of his life and career, he fairly soon forgets the purpose of his writing as a preliminary to therapy. After the third section, "The Death of My Father" (49-73), the theme of psychoanalysis disappears completely from the narrative until the closing chapter, "Psychoanalysis" (350-78), only about a third of which is devoted to his analysis and his precipitous apostasy.

However, despite the relatively small space given to psychoanalysis, it is of crucial importance to *The Confessions of Zeno* in forming the frame for the whole narrative, a kind of scaffold for Zeno to construct his life story. Corresponding to the preamble in *Portnoy's Complaint*, the "Preface" emanates from the analyst, the anonymous Dr. S., who introduces himself as "the doctor who is sometimes spoken of in rather unflattering terms in this novel" (25). He explains the unusual circumstances that have led to the writing of Zeno's autobiography at his instigation as well as to its publication on his initiative. Obviously, the entire situation is a breach of professional etiquette and confidentiality that throws Dr. S. into an even worse light than Zeno's "unflattering terms" that prompted this action on his part. His first line of defense is by reference to the recognized phenomenon of resistance when he asserts that "anyone familiar with psychoanalysis will know to what to attribute my patient's hostility." In his apology for having persuaded Zeno to write his autobiography, he concedes that "students of psychoanalysis will turn up their noses at such an unorthodox proceeding," yet he still believes the idea to have been a good one. The responsibility for the poor outcome is shifted onto the patient, who suddenly threw "up his cure just at the most interesting point, thus cheating me of the fruits of my long and patient analysis of these memoirs." Although Dr. S.'s "Preface" comprises a mere half-page, he discredits himself more and more in the course of his explanation, revealing himself to be egocentric, unethical, and spiteful to boot, for he has taken the step of publishing his patient's memoirs as an act of revenge. But he still harbors the hope that Zeno will resume his treatment, and on this condition he declares himself ready "to share the financial spoils with him." This proviso totally subverts the idea of the therapeutic alliance, basic to any form of psychotherapy, into a commercial partnership to reap the profits of a disreputable venture.

The "Preface," though it stands at the opening, functions as a retrospective structural device for the ensuing narrative in much the same way as the preamble to *Portnoy's Complaint*. However, it impinges more directly on the therapy than in Roth's novel. For whereas Dr. Spielvogel is characterized by his article as a serious, at worst somewhat too solemn analyst, his counterpart in *The Confessions of Zeno* is so unprofessional and despicable as to warrant his patient's resistance. If it is the analysand who accuses himself by excusing himself in *Portnoy's Complaint*, here it is the analyst who incriminates himself. The "Preface" to Svevo's novel can be read as a jocose, farcical, preposterous image of the relationship between analyst and analysand, a debunking of the process of psychoanalysis as resulting in reciprocal hostility instead of healing. But the irony has a sinister aspect too in projecting the negative potential of psychoanalysis. "The strategies of Svevo's irony are so elaborate . . . ," readers have been warned, "that it is important not to mistake his tone."[2]

But precisely because of the complexity of those strategies, it is difficult at times to determine a single particular tone when more than one is a possibility, as in the "Preface." Is the irony here directed locally against Dr. S. or globally, as it were, against psychoanalysis as a therapy?

Nor is it very clear why Zeno entered into analysis in the first place. His avowed reason, about which he speaks to Dr. S. at the outset, is his "weakness for smoking" (29). At the time of the novel's action, this would be a minor peccadillo, since the health hazards of smoking were not suspected. Zeno himself has the shrewd intuition that his addiction to cigarettes has been a convenient subterfuge for him:

> While I sit here analysing myself a sudden doubt assails me: did I really love cigarettes so much because I was able to throw all the responsibility for my own incompetence on them? Who knows whether, if I had given up smoking, I should really have become the strong perfect man I imagined? Perhaps it was this very doubt that bound me to my vice; because life is so much more pleasant if one is able to believe in one's own latent greatness. I only put this forward as a possible explanation of my youthful weakness, but without very great conviction. (33)

His "youthful weakness" is primarily indecisiveness as he switches from the study of law to chemistry, and back again to law. Later he shuttles in similar fashion between his wife and his mistress, making promises to himself about each of them that he cannot keep. His lack of resolution, together with his notorious absentmindedness, leads his father to order that he be excluded from the family business. From a Freudian perspective, the recondite source of Zeno's discomfort lies in the father/son conflict. When Dr. S. comes up with the diagnosis "exactly the same as the one that Sophocles drew up long ago for poor Aedipus: I was in love with my mother and wanted to murder my father" (351), Zeno feels in part "enraptured" and "exalted" at being placed in such an illustrious pedigree reaching right back to the mythological age; but he also dismisses this diagnosis with a wholehearted laugh as he recalls "my love for my mother, and the great respect and affection I had for my father" (351). Is this resistance or denial or an example of the mixture of "truths and falsehoods" (25) that Dr. S. discerns in his patient's confessions? In contrast to the narrator in *Les Mots,* whose self-image is profoundly amended by her discoveries in analysis, Zeno remains obstinately entrenched in his stance, scoffing at his analyst's interpretation.

Dr. S.'s diagnosis seems at first sight to smack of cliché. On the other hand, Zeno's recollections in the chapter "The Death of My Father" (49–73) lend more credence to the analyst's hypothesis than the analysand is willing to grant. For, in one of the cardinal ironies of this narrative, the extent to which Zeno was implicated in his father's death is uncertain. He admits that they had always been distant: "Up to the time of my father's death I had never devoted myself to him. I made no effort to get in touch with him; I even avoided him as far as I could without giving offence" (50). His father disapproves of him, deploring especially his "supposed contempt for serious things" (52). The scene of his father's dying is fraught with ambiguity:

> He sat straight up. I in my turn was startled by his cry and re-laxed the pressure of my hand, so that he succeeded in sitting on the edge of the bed, facing me. I think he was furious at finding himself held down by force, even for a moment, and that he had the impression that it was I who was depriving him of the air he needed so much, just as I was shutting out the light by standing, while he was sitting down. With a supreme effort he struggled to his feet, raised his arm high above his head, and brought it down with the whole weight of his falling body on my cheek. Then he slipped from the bed on to the floor and lay there—dead! (71)

Did Zeno, at least figuratively, murder his father? Was the anger that the son aroused an immediate precipitating factor in the death? Even though he does not realize at first that his father has expired, Zeno feels his heart contract with grief—and guilt as he cries "like a child who has been punished" (72). Since his father is gone, "it was impossible for me to prove my innocence" (72). Reasoning is inconclusive: "it was out of the question that my father, who was not in his right mind, could have taken such perfect aim at my cheek with the direct intention of punishing me. But how could I ever know for certain that my reasoning was just?" (72). The episode is cleverly designed to leave an aperture of doubt that provides some basis for Dr. S.'s postulate. In resisting the possibility that he maybe wished for his father's demise, Zeno refuses to confront a very painful issue. Instead, he lays the blame on the attending doctor whose orders he had been carrying out. "All that remains to me of those days is my hatred of the doctor, and that will never die" (65). The hatred for that doctor prefigures his negative transference to Dr. S.

Zeno's resistance to troubling interpretations of crucial incidents in his life nurtures his chronic hypochondria. He somatizes his psychological malaise, converting it into a series of physical symptoms. The most striking of these is the imitative limp he suddenly develops after a chance meeting with an old friend who has to use a crutch because of rheumatism in his leg, and who expostulates to him the complicatedness of the fifty-four muscles involved in movements of the leg: "I limped as I left the café, and for several days afterwards walking became a burden to me and even caused me a certain amount of pain" (108). The limp follows immediately on a setback in his courtship and reasserts itself thereafter as an expression of frustrated desire, but it wanes once he is successfully established. Other complaints exhibit a similar psychosomatic pattern. He is subject to sporadic attacks of an intense pain that darts about "from my thigh to the back of my head" (137). As in the limp, there is a distinct correlation between the bouts of pain and an unavowed psychological injury. The "turmoil of the nerves" (135), for example, is first provoked by two caricatures of him executed by his handsome and manipulative brother-in-law. Zeno's gastric disturbances, though on the whole less bothersome, fall into the same category of vague, fluctuating physical ailments. The bad taste he has in his mouth for several days after uttering an indiscretion can be interpreted as a punishment fantasy, a guilty conscience made palpable in a symbolic, corporeal form. A compensatory mechanism of another type underlies Zeno's overeating and constant indigestion during his engagement to Augusta, the ugly sister, whom he marries with considerable hesitation. His own pseudorationalization is that he feels compelled "to act a passion I did not feel" (146). By causing himself indigestion he is transmuting and objectifying his mental unease at the forthcoming marriage into bodily discomfort.

The multiplicity and instability of Zeno's symptoms, their defiance of diagnosis or treatment, and their repeated coincidence with psychological hurts all strongly point to what would at that time have been designated as hysteria. While the condition was ascribed primarily to women, Charcot already documented some cases among men, and Freud was certainly aware of its occurrence among males. However, this view was by no means widely accepted. The talk that Freud gave to the

Viennese Medical Society in 1886 on his observations of Charcot's work in Paris met with a mixture of contempt and incredulity because he reported that one of the things that had impressed him most was "der Nachweis . . . des häufigen Vorkommens der Hysterie bei Männern"[3] ("evidence of the frequent occurrence of hysteria in men"). Only gradually was the concept of hysteria dissociated from the old notion of the wandering womb as the etiology of the syndrome.[4] "Hysteria" is now in eclipse, dropped from *DSM-IV* (1994) as a separate disease and replaced in psychiatric terminology by designations that are at once more open (that is, devoid of judgmental overtones) and more specific. Zeno's complaints meet all the differential diagnostic criteria in *DSM-IV* for conversion disorder, namely: one or more symptoms affecting voluntary motor or sensory function that suggest a neurological or other general medical condition (the limp); psychological factors associated with the symptom because the initiation or exacerbation of the symptom is preceded by conflicts or other stressors; the symptom is not intentionally produced or feigned; it cannot after appropriate investigation be fully explained by a general medical condition; and it causes clinically significant distress or impairment in social, occupational, or other important areas of functioning (457). Conversion disorder itself falls into the wider class of anxiety disorders, a rubric into which Zeno's additional episodes of insomnia, dizziness, and sensations of suffocation would fit well. His "disease" (36) would therefore be acknowledged in contemporary psychiatric practice as a recognizable mental disorder in need of therapy. But that therapy would not nowadays take the form of psychoanalysis, as it did in Svevo's time, nor would the diagnosis be an Oedipus complex. Zeno's resistance can thus be seen from the vantage point of today as an instinctive defense mechanism against a treatment he senses to be inappropriate.

Nevertheless, he does make some efforts for a while to comply with Dr. S.'s instructions to recollect his past by writing his autobiography. His "Introduction" opens with the interrogative, "See my childhood?" (27). His tone is querying because his childhood lies over fifty years back, and to his aging "presbyobic eyes" it is obscured by many obstacles. The comic aspect as well as the artificiality of his endeavor is in the forefront here. His difficulties confirm the analyst's fears that the patient's age might be a hindrance. To circumvent this problem, Dr. S. has advised his prospective analysand "not to insist on looking so far back" (27) since recent experiences could be equally valuable. It is important to note that in the beginning Zeno is not at all uncooperative, although he sets about his assigned task in a misguided manner; he buys and reads a textbook about psychoanalysis in hopes of making the doctor's work easier. The book, while not hard to understand, proves "very boring" (27); what is more, reading about psychoanalysis may have been a counterproductive strategy tending to impede Zeno's spontaneity. Stretched out after lunch in an easy chair, pencil and paper in hand, he feels wholly relaxed: "I tried to let myself go completely. The result was that I fell into a deep sleep and experienced nothing except a great sense of refreshment, and the curious sensation of having seen something important while I was asleep. But what it was I could not remember" (27). There is a whimsical irony in this contrary but by no means unpredictable failure of free association: when an elderly man stretches out in an easy chair after a probably substantial Italian lunch, he is more likely to go to sleep than to recuperate his past. Yet Zeno's wholly normal reaction is an inauspicious, even an ominous start to his analysis, not least because his equanimity indicates an absence of inner turmoil. So his initial experiment foreshadows his resistance and the precipitous termination of his analysis. At his second attempt the next day, in a half-waking state, he invokes the textbook's assurance that psychoanalysis enables recall of earliest childhood. This time he does see "an infant in long clothes," but as it "does not bear the slightest resemblance to me" (28), he concludes it must be his sister-in-law's baby, born a few weeks previously. The "Introduction" moves toward a close with a reprise of its opening theme, now, however, in the disbelieving, exclamatory rather than the hopeful, interrogative mode: "Remember my infancy, indeed!" (28). The droll deflation is intensified by Zeno's regret that it is not in his power to warn the infant "how important it is for your health and your intelligence that you should forget nothing" (28). With his resolution "to try again tomorrow" (28), the chapter ends with the prospect of a third attempt after two failures to induce the memories essential to psychoanalysis.

Zeno's lack of success in remembering his childhood results in the absence in the "Introduction" of the live flashbacks that form a major means to portray the processes of psychoanalysis in *Les Mots* and *Portnoy's Complaint*. Such flashbacks and the associated dialogic scenes do occur in the next two sections of *The Confessions of Zeno*, "The Last Cigarette" and "The Death of My Father." At the beginning of both these chapters the enframing fiction of the forthcoming analysis is mentioned; in one instance, Zeno invokes the doctor's advice, and in the second he regrets not having asked him about another technical matter. So the doctor is present *in absentia*, as it were ("away on a holiday," 49), just as he is there but not visible in an actual analysis, seated behind the couch. His injunction to "Write away!" (29) clearly corresponds to the customary exhortation to free associate. References to the writing process and with it to the analysis punctuate the first of these two sections as Zeno notes, "I come back discouraged to the table" (29) where he works, or "while I sit here analysing myself" (33). No such phrases interrupt the account of his relationship to his father in the second chapter; we may conclude either that writing has become more of a habit to him so that he no longer needs to reflect on the immediate activity, or that his recollections of his father are so engrossing as to shut out other thoughts, or perhaps a combination of the two. Either way, after the opening of the second chapter the theme of psychoanalysis disappears utterly for nearly three hundred pages. In this respect *The Confessions of Zeno* differs significantly from *Les Mots* and *Portnoy's Complaint*, where the analytic situation is kept in the foreground throughout. The divergence stems from the discrepancy in the fiction's format: both Cardinal's narrator and Portnoy are actually in the process of undergoing an analysis, whereas Zeno is writing his autobiography in preparation for therapy. Consequently, as he grows more absorbed in the happenings of his life, he forgets, in the doctor's absence, the original purpose of his writing as a mere preliminary exercise and with it the projected analysis. The central part of the novel conforms more to the genre of a fictive autobiography than to that of a narrative of psychotherapy; the present time of the action coincides with writing, not with therapy sessions.

Dr. S.'s prediction that by writing Zeno "will see soon how you begin to get a clear picture of yourself" (29) is indeed fulfilled, though ironically, in a manner very different from what the doctor anticipated. Presumably Zeno's confessions were to uncover his weaknesses; his presenting symptom of addiction to cigarettes was to lead to the unearthing of other obsessions, inhibitions, or complexes. And at first this seems to be happening when Zeno starts to wonder, in the passage cited earlier, whether his smoking is not just an excuse for his failure to achieve his "latent greatness" (33). But the act of recording his life induces a change of self-image in a direction certainly not expected by Dr. S. Instead of revealing weaknesses, as Portnoy's psychological stocktaking does, Zeno's shows more and more that he has actually been far more successful than he himself believed. Already in his efforts to woo the beautiful Ada, he asserts, "I am not a bad man. . . . I am rather eccentric, but I can easily cure myself of that" (129). Here for the first time the possibility of a self-implemented "cure" is held out, even though the idea needs to be taken with a grain of salt since it is part of a courtship campaign. Yet a self-cure is precisely what Zeno achieves in the long run by the cumulative correction of his self-perception as a result of his examination of his life. The pejorative view of himself, which he has unquestioningly derived from his father's disapproval of him, is superseded by a much more positive self-concept as he comes to realize how well his life has turned out. The plain Augusta, whom he marries almost by accident (having flirted with her foot under the table instead of with her sister's, as he intended), proves an excellent wife and mother, while the beautiful Ada rapidly declines into illness so that she has to be sent away to a sanatorium. In business, too, he is more astute and lucky than his flashy brother-in-law, Guido, who lands the family in debt and commits suicide. When Zeno takes charge and by adroit speculation manages to restore financial stability, he is hailed by his in-laws as "the best man in our family, all our hope and trust is in you" (302). Even his absentmindedness produces a felicitous mishap when he forgets to sell sugar shares, as he had been instructed, and they rise astronomically to yield a handsome profit. Thus the outcome of his writing is not the disclosure of a burden of deficits, as happens with Portnoy's overtalking, but rather the development of a wholly new self-esteem. His hypochondria is corrected by his wife's laughing comment that he is "a *malade imaginaire*" (162), a judgment that he gradually comes to accept. In the end, Zeno, the clown whom no one—including himself—takes seriously, and who is constantly ailing, emerges with a happy marriage, reasonable health, and a respectable business. A series of reversals of fortune in the downfall of the initially glamorous Ada and Guido, and the concomitant ascendancy of the Chaplinesque bungler Zeno, shape the novel's essentially ironic structure.

The clarification and revision of his life history, effected by his writing, ultimately render psychotherapy superfluous. The negative transferences that have developed from Zeno's bad experiences with doctors through the years of his hypochondria are all finally projected onto Dr. S., who becomes the butt of his rising anger. Finding himself "worse than before" after six months of analysis (350), he abruptly breaks off the therapy by sending a note to say that he is prevented from coming for a few days: he dare not face the doctor because his "rage" is by then so intense that "I am afraid I should end by assaulting him" (350). Dr. S.'s diagnosis of an Oedipus complex prompts not only scorn for him, but a radical disillusionment with psychoanalysis in its entirety: "now that I have seen through it, and know that it is nothing but a stupid illusion, a foolish trick that might take in an hysterical old woman, how can I any longer endure to be in the company of that ridiculous man, with his would-be penetrating eye, and the intolerable conceit that allows him to group all the phenomena in the world round his grand new theory?" (350-51). The very vehemence of the patient's resistance could itself be interpreted in a Freudian vein as confirmation that a distressing trauma has been exposed. However, the first-person narration of *The Confessions of Zeno* precludes any information about Dr. S.'s responses or surmises at this juncture other than what Zeno chooses to tell. The therapist is here silenced while the patient has the freedom to overtalk. The doctor is made to appear pusillanimous as well as ludicrous. According to Zeno, the doctor confesses "that during the whole of his long practice he had never before met with such violent emotion" (351), to which Zeno adds, "That was why he was in such a hurry to say that I was cured" (351). The antipathy is evidently reciprocal; the "Preface" already shows Dr. S.'s strong negative countertransference to this patient. Both are eager to terminate the therapy, a necessary step, for "all sincerity has disappeared between the doctor and me" (351). Zeno takes to inventing dreams and shamming feelings till "in the end I felt quite worn out by this incessant duel with the doctor whom I was paying" (360). It is another of the ironic reversals in this novel that the therapeutic alliance here inverts into a "duel," aggravated by resentment at the cost of a treatment Zeno has come to regard as harmful. As the analysand's resistance escalates, he brands the analyst's theory an "edifice of false charges and suspicions" (360). In its place he advances his own version, a parodistic echo of Dr. S's diagnosis of him: "I wonder why he took such a violent dislike to me. He is probably an hysteric, who avenges himself for having lusted after his mother, by tormenting innocent people" (360).

But things are never simple in Svevo's novel; Zeno's abandonment of psychoanalysis still has a sting-in-the-tail sequel. The "duel" between him and Dr. S. has precipitated an increase in his smoking as well as insomnia. The circularity is obvious: the addiction that was his initial presenting symptom has only been heightened by the stress of the analysis. His "one thought now is how to recover from the treatment" for "I must put a stop to all this folly, unless I want to end in a lunatic asylum" (362).

The overstatement may be crass, but the point is made: psychoanalysis has been making him more unbalanced mentally. His first step is to avoid all dreams and memories, and his second is to consult old Dr. Paoli, to whom he dare not admit that he had made a fool of himself, at his age, by being "taken in by such quackery" (360). Yet it is the shrewd and cunning family practitioner who, at one fell swoop, frightens him into giving up smoking by telling him that he has developed diabetes. If the ethics of such a maneuver are dubious, its efficacy is beyond doubt. In another typical irony, Dr. Paoli's primitive trick accomplishes what Dr. S.'s sophisticated method had been unable to achieve. Zeno's final verdict on psychoanalysis is pronounced with the new name he gives it: "psychical adventure, . . . that is just what it is. When one starts such an analysis, it is like entering a wood, not knowing whether one is going to meet a brigand or a friend. Nor is one quite sure which it has been, after the adventure is over" (361).

So is Dr. S. "a brigand" or "a friend"? This is one of many ambiguities resistant to resolution because the narrative is entirely from the patient's perspective so that readers come to experience frustrations corresponding to the narrator's. Arguments can be adduced for either view: on the one hand, Dr. S.'s demeanor, as revealed in the "Preface," is certainly that of "a brigand." On the other hand, Zeno's bad relationship to his father and his guilt at his own possible role in his death suggest that Dr. S. may not have been so far off the mark. Perhaps his eye was not "would-be penetrating" (351) but genuinely so; we have, after all, only Zeno's word for it, and he is by this stage so full of anger as to be very suspect in regard to the reliability of his judgment. The analysand's "weaknesses," notably his lack of seriousness and his absentmindedness, may have provided him with the grounds for avoiding the adult responsibilities in business, for instance, for which he has been made to feel inadequate. His subsequent success shows that these weaknesses were misprisions that could have been amended by effective analysis.

The prospects for a favorable course of analysis are stymied, in yet another irony, by the very strategy that Dr. S. devises to get it started: writing. The writing that was to be an overture to the talking cure displaces the cure itself. For Zeno becomes addicted to it. He is extremely frustrated by the doctor's prohibition on writing once the analysis proper gets under way: "he asserted that during the cure I must not examine myself except in his presence, as any self-examination not controlled by him would only strengthen my resistances, and prevent me from being able to give myself up completely" (350). By then he cannot "give himself up completely," and develops resistances because he had already become accustomed to confiding in his "beloved notebooks" (350); significantly, he returns to them as soon as he abandons the analysis. The provisional substitute, introduced to bridge the time of the doctor's absence, turns out to be so productive a vehicle for self-exploration that it ousts the orthodox procedure. Finally Zeno proclaims, "I am cured. I not only have no desire to practice psychoanalysis, but no need to do so. . . . I have realized that being well is a matter of conviction, and that it is a mere day-dreamer's fantasy to try and get cured otherwise than by self-persuasion" (376).

The Confessions of Zeno offers another image of "just talk" alongside its serious endorsement in *Les Mots* and the grotesque raillery of *Portnoy's Complaint.* Svevo's ubiquitous irony forecloses any univalent interpretation so that readers are left with a range of options: is Zeno so recalcitrant a patient as to thwart the analyst's every approach? is he successful in attaining self-transcendence through his writing and his own irony? is Dr. S. a well-intentioned but inept analyst driven to desperate extremes by his patient's evasiveness? or does his vindictiveness indicate that he is poorly suited to his profession? The only certainty is the satirical momentum that animates this novel and ridicules any therapy other than that achieved by self-persuasion. The central flaw in this ideal is its refutation of a cardinal principle of psychotherapy: the necessity of a detached listener with the capacity to assess and respond to the patient's utterances. In *The Confessions of Zeno* we as readers are, by the analyst's default, thrust into that role and left to figure out as best we can the perplexities we face. So the narrative replicates its patient's resistance to full analysis.

6

Game for Therapy

David Lodge's *Therapy*

Only the insane take themselves quite seriously.
—Max Beerbohm

"I'm game for almost any kind of therapy except chemotherapy" (67), Laurence Passmore declares, and indeed he has a full schedule: "On Mondays I see Roland for Physiotherapy, on Tuesdays I see Alexandra for Cognitive Behaviour Therapy, and on Fridays I have either aromatherapy or acupuncture. Wednesdays and Thursdays I'm usually in London, but then I see Amy, which is a sort of therapy too, I suppose" (14-15). He has even tried "Inversion Therapy" (27) as one of several treatments for baldness; it consists of hanging upside down for several minutes to make the blood rush to the head so as to stimulate hair growth. Although he attends to all these varieties of therapy regularly, none of them appears to do him much good. His random, almost scattershot approach raises the question whether he takes therapy at all seriously. The alignment of his psychotherapy with aromatherapy and inversion therapy immediately reduces its stature and potential significance in Passmore's life. The seriocomic brio of Lodge's latest novel, published in 1995, captures the antics of a man who has achieved great worldly success but who has so little self-knowledge that he is hardly capable of beginning the search for his real self, and grasps for help from any kind of therapy that crosses his path. His credence, however temporary, in "Inversion Therapy" conveys in farcical guise his particular mixture of desperation, gullibility, and cheerful resilience.

In early middle age, with a figure that has earned him the nickname "Tubby," Passmore, has rocketed to fame and fortune with the popularity of the television serial "The People Next Door," which he has devised and for which he is the scriptwriter. He owns a fine house in the Midlands, an apartment in London, and a luxurious car; his two children are launched in adult life, and his wife has a fulfilling career. He has risen to these heights from a lower-middle-class background despite the fact that he took little advantage of his educational opportunities, leaving school early to work as a glorified errand boy in the office of a big theatrical impresario. He loves show business with "its febrile excitements, the highs and lows of hits and flops" (245). The very instability of this environment with its universal role-playing is congenial to a man who has always been uncertain of his own personality. In his adolescence, for instance, though a Protestant, he joined the youth club of the local Catholic church in order to pursue Maureen, a girl to whom he was attracted. Currently, his business associate and (mostly) Platonic girlfriend, Amy, is a gifted casting director, who can envisage any actor in other roles. Tubby's chameleonlike character makes him on the whole easygoing and good-natured; it also makes him "game for almost any kind of therapy."

The immediate impetus to seek out his therapies is a pain in his knee, which had begun about a year before and has troubled him sporadically ever since. An arthroscopic procedure with a ninety-five percent success rate has provided relief for only a short time. His surgeon, assuring him that there is no reason for the continued pain, describes it as "idiopathic patella chondromalacia," which is translated into "pain in the knee, and idiopathic means it's peculiar to you, old boy" (12). He prefers his physical therapist's explanation: "You've got Internal Derangement of the Knee. That's what the orthopaedic surgeons call it amongst themselves. Internal Derangement of the Knee. I.D.K. I Don't Know" (13). The vacuity of this diagnosis, beneath its grandiloquent phraseology, both satirizes the medical profession and introduces the theme of lack of knowledge. The vague, initial physical presenting symptom is immediately linked to the psychological as Tubby wishes he knew "what's the matter with me. I don't mean my knee. I mean my head. My mind. My soul" (4–5). He finds the knee a useful cover: when "you don't want to say 'terminally depressed,' but don't feel like pretending that you are brimming over with happiness either, you can always complain about your knee" (13–14). So the psychosomatic dimension of the knee is early on strongly hinted.

That Tubby had some four or five years previously had psychotherapy

for depression is not revealed until midway through the novel when his
wife tells how a marriage counselor whom they had consulted had recommended that he should have treatment. Then he saw a Dr. Wilson
for some six months, and seemed better for a while. Now his general
practitioner has referred him to Dr. Alexandra Marples, who insists on
designating herself not as a psychiatrist but as a cognitive behavior therapist. Her orientation is categorically non-Freudian; instead of trying to
uncover the hidden causes of a neurosis, she treats the symptoms that
are making the patient feel miserable. As Tubby's doctor puts it, "She's
very practical. Doesn't waste time poking around in your unconscious,
asking you about potty training, or whether you ever saw your parents
having it off together, that sort of thing" (16). She conducts therapy in a
handsome, high-ceilinged office, seated across ten feet of deep-pile grey
carpet from the patient on either side of the fireplace, where a gas fire of
imitation coals burns throughout the winter months, and a vase of fresh
cut flowers stands in summer. Tubby relates well, almost fondly to her,
partly because she is a fine-looking woman, "a rather beautiful, long-
lashed female giraffe drawn by Walt Disney" (17). He thinks of her as
"my current shrink" (14), although he realizes that she would resent that
word. He enjoys punning on her name, playing with "Marbles" for
"Marples" and with the notion that if she were to move or retire, he
could claim to have lost his Marbles. By comparing her to a giraffe and
toying with her name, Tubby asserts his own power and diminishes hers.
Her gender is important insofar as he sees her as a woman ("beautiful,
long-lashed") more than as a professional. Is his flippancy continued or
counteracted by the compulsive care with which he chooses a tie for his
next session with her? A plain dark blue might signal giving in to depression, whereas a bright one might be taken as a sign that he had got
over it. Here the satire is aimed at the tendency to the overinterpretation
of minor details in psychotherapy. But the choice of tie (and the refusal
to dispense with one altogether, an option the therapist puts forward)
denotes too that Tubby has some measure of respect for her. He does not
play games with her elegant first name which carries resonances of
Alexander the Great as well as intimations of Britain's revered Queen
Alexandra (1844-1925, consort of Edward VII) and her namesake, the
well-liked princess of our day. The fact that Tubby always refers to her
by her first name shows a certain familiarity that partakes of both affection and slight condescension.

Tubby's agonizing over the appropriate tie is open to several differ-

ent readings: as an indication of his fastidiousness, of his desire to con-
form to the norms of the class into which he has risen, of his perspicacity in realizing the implications of the signals he might be sending, or,
finally, as he sees it, of his "pathological indecision" (17). The therapist
straightaway pounces on the negative self-image projected in "pathological," but Tubby defends his term on the grounds of the triviality of
wasting half an hour of his life anguishing about apparently so slight a
matter. Indecision is one of the complaints that has sent him into therapy.
Beyond that, he suffers from a diffuse malaise, a dissatisfaction with
himself that is in crass contrast to the success he has achieved. Perhaps,
however, that very success has contributed to the mid-life crisis he has
begun to face at this point. The comfortable, though slightly stale routine of his weekly commute from Rummidge to London, his stolid marriage, his nonaffair with Amy, his formulaic television serial: all are
disrupted in the course of the narrative. His wife leaves him and eventually opts for another man; the leading lady of his show is determined to
return to the theater, and the soap opera can hardly survive without her;
his attempt to sexualize his relationship with Amy leads to the end of
their expedient friendship. The augury of this widespread dislocation is
the pain in his knee, the transparent symbol of all manner of unspecified
internal derangements. His loss of "the knack of just living, without being anxious or depressed" (16) is as puzzling and sudden an affliction as
that in his knee. The connection between the two is spelled out when he
experiences "two spasms in the knee, . . . one sharp enough to make me
cry out" (69) as he recalls the earlier episode of anxiety when he had
developed irritable bowel syndrome, another conversion reaction. The
parallelism is confirmed when Amy asks in the same breath, "How's the
knee? . . . And how's the *Angst*?" (43); the one is the cipher for the other
since Tubby has become "a really dedicated worrier" (28).

Alexandra's assessment of what ails Tubby is commonplace to the
point of banality: perfectionism and lack of self-esteem. He concedes
both rather grudgingly in the debunking, anticlimactic mode characteristic of *Therapy*. Show business, he asserts, is essentially "crap," and therefore has to be "*perfect* crap" (22). As for lack of self-esteem, "She's probably
right, though I read in the paper that there's a lot of it about" (22). Only
later, when he has against his will allowed a cut in his script does he
admit, "I feel self-esteem leaking out of me like water from an old bucket"
(60). Whether Alexandra's "rational-emotive therapy, RET for short"
(16), helps Tubby is more than doubtful. He subscribes to the principle

of getting "the patient to see that his fears and phobias are based on an incorrect and unwarranted interpretation of the facts," but, as he adds, with a correct and warranted skepticism, "In a way I know that already" (16). The breathing exercises she teaches him are "quite effective, for about five minutes after I've done them. And I always feel calmer after I've seen her, for at least a couple of hours" (16). Even as Lodge has Tubby grant the benefits he derives from the therapy, he undercuts, indeed virtually denies them in the second part of each sentence: five minutes and two hours are hardly positive outcomes worth the time, effort, and money invested. The greatest boost to Tubby's self-esteem comes from giving "a neat answer, like a clever kid in school," yet he recognizes even this "lift of the spirits" as "deceptive" (17); the comparison to a childish gratification carries reductive implications too. Undermining the psychotherapy further still is the somewhat longer comfort, both emotional and physical, that Tubby derives from acupuncture and aromatherapy. Miss Wu, the acupuncturist at the Wellbeing Clinic, shows tact and concern for him and his children as she delicately manipulates her needles; after this intervention he feels better "for the rest of the day, and maybe the next morning" (65). He switches to aromatherapy from yoga on account of his bad knee and to fill "a vacant slot in my therapy schedule" (98). The aromatherapist's double-barreled name, Dudley Neil-Hutchinson, suggests a certain pretentiousness, as does his practice of this "very ancient form of medicine" by computer on a "personally devised aromatherapy programme" (99). Tubby is unconstrained in confiding his sexual problems with ejaculation to a male. But when he asks "how you rub your mind," he receives only the evasive answer, "Ah, that's where the essential oils come in" (99).

So all forms of therapy are exposed to a benign though systematic ridicule in this novel. This is illustrated again in the most sustained conversation Tubby has with Alexandra when he expresses his guilt at being rich after seeing the homeless huddled in an arcade. Applying rational-emotive therapy, she argues that he is not responsible for the recession, especially as he had not voted for the governing party. He responds by divulging his secret relief when they won because it meant he would not have to pay higher taxes. At this confession he is "flooded with a mixture of shame and relief at having finally uncovered a genuine reason for my lack of self-esteem. I felt as I imagine Freud's patients felt when they broke down and admitted that they had always wanted to have sex with their mummies and daddies" (87). The discrepancy between the unnatural

temptation to incest and the rather natural desire to protect one's financial advantage shows the exaggeration to which Tubby is prone in regard
to his fairly minor depression. The parallel he draws is wholly incom-
mensurate, just as his rendition of Freudian theory is absurdly simplistic.
His verbal sparring with Alexandra on this occasion is evidence of the
futility of the cognitive behavior therapy; far from being induced to change
his thinking, Tubby concludes that her "talents are wasted on me. She
should be working in the City of London convincing people that Greed
is good" (87). The irony arises here from the contradiction between
Tubby's apparent praise of Alexandra's powers of persuasion and his own
resistance to them. In the last encounter portrayed between them, the
roles of patient and therapist are reversed as Tubby advises Alexandra,
who has a terrible cold, how to blow her nose in such a way as to avoid a
sinus infection. It is the one thing, he comments, that has stayed with
him from yoga. Her "blowing ineffectually, like somebody learning to
play the cornet" (110), is emblematic of her ineffectiveness as a therapist. The discourse plummets here from the lofty emotional level of
Tubby's life and its discontents to the severely practical technique of
nose blowing, on which the patient instructs the doctor. Like so many of
the happenings in *Therapy*, this incident is superficially funny but also
laden with symbolic significance. At this, their last meeting, patient and
therapist part laughing, though "rather despairingly" (111). The therapy
peters out unfruitfully; the office, the doctor, and the principle all look
good, but prove to be unavailing.

As in *Portnoy's Complaint*, a secondary therapy is also in progress in
Therapy, reminiscent of the Monkey's analysis with Dr. Morris Frankel.
But while both figures in Roth's novel are undergoing classical Freudian
psychoanalysis, Lodge sets up a contrast between Tubby's cognitive behavior therapy and Amy's orthodox psychoanalysis with Dr. Karl Kiss,
to whom she goes every morning. Although the proper pronunciation
of his Hungarian name is "Kish," Tubby prefers to call him "Kiss," and at
times almost envies Amy "her daily Kiss" (16). As with "Marbles" for
"Marples," the game with the name diminishes the therapist from the
outset. Like Dr. Frankel in *Portnoy's Complaint*, Dr. Kiss never actually
appears in the novel; he is merely the projected listener to Amy's lengthy
monologue on the couch (137-62). The analysis, which has been underway for three years, started after Amy's divorce "primarily to discover
what went wrong between herself and Saul. In a sense she knew already
that it was sex" (30). This phrase is a close echo of Tubby's when he

entered therapy: "In a way I knew that already" (16). Despite the different versions they try, neither really discovers anything new in therapy. Notwithstanding his occasional hankering after "a bit of old-fashioned Viennese analysis" (16), Tubby mostly condemns psychoanalysis as having "a way of unraveling the self: the longer you pull on the thread, the more flaws you find" (31). This negative view is borne out by the more adversarial relationship Amy has with Karl (although she always addresses him by his first name) than Tubby has with Alexandra. Amy is irked by Karl's habitual silence; she sees no reason for his canceling when he has a sore throat "because sometimes he doesn't say anything by choice" (43). Amy's monologue is full of rhetorical questions, or rather questions put to Karl, to which she gets no answer. She exhorts him at one point, "Oh, go on, Karl, let yourself go for once, give me an interpretation" (143). The latent sarcasm is blunted by Amy's somewhat flippant garrulousness, but her plea is a not altogether humorous comment on the disposition of psychoanalysis, in which the analysand is enjoined to free associate while the analyst holds back.

In an inversion similar to Tubby's teaching Alexandra how to blow her nose, Amy has to learn to "read between the lines" (147) of Karl's scant remarks since he never says anything explicitly. What little he does say has to be deduced obliquely from Amy's responses: "Just my little joke, Karl. Yes, of course I know that jokes are disguised forms of aggression" (141). Although Amy is on the whole a more docile patient than Tubby, she is provoked to resistance by Karl's coldness, to the very verge of outright rebellion: "No, I know you haven't *said* as much, Karl, but I can tell. Well, of course, if you insist, I must take your word, but I suppose it's possible that *subconsciously* you disapprove. I mean if *I* can suppress things, I suppose it's possible you can too, isn't it? Or are you sure you're absolutely completely totally superhumanly rational?" (137). The verbal crescendo at the end catches the patient's angry exasperation, and leaves the analyst with a pejorative image on account of his silence. Dr. Kiss comes across as distant, supremely self-assured, and rather haughty; it is a measure of Lodge's brilliant narrative strategy that his personality and style are made to emerge quite distinctively without his ever speaking directly. He is a satirical representation of the hovering, unforthcoming psychoanalyst as well as a foil to the warmer, more genial Dr. Marples. Yet neither one manages to effect a significant improvement in their respective patients.

Nonetheless, Dr. Marples acts as a catalyst to change in Tubby, albeit unwittingly. She asks him to write a short description of himself, presumably in order to make him aware of his self-image. From a factual beginning about his age, height, and weight, he runs on associatively without any paragraphs for nearly three pages, more about his physical characteristics than his psychological traits. It is this exercise that "got me going on the idea of writing this . . . whatever it is. Journal. Diary. Confession" (17). As a television scriptwriter he had always previously written in dramatic form so that he muses throughout *Therapy* on the process of learning to write what he calls "a book" (18). At first he is daunted at having "nothing but words for everything" (18), but as he gathers momentum and confidence he is astonished at "the torrent of words" released by "Alexandra's idea" (210). He reflects on the "mixture of monologue and autobiography" in his journal, which seems "like talking silently to yourself" (285). He wonders too about the absence of an addressee, but precisely this gap leads him to understand better the nature of his writing as an endeavor "to recover the truth of the original experience for myself, struggling to find the words that would do maximum justice to it" (260). This theme of recuperating the past is reiterated in his decision to write in longhand rather than on the typewriter: "Somehow it seems more natural to try and recover the past with a pen in your hand than with your fingers poised over a keyboard. The pen is like a tool, a cutting or digging tool, slicing down through the roots, probing the rockbed of memory" (260). In assigning to writing the function of excavating the past *Therapy* clearly resembles *The Confessions of Zeno*, although the circumstances are somewhat different.

However, as in the Italian work, so also in Lodge's novel the writing displaces conventional therapy as the remedy of choice; this is explicitly stated in one of the epigraphs to *Therapy*, drawn from Graham Greene: "Writing is a form of therapy." While Tubby harbors no ill will against Alexandra, she simply fades out of the plot, together with his various other therapists, as no longer necessary to him when he becomes increasingly preoccupied with self-exploration through writing. His extreme absorption in the stream of his own thoughts and words is objectified in the ludicrous episode when he misses two trains in a row because he is so engrossed in listening to the overtalking of his inner voice. Like Zeno too, Tubby eventually hits upon a self-devised cure of sorts as a result of discovering his truer self in the course of writing. He recalls with great fondness his first girlfriend, Maureen, and sets out to find her again. When he hears that she is on a pilgrimage on foot to

Santiago de Compostela, he catches up with her and joins her, admittedly traveling mostly in his ultracomfortable, air-conditioned "Richmobile." The pilgrimage is "a kind of therapy" (277) for Maureen after the death of her son, and it assumes some of the same significance for Tubby once he realizes the many griefs and losses with which she is contending. Through the kindness, understanding, and consideration he extends to her, he attains "forgiveness," perhaps even "absolution" (278) in the religious sense, as well as release from the self-absorption that has made him shut out his wife's conversation. He becomes more gently human, more attuned to the needs of others, and consequently more at peace with himself. In the importance of the pilgrimage the novel's religious, specifically Catholic coloration becomes apparent. That Tubby ceases to have a single twitch in his knee confirms the psychosomatic etiology of this complaint as of his sexual dysfunction, which disappears just as easily. "It's extraordinary," he concludes, "what a difference this quest for Maureen has made to my state of mind. I don't seem to have any difficulty in making decisions any more. I no longer feel like the unhappiest man" (280). "Extraordinary" is the right word here, for the ending of *Therapy* is more acceptable on the psychological plane than are the rather strange plot mechanics of the pilgrimage. Lodge's strength definitely lies more in social satire than in plot closure, as his other novels also show.

The plot of *Therapy* is considerably complicated by the subplot of Tubby's fascination with Kierkegaard. He comes upon the Danish philosopher when he looks up *Angst* in his English dictionary, and is referred to existentialism and the concept of dread expounded by Kierkegaard. Although he finds his ideas most perplexing at first, Tubby perseveres in his efforts to learn about Kierkegaard's life and to read some of his works. His curiosity is as much personal as intellectual. In the theories of the gloomy Dane he discerns at once a model and a sort of rationale for his own plight. "The purest form of depression," he deduces from Kierkegaard's essay "The Unhappiest Man" and from *The Seducer's Diary,* "is when you can give absolutely no reason why you're depressed" (107). Prefiguring Maureen's pilgrimage, he makes his own clumsy pilgrimage to Copenhagen with his beautiful assistant scriptwriter, Samantha, whom he plans to seduce. But "something held me back, and it wasn't fear of impotence, or of aggravating my knee injury. Call it conscience. Call it Kierkegaard. They have become one and the same thing. I think Kierkegaard is the thin man inside me that has been strug-

gling to get out, and in Copenhagen he finally did" (209). Tubby's identification with Kierkegaard becomes a powerful determinant of his conduct from this point on. For he reads into Kierkegaard several layers of
meaning for himself: he is a mirroring alter ego as the unhappiest man
for no reason, the sufferer from *Angst*, but he also functions as a surrogate therapist through his ability to analyze the illness and therefore to
live with it. The analogy with Kierkegaard is sometimes pushed too far,
notably in the correspondence between the philosopher's abandonment
of his fiancée, Regine, and Tubby's cruelty to Maureen in his adolescence. When Tubby finds Maureen again and shares her happily (?) with
the husband she no longer loves but will not leave, he is not only re-
deeming his own youthful lapse but also rewriting Kierkegaard's life.
The artifice is somehow too schematic and too self-consciously literary.
But it does suggest fairly convincingly that reading as well as writing can
be more conducive to change of behavior than traditional therapy.

Kierkegaard is an exemplar to Tubby in another respect too, as the
keeper of a journal. Even before Alexandra asks him for a self-descrip-
tion, Tubby had begun to make dated journal entries. *Therapy* starts with
"RIGHT, here goes," followed by "*Monday morning, 15th. Feb., 1993*"
(3). This format is maintained throughout parts 1 and 3 of the novel so
that it is, like the narratives of the three other overtalkers, a first-person
account. It has a greater degree of self-reflexivity than *Les Mots, Portnoy's
Complaint,* or *The Confessions of Zeno* because of Tubby's pronounced
awareness of his engagement in the act of writing a book. The writing is
subsumed into the therapy, of which it becomes the key element. The
last part also opens with a dated journal entry, but then switches from
the present tense to "a more coherent, cohesive narrative" (286), constructed from rough and rambling diary jottings made during the pilgrimage. External reasons are given for the change: Tubby had been too
tired, or had drunk too much wine, or the laptop had failed, and so forth.
But the crux lies in the modulation to the past tense, for he writes this
part of the story retrospectively, "knowing, so to speak, how the story
ended. For I do feel that I've reached the end of something. And, hopefully, a new beginning" (286). So *Therapy* closes, as it had opened, with
an end and a new beginning; the therapy initiated at the start is over, and
another phase of Tubby's life is beginning. Though complex, the novel's
structure is well designed.

The most surprising section is the second (133-98), which continues the first-person narration but seemingly from the perspective of sev-

eral of the people surrounding Tubby. Brett Sutton, the tennis coach at
the country club, gives a legal deposition (133-36) concerning Tubby's
illegal entry to his apartment at night, wielding scissors as a weapon,
because he suspects him of adultery with his wife. Tubby in fact finds
him in bed with another man. This is followed by Amy's extensive monologue (137-62) of her therapy session with Karl when she tells of the
break-up of Tubby's marriage and of their botched dirty weekend in
Tenerife. Next comes Louise (163-69), a production assistant whom
Tubby had earlier met on a business trip to Los Angeles and whom he
visits unannounced in search of a sexual relationship. Then there is Ollie
(170-76), the director of "The People Next Door," who meets another
associate over lunch at a pub to discuss the serial's future. The account of
the trip to Copenhagen is given by Samantha (177-90) in the course of
a visit to a friend in hospital recovering from surgery for impacted wisdom teeth. Finally, Tubby's wife, Sally, goes to see Dr. Marples (191-98)
to tell of her meeting with and marriage to Tubby "such a long time ago"
(194). Each of these speakers is endowed with a highly individualistic
voice, each speaks of his or her problems with Tubby, and each is placed
in a very specific situation. Louise, the American, for instance, discourses
exclusively by telephone to a woman friend. In every episode the interlocutor is addressed but does not answer: Brett's is a formal deposition
for the police; Karl has to be urged to venture an interpretation; the
responses of Louise's friend have to be conjectured from what she says,
as do those of Ollie's lunch partner; Samantha's friend cannot speak
because of her sore mouth; and Dr. Marples functions merely as the
listener to Sally's story. Each of the episodes has a decidedly comic aspect in revealing new dimensions of Tubby's antics, which form the link
between the diverse segments.

What is really startling, however, is the subsequent disclosure that
all these pieces have been written by Tubby himself. Alexandra had suggested, to counter his "*fear*" of other people's opinions (212), that he
write them down as he perceives them: "Being the sort of writer I am, I
couldn't just summarize other people's views of me, I had to let them
speak their thoughts in their own voices" (212). He maintains that he
had tried to see himself truthfully through others' eyes and had not made
up a lot. Only Samantha's hospital visit is conceded as "all my invention"
(213). So the second part of *Therapy* is not, as it initially appears, an
interruption of Tubby's first-person narration. As a dramatic scriptwriter
he is mimicking others' voices as an additional way to explore his self-

image. Lodge has resorted to a very clever narrational strategy that lends variety to the novel in its departure from the journal entries without jeopardizing the consistency of the narrative disposition. The series of overtalkers in this section is assimilated into Tubby's writing as therapy. The only significant modification effected by this tactic is the further distancing of Dr. Kiss through the realization that he is a double projection: of Tubby's imagining how Amy experiences him.

The virtuosity of Tubby's—and of Lodge's—performance in part 2 is convincing evidence of his capacities as a writer. Tubby has a passion for words as well as a gift for coining striking turns of phrase. He envisages the frolicsome squirrels as having "knee-joints like tempered steel" (3); taking a sleeping pill is "buying a few hours' oblivion at the cost of feeling next day as if my bone marrow had been siphoned off in the night and replaced with lead" (24); "Jake's eyes light up like an infra-red security scanner every time a pretty girl comes in range" (49); and at his first anxiety attack he had been "a Valium virgin" (68). For all his insouciance (a word he would love!) in some other respects, Tubby is extremely meticulous in his verbal usage—or, alternatively, as obsessive-compulsive as in his choice of tie. He habitually consults his dictionary to ascertain an exact meaning or spelling: "Gingerly I got to my feet. (Should that be 'gingerlyly'? No, I've just looked it up, adjective and adverb both have the same form)" (4); "(Incidentally, I just looked up 'paraphernalia' in the dictionary because I wasn't sure I'd spelled it right, and discovered it comes from the Latin *paraphema,* meaning 'a woman's personal property apart from her dowry.' Interesting)" (30). When Amy describes a place as "*louche,*" he is "not sure that's the right word. (I looked it up, it means shifty and disreputable, from the French word for squint)" (39). "After Sally dropped her bombshell that evening (what exactly is, or was, a bombshell, incidentally? And how do you drop one without blowing yourself up? Is it a grenade, or a mortar shell, or was it a primitive kind of aerial bomb that they lobbed out of the open cockpits of the old biplanes? The dictionary isn't much help)" (202). "My knee was giving me gyp too: sitting in one position for long periods is bad for it. (What is 'gyp,' I wonder? Dictionary says '*probably a contraction of* gee up,' which doesn't sound very probable to me. More likely something to do with Egypt, as in 'gyppy tummy,' a bit of army slang from the days of the Empire)" (214). He befriends Grahame, who sleeps in the entrance to his London apartment house, largely because he is "another looker-upper" (116), and he is attracted to Kierkegaard partly by his name: "Søren

Kierkegaard. Just the name on the title page has a peculiar arresting effect. It's so strange, so extravagantly foreign-looking to an English eye—almost extra-terrestrial. That weird *o* with the slash through it, like the zero sign on a computer screen—it might belong to some synthetic language invented by a sci-fi writer. And the double *aa* in the surname is almost as exotic" (122). Sometimes he just comments on his own choice of words when he takes a special delight in a term: "(I think that's the first time I've ever used the word 'disabuse.' I like it—it has a touch of class)" (54). Or he gets carried away browsing in the dictionary: "I just opened the dictionary to check the spelling of 'glowered,' and as I flipped the pages the headword 'Dover's Powder' caught my eye. The definition said: '*a preparation of opium and ipecac, formerly used to relieve pain and check spasms. Named after Thomas Dover (1660-1742) English physician.*' I wonder if you can still get it. Might be good for my knee. It's amazing what you can learn from dictionaries by accident" (81-82). The effect of these many interjections, often parenthetical, is not only to establish Tubby as a committed wordsmith but also to draw repeated attention to the novel's linguistic texture and to the act of writing in progress.

As a narrative of psychotherapy, *Therapy* is at the opposite end of the spectrum from *Les Mots*. In the French novel, the entire process of therapy is portrayed with a high seriousness as a matter of life and death. The foregrounding of the sessions with the analyst conveys their central importance to the narrator as the very fulcrum of her existence, certainly in the first few years of the analysis. By contrast, psychotherapy is just one of a whole range of therapies that Tubby tries, approaching them all with a mixture of hope and doubt. His skepticism extends even to his own state of mind; sizing himself up against a figure in Kierkegaard, he asks, "Am I really in despair?" and immediately replies, "No, nothing as dramatic as that" (111). His is unquestionably a much milder disturbance than that of Cardinal's narrator, who is totally incapacitated in an emotional dead-end, or of Portnoy, who is destroying himself in a vituperative, diffuse anger directed as much against himself as against his parents. Tubby's depression is of far shorter standing, and has been triggered by a concatenation of newly changed circumstances. Already bored with the repetitive weekly rhythm of his life, bored even with the predictability of his show's favorable reception, he is wounded by the blow to his ego of his wife's unexpected request for a separation, which comes, ironically, just after his paean to marital sex. His distress is compounded by the dilemma created by the defection of the serial's outstanding actress. Both his personal and his professional security are severely shaken at the same time by the double desertion of the two women whose loyalty he had taken for granted.

Because of the recent manifestation and the extraneous (rather than endogenous) sources of his depression, Tubby's prospects for recovery are good. Cognitive behavior therapy might be quite appropriate in his situation as a corrective to the negative self-image prompted by the reverses he has been experiencing. Given the nature and origins of his depression, it is credible that it should be self-limiting, with a more or less spontaneous improvement. However, it is not achieved without an input of considerable emotional, cognitive, and even physical effort on his part—greater indeed than he had ever been prepared to make before when he had usually taken the path of least resistance. That he derives more significant impetus for these efforts from his writing, from his reading of Kierkegaard, and from his reconnecting to Maureen than from his formal therapist is wholly consonant with the comic, satirical thrust of *Therapy*. In the context of the novel's sometimes black humor, its deflating irony, and its rhetoric of anticlimax, psychotherapy is, literally, a game to be played as one of a set of tentative experiments alongside such dubious remedies as aromatherapy and inversion therapy. None is as effective a pathway to recovery as salvation by personal soul-searching, expiation, and a recuperation of a genuine tenderness that is in striking contrast to the inauthenticity of show business role playing. Beneath its witty dissection of the contemporary scene, *Therapy* returns to a concept of healing devolving from religious belief and human compassion.

PART II

UNDERTALKERS

Undertalkers are often reluctant to just talk as a result of an upbringing that has conditioned them to reticence and repression. They find it extremely difficult to overcome a trait that has become ingrained in their personality because it is regarded as a virtue in their social context. They may also, consciously or unconsciously, shy away from confronting the potentially threatening revelations that might emerge from their talking freely. Frequently they are entrapped in unsatisfactory or destructive relationships, yet fear further destabilization, and cannot hope for radical reconstruction of their situation. But like the overtalkers, who seem to be pursuing greater self-knowledge while simultaneously shying away from possibly unpleasant discoveries about themselves, the undertalkers are torn between the desire for deeper understanding and apprehensiveness at the mere prospect of delving into their problems.

While the overtalkers enter readily, even avidly into therapy, the undertalkers tend to be much more skeptical, though by no means wholly resistant. The profile of the therapist is far more differentiated in their narratives than in those of the overtalkers partly because their reserve naturally endows the listener with a larger role in eliciting words. The nature of their relationship with the therapist therefore proves of crucial importance for undertalkers: the establishment of a positive transference—or its absence—is decisive for the outcome.

In contrast to the overtalkers, who are generally men, the undertalkers are predominantly women. Given the role of conditioning in personality formation, the connection between gender and men's at least superficial confidence to talk is hardly coincidental. The characters' stage in life is also of some significance, the undertalkers being on the whole younger than the overtalkers. In both groups two are in their thirties, but the undertalkers include two in their early twenties in contrast to the two middle-aged to elderly overtalkers. The undertalkers' sociogeographical context (two British, one New Englander, and one Canadian) is traditionally more associated with reticence than those of the overtalkers (New York, Italy, France, with the Briton in show business).

However, in literary presentation the undertalkers parallel the overtalkers in the predilection for the first-person disposition. Even where the protagonists are invested with a name, as are Esther Greenwood in *The Bell Jar* and Mrs. Armitage in *The Pumpkin Eater,* the angle of vision is still subjective. But instead of the overtalkers' extensive monologues, among the laconic undertalkers the format is more scenic with a higher proportion of dialogue that reflects their need for prompting to talk.

The four narratives of undertalking are quite diverse. Josephine in Jennifer Dawson's *The Ha-Ha* (1961) is given almost no opportunity to talk; Mrs. Armitage in Penelope Mortimer's *The Pumpkin Eater* (1962) is badly mishandled by a gauche, rigid therapist; so is Esther Greenwood in Sylvia Plath's *The Bell Jar* (1963) by her initial mechanistic male doctor before she receives understanding treatment by a sensitive, supportive woman. The only male undertalker, David in Robertson Davies's *The Manticore* (1973), undergoes a Jungian analysis by a female therapist.

7

Amateurish "Heart-to-Hearts"

Jennifer Dawson's *The Ha-Ha*

The loud laugh that spoke the vacant mind
>—Oliver Goldsmith

The *ha-ha* in the title of Jennifer Dawson's novel, which won the 1961 James Tait Memorial Prize in Great Britain, has a dual meaning. On the primary level it denotes a place, a sunk fence that forms a boundary to a garden.[1] The first-person narrator chances upon it on the perimeter of the hospital where she has been institutionalized in her early twenties after a breakdown while an undergraduate at Oxford.[2] The ha-ha is a refuge for her, a haven of privacy: "It was not hard to climb this wall, and you dropped down easily into the soft, long grass of the ha-ha on the other side. There was no pleasure like this dropping down from the road, and lying there in a rough patch of land that had been overlooked by the gardeners, and was full of poppies" (24). The word *pleasure* is conspicuous in this quotation because it occurs in this novel solely in relation to the ha-ha. It represents not only a temporary release from the constraints of the institution, but also an important crossing of the zones through its intermediary position between the normal world of reality beyond the hospital and the artificial realm of the sick within its confines. The novel's underlying tension is between involuntary incarceration "under certificate [of insanity]" (17) and escape into self-determining freedom. On this path the ha-ha is a midway station. But its role as a secret and safe place changes fundamentally when Alasdair, another patient, comes upon the narrator there. So the ha-ha is instrumental in initiating the central episode of the novel's plot.

But on a secondary, more sinister level ha-ha designates too the narrator's disconcerting propensity to incongruous laughter. For etymologically ha-ha is thought to derive from ha! an exclamation of surprise. The narrator's inappropriate laughter is directly connected to her illness the very first time it is mentioned: at a tea-party at her Oxford college "the laugh I gave shocked even the Principal" (12), who summons her afterwards to suggest that she see "a specialist" (presumably a psychiatrist). It is but a short step to the hypothesis that her abnormal laughter eventually led to her institutionalization and certification. When Alasdair asks her point-blank why she had laughed so much and whether she had been hospitalized to be cured of her laughter, she can only answer, "I don't know. Just that it seemed so funny being alive at all" (31). The incidence of her uncontrollable laughter acts as a marker of her mental health. In the course of her hospital stay the laughter subsides enough for her to be "regraded" (17) so that she is allowed out into the town in her own clothes and is placed in transitional work cataloguing a retired colonel's books. But at a party given by an acquaintance from her Oxford days, where she feels awkward and out of place, she again laughs in such a way as to embarrass others. Indeed, as she leaves, she overhears snide comments and "a titter of laughter" (80) at her expense. Even with Alasdair outbursts continue that he describes as sounding "like a disused lavatory cistern" (62). The recurrent laughter is clearly both a symptom and a mask for her illness; however, not until the end of the narrative does she intuit that the laughter is a displacement of weeping (155).

But the laughter also functions as a substitute for talk: "I did not know how to talk about myself" (43). Nor has she ever been able to engage in social communication: "unfortunately," she explains, "I did not seem able to learn exactly how the appropriate reply fitted on to the prior remark, and a lot seemed to depend on this in undergraduate circles. With me the two never seemed to dovetail" (10). However hard she struggles with the words, she cannot find the responses her interlocutors seem to expect. She recalls how she "used to get into trouble for thinking of the wrong things and letting them loose verbally, and as no one ever told me what the right ones were, I was in the dark most of the time" (8). In her attempts at conversation she "can't quite hear across the gap" (70) so that she comes to wonder "what words were *the words*, the things that carried, the words that counted, and qualified you for the world of other people" (86). Her ineptitude makes her ludicrous in social situations: "Mouths clapped up and down; words shot in and out, but the room full of people seemed to have escaped me. I tried to stretch

out and get caught up in it, but each time my turn came to lay a contribution, I found myself catapulted into this empty space in the middle of
nothing, discussing with no one but myself the longevity of badgers or
Myra's thorny spider" (77). When her old college acquaintance, who
sees her on the street, wants her to get into her car and "then we can talk"
(43), she is petrified into utter silence.

This incapacity for verbal exchange is rooted in deeper doubts "about
the nature of reality" (50), doubts of which she is just as aware as of her
handicap in talking. Her problem, kindly designated as "non-alignment"
(51), comprises not merely her position as an awkward outsider but also
her floating in a strangely dissociated state. Even her name, not disclosed until a third of the way through the novel when she receives an
invitation addressed to "Miss Josephine Traughton," strikes her as alien:
"It was the hit-or-miss of these words that struck me most. I knew the
collocution was supposed to represent me and no one else, but it always
seemed odd that so loose an approximation as a name could have a claim
on you, could intervene in your life" (49). At a later stage she actually
disowns her name completely, just laughing because "it sounded so funny.
So inexact and so improbable" (133). This dissociation from her very
name signifies the absence of any sense of self as a distinct person. Since
she does not know what to say, what to wear, how to behave, she feels
that the world of ordinary people "had never had anything much to do
with me" (48). In a burst of insight she concludes that "it wasn't the
party that was wrong. It was me. . . . I don't know the rules of life, and if
I kept a phrase-book for twenty years I would not know the right answers. It's a thing I shall never learn. I am odd, incorrect" (91). That this
is beyond just late adolescent self-doubt or low self-esteem is conveyed
in the crucial concept "hollowness" (131) that comes to haunt her. The
failure of words is exposed ultimately as a terrifying inner emptiness
despite the brilliant intellect she had shown at Oxford.

In creating a narrator who is so tongue-tied—and so lacking in self-
knowledge—Dawson confronts a difficult challenge. For Josephine has
to tell her story and to reveal herself without infringing her basic characteristic. Dawson handles the problem by making the narrative short
(159 pages) and its voice laconic. Though Josephine uses long sentences
(she had, after all, already distinguished herself at Oxford as a likely
future scholar of Anglo-Saxon), they serve primarily to capture her puzzlement as she gropes tentatively for suitable expressions to probe her situation. The longer sentences contain her private thoughts; her voiced

statements tend to brevity, and if she does say more, she immediately backs into self-recrimination: "'Excuse me,' my hand went to my mouth apologetically. 'Excuse me; I seem to have made rather a long speech about a trivial story'" (12-13). Equally tricky is the divulgence of the nature of her illness, of which she long remains ignorant. It is Alasdair who heedlessly names her disease when he mentions "'watching and talking to the schizies on the ward.' He opened his mouth as though he could snatch back and swallow what he had said" (92). Dawson's discretion and skill as a writer in dealing with the topic so delicately are well illustrated in this telling incident. Alasdair does not directly conjoin Josephine and schizophrenia, yet his evident compunction at having even uttered the word in her presence alerts readers to its relevance. In light of this clue, Josephine's detachment, her indifference to her fate, her affective passivity, her tendency to dissociation, her inability to talk, to connect with others: all these traits coalesce into an identifiable syndrome. The diagnosis is imparted to readers with the utmost tact, indeed with a reticence that seems fittingly to echo Josephine's own style.

Like most narratives of psychotherapy, *The Ha-Ha* has extensive recourse to scattered flashbacks to fill out the protagonist's history and, possibly, the etiology of her illness. At the novel's opening Josephine has already been in the hospital for an indeterminate period; she has made such improvement that she is about to be granted the major privileges of permission to go out on her own and to start modest rehabilitative work. What had happened previously is slowly disclosed through Josephine's memories, which sometimes remain just her inner thoughts but often are dramatized into dialogic scenes.

While the immediate impetus to her hospitalization is her unseemly laughter at the Principal's tea-party in her Oxford college, anterior episodes are gradually uncovered too. The recurrence of her inapposite laughter forms the linking motif. The laughter is especially prominent throughout her relationship to her widowed mother which she describes as "very 'thick'" (32). The added quotation marks in that phrase are a further example of Dawson's oblique manner of narration. The colloquialism, *thick*, foreign to Josephine's usually rather formal vocabulary, and its typographical emphasis endow it with a conspicuousness that hints at the peculiarity of the mother's role in her daughter's life. She emerges as inordinately controlling as well as patronizing, infantilizing and diminishing an exceptionally bright college student who has, however, been conditioned into a cowed submissiveness. The recalled scene that shows the relationship centers, significantly, on the choice of dress for a party—a quandary that will later again beset Josephine. The mother's overbearing management in this instance maps the ground for the daughter's subsequent extreme diffidence; it becomes obvious how her independence has been wholly smothered. It is also her mother who has inculcated into her reticence to the point of repression as a guiding principle: "I don't think about it. Mother used to say there were some things it was just not right to remember" (30). Again it is mother who calls her "'her giggly girl,' or if it [the laughter] grew excessive 'the giggly one'" (31). As with *thick*, the combination of colloquialism and quotation marks highlights a cardinal element in the narration by indirect means. We are made to realize that the source of Josephine's oddness resides at least partly in the upbringing she has received.

Josephine's bizarre laughter is, in her mind, somehow implicated in her mother's death as a result of an accident with an electric blanket. Long before the details become known, we learn that Josephine regards the hospital as her home since her mother's death. Later it transpires that the accident occurred on the night after her mother had bought her a dress for a party—a dress that under the circumstances was never worn. The entire shopping expedition is under the shadow of Josephine's compulsive laughter, of which her mother severely disapproves: "Try to pull yourself together. I have not seen the giggly one for such a long time! What has happened to all our good resolutions?" (56). The mixture of pain and rebuke evokes a tone that might be used toward a naughty child. To no avail: "at that stage of my laughter, neither her reproaches nor her sadness could check me. It was existence itself I was laughing at" (57). In an apparently irrational assumption of guilt Josephine adds, "It was as though my laughter had killed her" (58). Her surprising reaction must surely be interpreted as a manifestation of her unconscious resentment against her mother. This reading is supported by a minor incident that delays the shopping: a blockage of the kitchen drain. Among the objects choking it is a snail: "It was naked. It had no shell. It just lay there flapping to and fro" (54). Her mother's confrontation with the snail, with "a look of consternation spread over her face" but also "as though she were at the battle-line" (54), mirrors her stance toward her daughter. The snail, which is of course vanquished, is an objective correlative to Josephine. By positing her hypothetical responsibility for her mother's death, Josephine is turning against herself the powerful, repressed aggression she feels against the person who had tyrannized and warped her.

If Josephine's life before she enters the hospital is reconstructible in its main lines, what happens to her in the institution prior to the start of the narrative remains somewhat hazy, possibly because her memory has been clouded by drugs or other treatments. In response to Alasdair's leading question, "What treatment did you have by the way? Just pills and heart to hearts, or the high jump?" (30), she tells him that she had been given insulin. This does not appear to have been backed by professional psychotherapy. The only doctor introduced by name is Dr. Clements, the superintendent, who makes weekly rounds. A "tall, masterful man who always looked you in the eyes, unflinchingly" (146), he is remote and could at best be deemed avuncular in a curiously impersonal way. Although he knows the patients by name and dispenses vague, clichéd advice about learning to manage their experiences, he never engages in talk *with* them. His distance is implied by the invariable presentation of his trite lectures in indirect discourse so that even during his rare appearances he is removed and unapproachable. He is definitely an authority figure to be feared rather than trusted. At the sound of his heavy footsteps the ward Sister sharply warns Josephine, "Don't sit there dreaming on the window-sill or he will decide you are withdrawn and preoccupied and not ready [for regrading and work]" (18).

Of the hospital personnel it is the Sister who makes the most sustained effort to draw Josephine out and to support her. The novel opens on a conversation between them just after Josephine has been transferred to a side room in another ward. Sister wants to sound out and get to know this new patient. Her motivations are complicated: partly to fulfill her professional obligations, partly out of a genuine human desire to befriend and encourage a lonely girl, and partly also to relieve her own exile. For like Josephine she is something of an outsider, having come to England from Germany to which she still thinks back with nostalgia. As Josephine settles into the room, she notices that Sister "wanted to talk" (8). The older woman's warm interest succeeds in loosening Josephine's tongue sufficiently to elicit some of her story. Thus talking to Sister serves a dramatic function here as a tool for exposition. Whether the talk on this and subsequent occasions is therapeutic is an open question. Sister announces that she will "want to drop in here for a talk about life" (18), and she keeps her word, coming every evening to chat after Josephine's return from work: "I would tell her about my day at the Mayburys', or about my life with Mother at Wookens Walk, or the little cottage we used to rent at La Charrue every summer. She in her turn would talk about her life in Munich and the opera that she was so passionately fond of, or of her escape to England, and her years in the internment camp and among people whose language she did not speak" (37). Josephine here comes closer to reciprocity than anywhere else in *The Ha-Ha*, yet even while exchanging reminiscences, each of the two women remains within her own orbit. Sister is certainly more maternal than Josephine's mother; in a parallel to an earlier episode she helps her to decide on clothes for a party in a supportive way. However, the medallion on a heavy chain that she lends Josephine for the party proves more of a burden than an asset, weighing her down as the evening wears on. In a novel replete with symbols, this detail suggests how well-meaning but also how misguided her proffered help is. Sister is too amateurish and also too captive to her own neediness in the heart to heart talks she instigates to be an effective healer. Later Josephine flees Sister's "passionate voice" as it "hunted me down" (84); the words *passionate* and *hunt* point to the urgency of Sister's want for a sort of companionship. Finally Josephine recoils wholly from her advances; in face of the six times reiterated "Tell me" (117), she stays doggedly silent. The connection is broken, perhaps because Josephine senses Sister's emotional needs and knows that she cannot meet them. As an amateur therapist Sister fails on account of the intrusion of her own unresolved problems.

While Sister is merely ineffectual, Josephine's other amateur therapist within the institution inflicts considerable harm. A medical student as well as a fellow patient, Alasdair has a certain amount of knowledge of mental disorders, which he supplements by reading. In contrast to Josephine, he is a talker, almost an overtalker, as he rants about the hospital's shortcomings and discourses on his anxiety neurosis, which has led to "too many emotional crises" (29), and for which he is being treated by analysis. Josephine is at a loss as to why he tells her so much not only about himself and his life but also about his women and his poor "performance": "'Your performance?' I thought of amateur theatricals, but I did not want to interrupt him" (29). This cross-communication at their first encounter is an ominous portent of their future misunderstandings. Whereas he recognizes—and welcomes—her "*sancta simplicitas*" (34), she is endangered by her total ignorance of sexuality. Presumably this topic would fall into the category of things her mother thought should not be talked about. When he squeezes her waist and puts his hands on her neck while dancing, she mutters something about needing roller skates so that he could just wheel her around. She seems wholly unaware of the implications of his touch: "He was still pressing me against him. Perhaps there was a specific purpose in the manoeuvres. Perhaps the gentleman was an athlete flexing and toning up and so on" (78).

Ironically it is in the safety and privacy of the ha-ha that Josephine meets Alasdair. At first she takes him for a male nurse, but then she remembers having seen him strolling about the grounds with a book under his arm. He is forward to the verge of brashness as he speaks to her in a firm, deep voice that "seemed to be full of amusement" (26). Apart from divulging his own complaints and difficulties, he promptly plies her with all sorts of questions about her situation. But his casual, flippant manner conceals a capacity for penetrating insight that surfaces as he suddenly asks her at the close of their first meeting, "were you fond of your mother, or did you hate her?" (32).

That startling question, which naturally shocks her, marks the beginning of his rather crude attempts to practice psychotherapy on her. When she cites one of her mother's sententious sayings in response to his compliment that she looks quite pretty when she smiles, he reiterates:

"Don't you hate your mother?"
The sweat was on my forehead now. I thought of the lighted rooms and the voices, and I was always outside. "I got used to her," I hedged.
"Aren't you glad she's dead?" he persisted relentlessly. There was silence. There was his clear, relentless face searching me. I could hear the modern jazz quartet, and the laughter from the college rooms. "You are free now," he seemed to be saying. I wanted to run away from him. "You are free now," something shouted at me, remorselessly. It seemed like my conscience saying that, and I blurted out at last. "I am glad! I'm glad she's dead. The future can begin." (61-62)

The ground is now cleared for the "radical break" (59) with her past that he has been urging on her.

At their subsequent meetings either in the ha-ha or in the deserted boardroom Alasdair's efforts at psychotherapy parallel Sister's, although he is far more outspoken, as his suggestion about her hatred for her mother shows. Asserting that "it's time someone enticed you back from the underworld" (58-59) and end her "exile" (59) from life, he strenuously deploys all his powers of persuasion. He represents himself here in the mythical role of the maiden's rescuer, but the word he uses early in his campaign to change her behavior, *entice*, has distinctive sexual undertones and is destined to assume great significance as the action unfolds. At first Josephine is less responsive to him than to Sister, whose gentleness was less frightening than his dogged insistence. "The more silent and thoughtful I became the more urgently and pressingly he talked" (95). Although his overtalking tends to intimidate and swamp her, she slowly comes to confide in him, even verbalizing the negativity of her self-image that forecloses friendships: "No one was unkind at Oxford, . . . ; it was just that I didn't have the knack of existing" (109). In such lapidary avowals the real tragedy of *The Ha-Ha* is adumbrated: that Josephine was never offered professional psychotherapy. Her candor in acknowledging her shortcomings, her assent to the idea that she had hated her mother, together with her high intelligence, make it likely that she would have been amenable to expert psychotherapy despite her schizophrenia if she had been given the opportunity.[3]

Alasdair lacks not just the training to help Josephine; he is wanting too in the altruistic goodwill necessary to a psychotherapist to withstand the frustrations inevitable in working with a patient whose self-perception is as distorted as Josephine's. Above all he is a bad therapist for her because he is pursuing a hidden agenda; the psychotherapeutic interaction is designed, ironically, not for her benefit but for his own. His insidiousness begins to become apparent when he changes his tactics from verbal persuasion to flattery and touch: "he caught hold of my arm, and drew me away to the right. I did not ask any more where we were going in the darkness. It was sufficient to be drawn along by the elbow, for it assured me that at least something existed; at least something was real, even if it was only my arm being drawn along, and something at the other end leading it" (89). To surrender to his directive will, to put herself in his charge is appealing to Josephine for the moment, though essentially antitherapeutic insofar as it weakens instead of strengthening the patient's ego. Their physical intimacy grows: "Alasdair would put his arm round my shoulders as we talked, and gradually drew me on top of him, and I would lie there as it grew dark . . . , comforted and assured, in some strange way I had never anticipated, that, enclosed within a strong circle, I existed. There was that aura surrounding people, and I had never stood within it before" (98).

When they go out by bus for a picnic on "the same hill [as the hospital], except that we were on the other side" (105), that is, in freedom, he seduces her sexually:

> As he stooped or stood erect, bent or fumbled, the world seemed to close in till it was like a room with walls and ceilings. It was because of that that I obeyed the summons to share what reality there was with someone else. It put a floor under your feet, and even though it was odd, inappropriate; even though it was painful, that seemed part of the mysterious instruction to use any means you have to cling to that which is real because it may establish something further.
>
> I felt nothing more, though, only the discomfort of this initiation ceremony and his heavy breathing and clutching, for life and death. (110)

Afterwards it is Alasdair, not she, who "talked and laughed all the way back to the road" (111). The motivation for his actions in befriending and seducing Josephine becomes abundantly clear in his comment: "Nice afternoon it's been. Very good for me, and for you too, I hope"(114). His needs take precedence over hers. Callously exploiting the "*sancta simplicitas*" he had from the outset recognized in her, he is able to overcome his anxiety neurosis by managing a good *performance* with a young woman who is absolutely nonthreatening to him because she has no expectations. In his selfishness he has used her to achieve a cure for himself. Once he has attained his end, he ceases to heed her feelings, addressing her condescendingly as if she were a small child or a pet: "Nice girl. Nice Josephine. Nice day" (114). The next day, looking for him in the hospital, she hears from a male nurse that he had left: "He had left without telling me" (125).

Predictably, the impact of his abrupt abandonment of her after a kind of courtship and intimacy is catastrophic for Josephine. In a continuation of her earlier misunderstanding of his sexual talk, she wholly misinterprets his intentions in having intercourse with her. With her usual naivety she regards the experience as the gateway to the new future to which he had been pushing her. Nonetheless, his palpable change of tone does not escape her:

He paused and looked at me and frowned. "You are not afraid of the future are you? . . . How are you feeling now? Hungry?"

"Not really. The other is more important."

"What other?" He frowned again and his voice had a sharp edge. I had never noticed it before and I was slightly afraid. I suddenly felt isolated and alone.

"What other?" he repeated impatiently.

"Our life together," I fumbled clumsily. "You have initiated me into a new life." The words sounded silly. "No one has ever loved me before," I added. "Perhaps that was why I got caught in the fowler's snare."

"Unworldly little Josephine." His voice softened and I was relieved. (112)

Indeed, "unworldly little Josephine" has begun to dream of a husband rather than the hostel or shared apartment that Sister envisions for her after she leaves the hospital. For if she represents to Alasdair an easy sexual conquest to end his anxiety, he denotes to her a bridge of access to the "solid things" (106), the everyday reality from which she had previously felt excluded. Curiously, at a basic level, they share the same aspiration: to regain normality. Only Alasdair can do so more readily because his disorder is functional whereas her crosses into the pathological.

The full extent of the damage wrought by Alasdair's antitherapy is indicated by Josephine's outrageous behavior after his disappearance. This part of *The Ha-Ha* is sketchy and disjointed as Dawson writes imaginatively from the viewpoint of her narrator's fragmented consciousness. Josephine's relapse is marked by her reversion to the old laughter and giggling, yet she also knows now "that there *was* a form of contact. I could not deny that. Something had changed in me, and I could not neglect it any more than I could deny having been to the other side of the hill" (127). The metaphoric charge of the hill, with the hospital on one side and the real world on the other, is invoked here to symbolize Josephine's new awareness of ways of life other than those her mother had taught her. Driven by "the need to keep alive, the need to hold on to what little reality there was" (127), she flees the institution and is picked up by a man in a car as she stands frightened at the roadside. To his conversational gambit she responds with a locution she has picked up from Alasdair: "Then I found that I must at last have learned a rule. ''Sright,' I found myself replying to him in a strange idiom that was not

mine, with a fatuous smile that was not mine" (128). The irony of the
living skills she has acquired from Alasdair mounts as she is shown moving from pub to truck to car, following any man who beckons her. "It
was all so simple," she muses. "Perhaps this was how things were done,
how Rome was built. It did not happen in a day, as Mother had been
fond of reminding me" (130). The perverted appropriation of one of her
mother's maxims for her current lifestyle is a brilliant means to convey
obliquely Josephine's drift into an aberrant confusion.

After her capture by the police and her enforced return to the institution, the narrative, filtered through her mind, becomes ever more shadowy and disconnected to express Josephine's decreasing grasp on reality
and understanding of what is happening to her. With an unspecified
"scientist" (134) standing at her bedside, she complains in a long interior
monologue about "all the questionnaires that were being put out, and
the sessions of guessing games which they seemed to be more versed in
than I" (135). Who are the reiterated "they"? She is quite befuddled:
"Once I heard them say something about consciousness—or was it constipation?—at any rate they thought I had a high degree of it, which
meant that there was a great psychic opportunity, which I was glad to
hear of" (135). Since "there was nothing actually that I wanted to say"
(135), "now I stay silent" (137). The repetition of "For a long time" (138)
conveys through its indeterminacy her retreat into an inner realm removed from the imperatives of the hospital world. Her bewilderment is
aggravated by the electroconvulsive treatment she is given. It is left to
readers to deduce this fact from her mention of "operatives . . . with their
needles and black boxes and rubber gags, and I had bad headaches afterwards and forgot where things were" (138). Unable to name or identify
things, she merely hears a series of instructions "they" shout at her. Dis-
oriented to the point of being unsure even of the month, she spends her
days knitting sweaters for the occupational-therapy sale while ponder-
ing this "metaphysical, ontological question": "What supported that room?
Was it bricks or iron, or just more rubble? It was precarious enough at
any rate, swaying there above the town, and all that laughter. The whole
thing rocked, I saw" (141).

She is still in this twilight state when she finally reads the farewell
letter Alasdair had left for her. The presentation of this incident is a fine
example of the subtlety and cleverness of Dawson's narrative technique,
especially of her success in remaining within a by now very limited mind.
The active agents are "they," and the occasion for the discovery of the

letter, which had apparently been there for a long time, is routine cleaning: "It was a certain Wednesday, the day they high-dusted in the dor-
mitory and went through the drawers with a basin and sponge. I was
sitting on the bed among a pile of things. They were down on their
knees beside the locker" (140). As the contents of her locker are cleared,
"they" call "Catch! . . . Wake up! Hold this!" (140). Thus a thoroughly
domestic, unromantic context is created as Josephine sits there gazing at
the strange jumble of her "meaningless things" (140) amidst wet rags
and the moan of the electric polisher. Above the din "they" keep shout-
ing: "You haven't opened your letter! Fancy not opening a letter!" (141).
When she realizes it is from Alasdair, "hope rose in me. I thought I saw
him coming down the drive to meet me" (142). Her arousal from her
stupor shows Alasdair's capacity, despite his arrant betrayal, to exercise
some of the power invested in a good therapist, whose influence continues *in absentia*. The letter, hypocritical, evasive, and egotistical, is another grotesque anticlimax, though hardly a surprise to readers.
Significantly, Josephine's reaction to it is not recorded at all, as if she
were so emotionally crippled as to be beyond thought or feeling. Straight
after the letter, comes this factual notation of the commonplace: "They
were still bending over the lockers a little way off. One was eating and
had biscuit crumbs round her mouth. A blackbird swerved at the window with a worm dangling in its beak" (143). Precisely through this
eschewal of any comment on her response and the return instead to the
scene of the weekly cleaning Dawson captures the pathos of Josephine's
extremity.

Nevertheless, she is dimly and dumbly affected by the letter, particularly by Alasdair's recall of "the first time I saw you sitting in that
ditch" (143). Even the exotic *ha-ha* has been degraded into an ordinary
ditch. She hears a voice calling her distinctly from the direction of the
ha-ha. As soon as she is able to avoid detection she rushes out "to the
field where we had sat. But, when I got there, it was bare. There was
nothing, no voice, no sound at all except the roaring of the poplars along
the frontier. The poppies had gone, I noticed, and they had cut the grass
back and it was short and stubbly and full of pools of light and black,
like a wet beach that the sea has just left" (143). The bareness, emptiness, and despoliation of the poppies and the long grass that had provided shelter for privacy in the ha-ha form a potent objective correlative
for the hollowness that benumbs Josephine.

But not totally. She hears the trite phrases uttered by Dr. Clements, "difficult things, these human relationships" (149), without registering them just as she spurns "those condoling, cajoling acts of love" (158), the sweetmeats brought by Sister Schwarz. For instinct warns her that these kindnesses are intended "to keep me resigned and contented with a certain way of life" (158), a way of life that "was death. I was being smothered to death" (156). What she had not been able to see in her mother she can now see in her caregivers. Alasdair's amateur therapy, notwithstanding its short-term negative effect, lingers in her mind: "If you could stay away for fourteen days, I remembered Alasdair had told me, they could not reclaim you" (158). In a surge of optimism and enterprise, she envisages her future as "a blank to do what I could do with. Who knew what possibility it held" (158). She climbs "over the pile of rubble that had been my wall and had enclosed my world, said good-bye to the hill, and ran and ran until I knew for certain that I had not after all been extinguished, and that my existence had been saved" (159).

Those are the closing words of *The Ha-Ha*. The open ending is upbeat, yet it must leave a residue of doubt. Is it credible that she can suddenly jolt out of her apathy into decisive, daring action? How will unworldly little Josephine fare in the world on the other side of the wall? Will this undertalker do better at her second attempt to connect with people and with reality? Will she surmount the inner wall bounding her? Probably the most positive sign is the crystallization, at long last, of the kind of healthy anger and independent resolution she had never before experienced. Anger, together with the urge to live a real life, is the spur to her rebellion and flight. With the help of properly supportive, reeducative psychotherapy her prospects would surely have risen.

8

Ritualized Roles

Penelope Mortimer's *The Pumpkin Eater*

To be direct and honest is not safe.

—Shakespeare

"'Well,' I said, 'I will try. I honestly will try to be honest with you, although I suppose really what you are more interested in is my not being honest, if you see what I mean'" (7). These are the intriguing opening words of Penelope Mortimer's short but complex eighth novel, published in 1962 and made into a film in 1964.[1] Addressed by the first-person narrator to her psychiatrist at her initial interview with him in his office, the phrase obviously serves to pique readers' curiosity by creating puzzlement. Who is the speaker? Why is she there? What are the suppositions about psychotherapy implicit in her cryptic comment? Does the interest she imputes to the psychiatrist in her "not being honest" allude to his aim of ferreting out what lies beneath the surface, what is buried in her subconscious? The reprise of the identical words in the past tense, "I have tried to be honest with you, although I suppose you would really have been more interested in my not being honest" (158), at the beginning of the novel's closing paragraph confirms their importance. By the end the "you" is no longer the psychiatrist but we as readers, onto whom has been shifted the onus of figuring out the actions and motivations in *The Pumpkin Eater*. In a work where all the protagonists are to some extent role-playing, the issue of honesty and authenticity is cardinal and insoluble. It is no coincidence that the titular pumpkin eater, Jake Armstrong, is a film scriptwriter whose next movie is the eagerly awaited comedy-thriller *The Sphinx*.

The narrating voice and the central figure is actually the pumpkin eater's wife:

Peter, Peter, Pumpkin eater,
Had a wife and couldn't keep her.
He put her in a pumpkin shell
And there he kept her very well.

The *Mother Goose* nursery rhyme infuses a certain irony into this novel, for Mrs. Armstrong is not "very well" in her pumpkin shell. On the contrary, she has had what the family physician describes as "a sudden collapse" (37) while her husband, with considerably less tact, fumes, "my wife's gone off her nut in Harrods. Harrods of all places" (38). Looking for something to buy for her children and finding nothing, she has burst into uncontrollable crying and been brought home. Despite the injection she is then given, "when [she] woke up the tears were still pouring out, a kind of haemorrhage of grief": "Now exhausted, I wondered if I was going out of my mind. Was this how it began, with this terrible sense of loss, as though everyone had died?" (36). This is the incident, cannily not recorded until the seventh chapter, that has prompted her referral to a psychiatrist. Since this hitherto "tough, sensible" woman, "full of life" is now "very unhappy" (36) and "very disturbed" (37), the family physician urges prompt treatment to "get this depression sorted out before it takes root" (38). The substance of *The Pumpkin Eater* is the painful exploration of the etiology of Mrs. Armstrong's surprising breakdown, which proves to be far more complicated than her psychiatrist suspects.

Mrs. Armstrong's three sessions with the psychiatrist neatly punctuate the first half of *The Pumpkin Eater*, occurring in chapters 1, 8, and 11. Interspersed among them are expository flashback scenes that fill out her life history up to the novel's opening. Thus chapters 2 through 6 are devoted to the thirteen years of her marriage to Jake from their humble beginnings in a house subsidized by her father through the radical transformation of their lives since his meteoric rise to success some eight years earlier. Affluence has brought many outer trappings of ease—furniture, cars, machines, help—but has also, paradoxically, somehow impoverished them: "we all began to live alone" (77), hiring people to do everything, down to the buying and wrapping of Christmas gifts for the children at London's foremost toy store, in place of the jolliness of the old communal washing up, painting, grating cheese, and making cookies. Just before the advent of wealth, nine years prior to the action, Mrs. Armitage recalls how an actress, Philpot, and her child had stayed with the family, a woman whom she had come to hate, as she tells her psychiatrist in the opening interview. The second flashback, in chapters 9 and 10, reaches even further back to Mrs. Armitage's adolescence, to the two other people she had hated: Ireen, a schoolmate who had made her feel ignorant and inadequate, and Mr. Simpkin, an elderly man who had made indecent advances to her. By amplifying matters brought up in the first session with the psychiatrist, the flashbacks not only uncover her past but are directly linked to the ongoing therapy.

The three meetings between Mrs. Armitage and the psychiatrist are characterized by fundamental similarities despite the ironic reassurance at the end of the second that "great progress is being made. Great, great progress" (47). All are presented in the form of lively direct dialogue with very little connecting narration so that a paradoxical sense of immediacy and repetitiveness is evoked. Thus the therapist remains undefined except through his utterances and the gestures and body language that his patient attentively registers. For he is consistently focalized through the viewpoint of the first-person narrator. Devoid of a name, he is called generically "the doctor," a largely inscrutable figure who fulfills the prescribed professional rituals and role. While Mrs. Armitage is alert to every nuance of his stance toward her—an occasional smile, a long silence as if he had gone to sleep, hearty laughter, blinking, a dreary stare, a look sometimes of interest, at other times a weary slumping in his chair—his perception of her can be pieced together only from his fragmentary remarks. So he appeals to her as "an intelligent woman" (46) and experiments with a number of interpretations such as hypotheses about her dislike of "messes" (12) and of sex without procreation, and her "will to self-destruction" (73). She is so unreceptive to his suggestions that when he bows his head, "for a moment I felt sorry for him. Poor man, the butt of everyone's anger. I should be nicer to him" (73). She is here trying through a deliberate effort to amend her predominantly negative transference to him. At the same time she is endeavoring to be honest with herself in owning up to her exasperation with him.

The issue of honesty is plainly articulated between them: she counters his urging to "be honest" (47) with "I don't honestly know what you are talking about" (73). This is symptomatic of the seriocomic cross-communication that pervades all their exchanges. The basic disparity between his normative assumptions and her life experiences puts them on a collision course as she refutes his expectations: bringing up her children had by no means been a "financial burden" (43) even during the years of poverty; her third marriage had ended without anything happening simply because she no longer wanted to "go to bed with him" (46); during her two divorces and short widowhood she "wasn't unhappy" (44), certainly not in the way she is now, notwithstanding her present overabundance of worldly possessions and comforts. From her responses an image gradually emerges of an unconventional woman who is totally unaware of her own unconventionality. Her resistance stems ultimately from her refusal to envisage the record of her life as in any way strange, as the doctor does: Jake, it turns out, is her fourth husband, and she has an inordinate number of children. Married at seventeen to a reporter who drank too much, she had three children before leaving him after five years for the Major, to whom she bore a daughter, Dinah. After his death in action, her third husband was Giles, a professional violinist who loved the children but whom she abandoned in favor of Jake despite her father's warning that he would be a "frightful husband" (13) in contrast to the others who had been "decent, adult, unselfish men" (31).

Yet she had broken loose from them "while escaping my childhood" (31), one of the most significant avowals she makes, though in internal monologue to herself, as it were, not to the doctor. Each of the previous husbands had been "readily left alone . . . while Jake waited for his maternal kiss" (31). Only in her relationship to Jake, however unreliable and unfaithful he may be, can she exercise the motherly role that is her dominant drive. So instead of exploring the reasons for her current depression, she wants to grasp repetitively at her customary panacea (or escape): another child. Her desire for another child is the overt arena of the battle of wills between her and Jake when the novel opens. Just how many children she already has at this point is never specified; glancing at his list, the psychiatrist "made do with 'a remarkable number'" (10), though he does ask whether it has not been difficult for her to find names for them all (none other than Dinah is named in the text). On her marriage to Jake her father had sent the eldest three, then nine, seven, and six, away to school, still leaving Dinah, Giles's uncounted "brood" (16), to which are added Jake's offspring, the youngest of whom is now three. When the family physician ventures, "I suppose . . . she'd like to have another child" (37), Jake explodes: "She's got a bloody houseful already" (37); he is "sick of living in a bloody nursery!" and cannot go on indefinitely with her "*obsession*" (38). She has to "face facts" (38), he argues, to "grow up," "go abroad, or make some friends or . . . make a life for herself" (38), in other words, an existence not validated exclusively by childbearing and rearing. She in turn concedes that as they grow older, the children "needed more and more of our lives" (100) so that they have come to stand between her and Jake. She goes so far as to admit that she had surrounded herself "with a bodyguard of children" (32). Functioning indeed as an insulating buffer, the children protect her from the world as well as from confrontation of her self. She asks herself "(why so many?)" and "—what was I frightened of?" (32).

Her sporadic soul-searching is not furthered by the psychiatrist, nor is he able to help her to clarify her compulsive commitment to her mothering role. His task is made considerably more difficult by her adamant denial that anything is amiss with her despite her weepiness and her distress at having "nothing to do" (34) and lacking "the faintest sense of direction" (35). Without breaching the first-person narration, these facts dispose readers to pay greater heed to the psychiatrist than she is willing to do. From the outset the therapy is for both of them an exercise in frustration because of her refusal to lower her guard—her resistance—sufficiently to allow him to connect with her. Far from a therapeutic relationship, let alone an alliance, theirs is a hard fought contest as she fends off his every proposition:

"I simply want to find out how you should be treated."

"Treated for what?"

"We don't know yet, do we?"

"For wanting another child? Is that why Jake made me come to you? Does he want you to persuade me not to have another child?"

"I am not here to persuade you of anything. You came of your own free will."

"In that case I do everything of my own free will. Crying, worrying about the dust, even having children." (10)

Her stubborn aggressiveness is so pronounced as to indicate defensiveness, a need to cover an underlying vulnerability that is served too by the "bodyguard" of her children.

In the face of her programmatic recalcitrance the psychiatrist has to work strenuously, yet discreetly, to induce her to talk. Abandoning the idea of "treatment of any sort," he suggests that her "immediate need, I feel, is for someone to talk to" (42). The interpolated "I feel" hints at a degree of tentativeness, or at least caution on his part as he amends his approach at the beginning of their second session. When he appeals for her consent with "shall we see how we get on?" (42), he invokes cooperation through the first person plural, which projects a greater measure of parity than he had granted her at their first meeting when he had used imperatives:

"Tell me about Jake."
"Tell you . . . ?"
"Yes. Go on. Tell me about Jake." He sounded as though he were daring me.
"Well, what . . . what do you want to know?"
"Whatever you want to tell me."
"Well, Jake . . . It's impossible to talk about Jake."
"Try."
I took a deep breath. I felt as though I could open my mouth and pour words out for ever. I felt as though I could open my heart, literally unlock it and fling it open. Now the truth would be told. The breath petered out of me. I said nothing. (11)

In lieu of opening her heart, telling the truth, being honest, and talking about Jake, she then launches into a lengthy, detailed description of their house.

This episode shows that Mrs. Armitage is not an undertalker in the literal sense that Josephine in *The Ha-Ha* is. Her verbal fluency, social aplomb, and quite firm opinions are amply revealed in her dealings with her psychiatrist. But her talk is evasive, as in the above instance when she elaborates digressively on the innocuous topic of the house rather than touch on the threatening nature of her current rapport with her husband. She resorts habitually to the same diversionary tactics. On the opening page she rambles on about her mother's collection of scraps of wool, kept in a drawer, that she used to be made to tidy on wet afternoons. This is a circuitous way of expressing her feelings about the futility of the therapy she is about to begin: "It's perfectly obvious why I tell you this. There was no point in tidying the drawer. The wool was quite useless. You couldn't have knitted a tea-cosy out of that wool, I mean without enormous patience. She just made me sort it out for something to do, like they make prisoners dig holes and fill them up again. You do see what I mean, don't you?" (7). The therapist's reply, "'You would like to be something useful,' he said sadly. 'Like a tea-cosy'" (7), is typical of the constant deflection into the comical in *The Pumpkin Eater* that distracts attention from the seriousness of her problem in the same way as her tendency to overtalk on marginal matters masks her undertalking about essentials. When the psychiatrist asks her specifically not only about Jake but also about her liking for children, she avoids a direct answer by posing a counterquestion until he ventures, "Could it be a question that you don't wish to answer?" (9).

Unproductive though they may appear on the surface, the therapeutic sessions cumulatively point to just how much Mrs. Armitage does not want to talk or think about. "I want to cry, and not think" (8), she bluntly asserts. Continuing this system of self-protective substitutions, she forefronts the trivial in order to displace the dangerous:

"What do you worry *about*, Mrs. Armitage?"
"Dust," I said.
"I'm sorry?"
"Dust. You know? Dust." (8)

Again the concern seems comic unless it is recognized as a strategy to sidestep truly alarming issues such as Mrs. Armitage's suspicions about Jake's unfaithfulness ever since Philpot's visit. How then can this ingrained evasiveness be reconciled with her advocacy of honesty? Does her introductory declaration that "not being honest" (7) might interest the psychiatrist more connote her knowledge, at some level, of her suppression of truth? Has such self-concealment become the only way for Mrs. Armitage to sustain her life? While she has no difficulty in verbalizing, she resorts to free association as an escape route. Not an undertalker, she is indeed a potential overtalker, and certainly an underthinker who knows that "to be direct and honest is not safe" (epigraph).

Since Mrs. Armitage is not able to open her heart and tell the truth, it falls to readers to "honestly try to be honest" (7) in constructing the reasons for her unhappiness. In so doing, we participate in the doctor's endeavor, becoming in a sense her vicarious therapist. By coming to share his perspective on her, we are forced to read not merely between the lines but against the grain of her first-person narrative in order to discover the frightened person who has taken refuge in the ritualized role of mother. Through a distanced disengagement from her overt story readers can acquire the detachment that she is unwilling to risk and that the psychiatrist is unable to activate in her. Symptomatic of her avoidance of her deeper problems is her choice of dust as her primary worry.

Her entrenchment in her role and her associated fear of "honesty" becomes most apparent in her reiterated rebuffs of the psychiatrist's suggestions. She is closed to any efforts on his part to get her to reconsider her life, to amend the self-image she has evolved over the years. If "it wasn't idyllic, . . . it was all right" (44), she insists. Her resolute self-justification can be interpreted in two opposite ways: either as she presents it, that is, as testifying to a mature acceptance of vicissitudes, an almost swaggering self-confidence, or alternatively, as a strenuous denial of the "messes" (12) in which she has landed herself, and particularly a shunning of an honesty that might unravel the entire edifice of happiness she has created in motherhood. The latter possibility is held in check through the preponderance of her voice, and hence her version, in the narration. But the extraneous evidence of "those little weeps" (46), of which the psychiatrist reminds her, refutes her rendition.

An essential part of Mrs. Armitage's strategy to uphold her version is to belittle the psychiatrist. He is made to seem well-meaning but unpersuasive. According to her, she manages to force him to retreat by her quick-witted rebuttal of his suggestions. She records his increasing discomfort as he moves from being "almost cosy" (42) to blinking, fidgeting with his pencil, muttering "valiantly" (43), to long pauses, when he slumps in his chair, "tired out" (46), and with an ever weaker smile. Yet her projection of herself as able to get the better of him is undermined by his reference at the end of their second meeting to her need for medication when he writes her a prescription. This is the symbol of his power, just as her weepiness exposes that, contrary to her argumentation, something is amiss.

Another facet of Mrs. Armitage's manipulation of the therapy is her injection of black humor to rob the process of a seriousness that is potentially terrifying to her. Her sarcasm, like her digressiveness, has an ulterior distracting purpose. A striking example of this defensive tactic[2] occurs when he asks whether "in spite of what might be called a very full life, it's sex you really hate?" (47). His circumlocution, "a very full life," for her sexual experience is carefully worded not to give offense. Her (non)-response is, "You really should have been an Inquisitor. . . . Do I burn now or later?" (47). Although he laughs heartily and praises her flourishing sense of humor, "everything about his face, except the jovial mouth, was as cold as mine" (47). The whimsical tone cannot wholly dislodge the perilous question that has been raised. Similarly, her sudden advice, "You ought to have a bowl of water in front of that gas fire" (12), is a ludicrous incursion of her domestic preoccupations at a moment when she would like to end the conversation. If psychotherapy is made to seem rather farcical in *The Pumpkin Eater*, it is so only within the context of the first-person narration as an expression of the patient's programmatic skepticism about the entire enterprise. Mrs. Armitage wants it to be a farce in order not to be driven into an honest self-scrutiny that might destroy the ritualized role she has established. Ridicule of the psychiatrist and his ideas is a means of self-assertion, a determined, maybe even desperate ploy to maintain control.

By the third session, however, there are signs of incipient change, though in part they are deceptive. It is surprising—and apparently encouraging—that she should want "to talk about myself," but then, having sat for a long time, she finds herself "unable to think of anything" (72). Undertalking prevails, as though she had no self beyond her function relative to her children; they are her whole raison d'être, providing a legitimate excuse for her failure to develop an identity outside her mothering role. But her momentary wish to talk about herself has a darker motivation too insofar as it is another example of her evasiveness. She wants "to attract his attention" (72) so as to steer him away from the subject he proposes at the beginning of the third session, Jake: "'I don't want to talk about Jake,' I explained. . . . 'What has Jake to do with me?' I asked, realizing too late that the question sounded biblical and absurd" (72). In the very absurdity of the question Mrs. Armitage betrays her desire to elude the matter closest and most frightening to her. When she does speak about him, it is to sketch his history rather than to examine their relationship. Nevertheless, after her concession, "we've managed it badly, I suppose. There's nothing left" (77), the psychiatrist presses her to admit that she loves but does not like Jake, and that she does not believe that he is "liable to change" (78) although change is necessary for the survival of the marriage.

Just as it seems as if they were starting to communicate better and on a significant level, as the "backward pupil" that she feels herself to be "is beginning, . . . to make a little progress" (78), the therapy breaks off. He exhorts her to think about what he has just said, to "chew it over during the next couple of weeks":

"Couple of weeks?"

"I shan't be seeing you again for a fortnight. Surely I told you?"

"No-"

"Oh, really- I'm tremendously sorry. I quite thought I'd told you last time. We're off to Gstadt on Friday for a spot of skiing." He grinned bashfully. "It's my great passion, I'm afraid."

"But. . . ." I couldn't believe it. "Leaving me? Leaving me now?" (78)

The therapist is here infringing a basic professional principle: "Springing a vacation or recess on a patient without prior notice is apt to precipitate anxiety and to stimulate conceptions of the therapist as a rejecting or irresponsible person."[3] This is precisely what happens. His beaming blandness, "as a salesman leaving a free sample" (78), provokes her to a violent outburst: "If I'm sane enough to be left alone with my *thoughts* for two weeks then I'm too sane to need these futile, boring conversations—because by God they bore me—at six guineas a time" (79). The ferocity of her resentment at what she sees as his abandonment leads to the conjecture that she has, despite her resistance, developed a deeper attachment than she dares to admit. Her overt anger points to a masked dependence.

Does the psychiatrist's carelessness in not giving due warning of his impending vacation cast aspersions on his competence? To what extent can he be held coresponsible for the unfruitfulness of the therapy? He is certainly remiss in his handling of his absence, but otherwise it is hard for a number of reasons to draw reliable conclusions about him. First, the contact between doctor and patient is limited to three meetings, hardly enough to establish a mutually trusting alliance. Secondly, the sense of his distantness is a product of her resistance and is further fostered by the first-person narrative disposition. Her largely negative transference to him is not so much prompted by anything he says or does (except his late announcement of his plans to go skiing), but stems ultimately from her fundamental repugnance to psychotherapy. Her antagonism is ideological, a form of protest against her need for any treatment, rather than personal. In order to attain a fairer picture of him, readers have to dissociate from her angle of vision, but such a move is made more difficult by the fact that he appears in *The Pumpkin Eater* only in interaction with her. His behavior is conditioned by her resistance; for instance, he has to adopt a querying stance, asking many questions. Mostly he shows tact, some flexibility, and a gentle persistence with a patient who is clearly exasperating. There is little evidence of a negative countertransference. However, he lacks empathy for her, notably for her desire to have another child, even though he deems it a "conviction" in amendment of her harsher word, "*obsession*" (10). On this central issue he sides more with Jake in a kind of male solidarity. In this respect he, too, plays out a ritualized role limited by gender dichotomization.

Perhaps it is his concurrence with Jake that blinds him to the locus of the major problem, which emerges only in the second half of *The Pumpkin Eater*. The therapy ends abruptly with his skiing vacation. Mrs. Armitage is so angry that she refuses to make a further appointment, but her comment from hindsight shows some regret and hence implicit hope that he might have been able to help her: "I heard later that he had broken a leg skiing. I thought then, blaming him, that if he hadn't gone we might both have remained undamaged" (79). The damage to him is obvious and immediate; that to her more devious and slower to unfold. After the therapist's disappearance the plot moves forward in a linear mode without the flashbacks in the novel's first half, necessary partly for the sake of narrative exposition but mainly to fill in the past in connection with the therapy. Abandoning pretense of honesty, Mrs. Armitage and her husband entrap each other in a reciprocal deceit: she deliberately lets another pregnancy happen, while he talks her into an abortion (and hysterectomy) on the grounds that another child is "tragic" (105) at this point in their lives when they would otherwise, with the children growing up, be free to travel together, enjoying "love and a good time" (105).

Interestingly, Jake also invokes the psychiatrist's judgment to support his arguments: "the doctor, that psych, did say that I shouldn't have another child. I'm in the middle of treatment, Jake says, for depression. An abortion would be perfectly legal. It wouldn't be underhand, nasty, anything like that" (105). This seems to be Jake's report of the psychiatrist's recommendation, and it fuses with his own statements ("Jake says")—and his own interests. By contrast, to her forthright question whether she should have had an abortion in the past, the psychiatrist twice "muttered valiantly, 'Of course not'" (44). Arguably, with her current acute depression, circumstances have changed, yet there is an important gap in the narrative here. There is no way of knowing whether Jake ascribes this opinion to the doctor to suit his own purposes, or whether indeed he ever specifically voiced such an opinion. If the latter, then the psychiatrist discussed Mrs. Armitage's state of mind with her husband, thereby heightening the possibility of collusion between them. This is not to invest the psychiatrist with duplicity; indeed, common sense dictates that he would go along with Jake. Ironically, through Jake's appeal to professional authority, the psychiatrist becomes pivotal to the action of *The Pumpkin Eater;* he comes to exercise greater power in his absence than he was ever able to do by his presence.

Jake's term, "tragic," is more apposite to subsequent plot developments. Mrs. Armitage learns that during her stay in hospital Jake has impregnated his leading lady, Beth Conway. This child will be born, as an act of revenge on the part of Beth's husband to ruin her career. After his daily dutiful visits to his wife's bedside and despite the daily flower deliveries arranged by his secretary, Jake has met Beth at a nearby hotel. This enormous infraction of honesty lends force to the novel's opening and closing phrases. In a searing confrontation Mrs. Armitage challenges her husband:

> "Did you sleep with Philpot?"
> "Oh Christ, why drag up that old thing again? It's centuries ago. It's ancient history."
> "Did you?"
> "Yes, of course I did."
> "But you told me . . . that you hadn't"
> "That's right. I lied to you. What else do you expect me to do?" (118).

While he wants only to think of the future, she is intent on "the truth" (118). The discrepancy between Jake's pursuit of expedient pleasure and his wife's ethos of honesty is made almost too plain at this juncture:

> "What's the good in ferreting out the truth all the time? It's always unpleasant."
> "Is it only lies that are pleasant?"
> "Usually. That's why people tell them. To make life bearable" (118).

But Jake's avowal of his philosophy only makes her life less bearable.

How much did Mrs. Armitage know, or guess, or intuit about her husband's philandering? That is the most pressing question in *The Pumpkin Eater*. When the psychiatrist asks her about Jake, she feels for a moment "as though I could open my heart, literally unlock it and fling it open" (11) to tell the truth, but then she says nothing. Does this passage imply that she knows "the truth" about his infidelities, for which he has easy opportunities away on location while she stays at home with the children? If so, it is a truth she cannot utter, or confront. So she fights off the therapist, resenting the sessions not because they are "boring," as she claims, but because they threaten the precarious security she has fashioned for herself in motherhood. The children, who are, like the doctor, unnamed with the exception of Dinah, do form her "bodyguard" (32). Yet in the long run her strategy of submerging herself in the role and not wanting to know the truth about her life has faltered. Early on already she wonders, "what was I frightened of?" (32). In a dream she has at the time of Philpot's visit, she and Jake are at a fair passing through a chain of caverns: "But we were going the wrong way. . . . When we came out, the party, the people, had all gone; nothing was left but icy water lapping against the walls, darkness and cold" (41). On a subconscious level she recognizes here "the wrong way" they have taken to land in iciness, darkness, and cold. On a conscious level that insight is too painful to acknowledge.

In reflecting that both the psychiatrist and she might have "remained undamaged" if he had not gone skiing and the therapy had continued, she intercalates the phrase, "blaming him" (79). She blames him not just for leaving her, but more for his inability to enable her to name and face the problem. For the therapist's function has been defined precisely as inducing patients to drop their masks or roles in order to perceive their situation more honestly. "If the patient could express simply and clearly what she felt and could give a perfectly accurate view of her relations with others, the therapist's problem would be simple. . . . The most difficult problem for the therapist is, therefore, to see through the many forms of masking and mitigating behavior that prevent the patient from seeing her own problem clearly and explaining it to others."[4] The doctor in *The Pumpkin Eater* cannot get beyond the resistance to see the problem behind the role.

On the other hand, "blaming him" is hardly fair after just three meetings in which she has done her utmost to thwart his efforts. Whether she is even trying to be honest with him, as she maintains, is a moot issue. Indeed, she may indirectly be warning him that she is doing exactly the opposite. She is not honest when Jake asks her before they have intercourse, "'You're . . . fixed up all right?' I didn't answer" (91). The silence of undertalking is also a want of honesty. Later, when Jake alleges that she had decided on the abortion "of your own free will" (121) in an eerie echo of the psychiatrist's "You came of your own free will" (10), she does have the honesty to reply, "{W]e both failed" (121). Accepting a share of the responsibility for the abortion marks the beginning for her of a self-scrutiny that leads to a more genuine honesty.

The Pumpkin Eater is too subtle to produce a facile solution; its ending is a compromise. The tower in the country that has been reconstructed for the family is nearing completion; it is the "pumpkin shell" in which the wife may be "kept very well." The intertextual presence of the nursery rhyme instills an element of hope that the failure when "Peter, Peter, pumpkin eater / Had a wife and couldn't keep her" may be succeeded by a phase and a place where amendment can be made. Mrs. Armitage spends three days alone there, the first time in over twenty years that "there were no children to identify me or to regulate the chaos of time" (152). Stripped of her role, she emerges as from a cocoon. The tower can be read symbolically as an elevated, detached vantage point where she works at shedding the past, at sorting out "the part of me that believes in things and the part that doesn't" (142). While she has to sift what she believes about Jake, even more so she has to examine herself.

> Those were the last hours . . . during which I tried to believe that it was Jake who was deluded and I . . . It's amazing how vanity clings to the very end, you open your dead eyes to look in the mirror which they are holding to your mouth. I still believed I was right. I still went on about avoiding evil; avoiding the messes in the street, the dust, the cruelty in one's own nature, the contamination of others. I still believed that with the slightest effort we could escape to some safe place where everything would be ordered and good and indestructible. . . . This belief wasn't strong any more, but it still clung to me, tried to comfort me through the night. I was convinced by now that it wasn't true. (156)

In the solitude of the tower she has finally stopped flight and evasion, thought her life through, and struggled in all honesty toward ma-

turity and truth. It is almost as though she were acting as her own therapist, if that were possible. In the closing repetition of "to be honest with
you" (7 and 158), the memory of the first meeting with the psychiatrist
is invoked. Although not much seemed to be accomplished in their sessions, perhaps his probing was after all the stimulus to her albeit delayed
self-actualization.

After the three days alone in the wilderness of reflection, she hears
the children coming up the hill, followed by Jake: "I was no longer frightened of him. I no longer needed him. I accepted him at last, because he
was inevitable" (158). So the psychiatrist proves right after all: "Great,
great progress" (12) is eventually made.

9

The Ogre and the Fairy Godmother

Sylvia Plath's *The Bell Jar*

somewhere east of Suez, where the best is like the worst
—Kipling

A bell jar is a cylindrical glass vessel with a rounded top and an open base used to protect and display fragile objects or to establish a controlled atmosphere or environment in a scientific experiment. Both these meanings apply approximately to Esther Greenwood, the first-person narrator-protagonist in Plath's novel. She sees herself and is seen by others as a fragile young woman in need of protection, and she lives in a controlled atmosphere or environment in a number of senses: under her mother's sway, under the peer pressures of the women's college she attends, under the cultural expectations for women in the early 1950s, and in the psychotherapeutic situations to which she is temporarily subjected. Bell jar has two additional connotations for her; first, negatively, it denotes the self-enclosure of depression as it descends on her: "To the person in the bell jar, blank and stopped as a dead baby, the world itself is a bad dream" (193). Second, positively, it can also allude to the transparency associated with the insights gained from self-narration. Like the psychotherapy she receives, the bell jar is therefore a two-edged instrument. In a movement initially downward and later upward, the novel shows Esther's imprisonment under the bell jar and her eventual liberation from it with the help of constructive psychotherapy.

Esther has certain similarities to Josephine in *The Ha-Ha*, although her illness, major depression, has a more hopeful prognosis than Josephine's schizophrenia. Like Josephine, Esther is at once an overachiever and an undertalker; she has a brilliant scholastic record but is awkward in human relationships, lacking in social self-confidence and very conscious of what she perceives as her inadequacies despite her standing as a straight A student. This fundamental contradiction is apparent at the beginning of *The Bell Jar* when Esther is spending the summer in New York as an intern at a women's magazine. That she has been selected for this honor in a national competition testifies to her outstanding ability. However, at the symbolically named Amazon Hotel, where she is staying with the other eleven winners, she feels gauche, inexperienced, strangely left out. "I was supposed to be having the time of my life," she ruefully comments, "the envy of thousands of other college girls just like me all over America." But far from "steering New York like my own private car," as she is assumed to be, she admits to herself that "I wasn't steering anything, not even myself. I just bumped from my hotel to work and to parties and from parties to my hotel and back to work like a numb trolleybus" (2). This confession points to the same disparity between intellectual capacity and life skills as besets Josephine. Esther has impressive verbal gifts, suggested immediately by the striking simile "like a numb trolleybus" (she aspires to be a writer), yet her communicative power is severely underdeveloped. She is well able to render a lively monologic account of herself while lacking facility in speaking—and relating—to others.

Esther also parallels Josephine in her family circumstances. She is an only child whose father had died when she was nine, and as she realizes in retrospect, she "had never been happy again" (61). Her mother, who had gone back to work as a teacher of shorthand to support herself and her daughter, constantly impresses on Esther how she had scrimped in order to give her all the costly extras—sailing camp, piano, watercolor, and dancing lessons, etc.—considered proper to a middle-class upbringing. Mrs. Greenwood thereby induces a sense of guilt in her daughter at her indifference to her mother's efforts in her behalf. Those efforts are wholly misdirected, stemming from a radical failure of any understanding or even inkling of her daughter's desires and ambitions. Mrs. Greenwood is not portrayed as intrinsically evil, only restricted in outlook and overly sure of the rightness of her beliefs. For instance, she is reported to take "care never to tell me to do anything. She would only reason with me sweetly, like one intelligent mature person with another" (99), a tactic that appears relatively unobjectionable, yet nevertheless imposes a burden on Esther by virtually blackmailing her into agreement. The pernicious effect of Mrs. Greenwood's conservatism and want of imagination is best revealed in the pressure she puts on Esther to learn shorthand: "My mother kept telling me nobody wanted a plain English major. But an English major who knew shorthand was something else again. Everybody would want her. She would be in demand among all the up-and-coming young men and she would transcribe letter after thrilling letter" (61). However well-intentioned, such pedestrian advice diminishes Esther by discounting her special giftedness and leveling her instead to a standard of dreary mediocrity.

The unmistakable note of irony in the overstatement at the end of Esther's rendition of her mother's words ("letter after thrilling letter") indicates her skeptical rejection of her mother's guidance. Yet the reaction triggered by this incident is characteristically contradictory. On the one hand, in a burst of spontaneous self-assertion Esther affirms, "The trouble was, I hated the idea of serving men in any way. I wanted to dictate my own thrilling letters" (63). On the other hand, even as she dismisses "those little shorthand symbols" (61) as of no interest whatsoever to her, she begins to compile an agonized list of the things she could not do, starting with cooking, dancing, carrying a tune, balancing a book on her head, and so forth. She feels "dreadfully inadequate" (62) as her list grows to include riding and skiing (too expensive), speaking German, reading Hebrew, and writing Chinese. While these latter attainments are frankly recondite accretions that reflect her intellectual ambitiousness, the primary accomplishments at the head of the list, such as cooking, dancing, music, and gracefulness, are those traditionally attributed to women. The necessity of knowing shorthand, posited by her mother as vital to a woman's economic survival, clearly derives from her own life experience, but in her daughter it raises deep doubts about her direction, her aims, indeed her viability.

In wanting to dictate her own thrilling letters and even more in her aversion to the idea of serving men Esther is bucking the societal and cultural expectations for a woman in New England in the early 1950s.[1] The ideal image of happiness through submissiveness to her husband and ministering to their children is almost repulsive to her. She sees her neighbor, Dodo Conway, who has a large brood of children, as a kind of human cow, a mindless nurturer. Her boyfriend's mother, Mrs. Willard, who devotes herself exclusively to her family's domestic needs, fills her with an emotion akin to pity rather than the admiration such a model housewife and mother would have aroused at that time. Esther's view of marriage is cynical: "And I knew that in spite of all the roses and kisses and restaurant dinners that a man showered on a woman before he married her, what he secretly wanted when the wedding service ended was for her to flatten out underneath his feet like Mrs. Willard's kitchen mat" (69). Her picture of marriage even to the glamorous Constantin is equally dismal: "It would mean getting up at seven and cooking him eggs and bacon and toast and coffee and dawdling about in my nightgown and curlers after he'd left for work to wash up the dirty plates and make the bed, and then when he came home after a lively, fascinating day he'd expect a big dinner, and I'd spend the evening washing up even more dirty plates till I fell into bed, utterly exhausted. This seemed a dreary and wasted life for a girl with fifteen years of straight A's" (68). Following Buddy's remark that a woman feels differently after being married and having children and would no longer want to write poems, she fears that the marital and maternal condition "was like being brainwashed, and afterward you went about numb as a slave in some private, totalitarian state" (69). Significantly, "numb" is the adjective she had applied to herself in New York ("like a numb trolleybus"). Numbness, the opposite to full possession of one's mental and emotional powers, is a state she abhors, but one that will befall her increasingly as she sinks into depression.

As a young woman with great achievements and potential she longs for more than the conventional path summarized so pithily and reductively in Buddy Willard's citations from his mother's belief system: "What a man wants is a mate, and what a woman wants is infinite security" and "What a man is is an arrow into the future, what a woman is is the place the arrow shoots off from" (58). These ubiquitous societal assumptions and pressures make it difficult for Esther, especially at her early age, wholly to jettison the ideal to which she is continually being conditioned. Not to have a date on a Saturday night is the ultimate mark of failure at her college. Her vision of the green fig tree, an allegory of her life, vividly conveys how torn she is between the multiple possibilities she sees as facing her:

> From the tip of every branch, like a purple fig leaf, a wonderful future beckoned and winked. One fig was a husband and a happy home and children, and another fig was a famous poet and an-

other fig a brilliant professor, and another fig was Ee Gee, the amazing editor, and another fig was Europe and Asia and South America, and another fig was Constantin and Socrates and Attila and a pack of other lovers with queer names and offbeat professions, and another fig was an Olympic lady crew champion, and beyond and above these figs were many more figs I couldn't quite make out. (62)

Dazzled by this overabundance of choices, Esther does not know what she wants to do. When the interns at the magazine are asked what they want to be, she can give no answer so that the editor says for her, "She wants to be everything" (83).

This witticism points to an irony, for in wanting to be everything Esther risks being nothing by having no specific goal. She vacillates, experimenting with a range of roles. Often she takes the easy road of passivity, notably with young men because that is what her culture mandates: "The reason I had a daiquiri was because Marco ordered it for me" (87). She responds to Buddy's dicta with an apparently compliant "I guess so" instead of the sharp answers on the tip of her tongue. Her habit of deference lands her in trouble when she obeys Buddy's exhortation to ski down a hill despite the fact that she does not know how, and ends up by crashing into a tree and breaking a leg. Her uncertainty as to her identity is clearly manifest when she imagines playing the role of Elly Higginbottom from Chicago. In the story she plans to write, the heroine Elaine, who has a name with six letters and the initial E like her own, is admitted to be "myself, only in disguise" (98). In the few phrases she cites from her draft she makes Elaine's—and her—dilemma readily apparent: "Elaine sat on the breezeway in an old yellow nightgown of her mother's waiting for something to happen" (98); "Inertia oozed like molasses through Elaine's limbs. That's what it must feel like to have malaria, she thought" (99).

Although Esther largely spurns the routes thrust at her—shorthand, marriage, motherhood—she does not have the ego strength to assert her independence on her own. Given the insidious control exercised by her mother and the ethos of her environment, it is not at all surprising that her self-confidence is at a low ebb. She sees herself "starving to death" (63) in the crotch of the fig tree because she is unable to make a decision. On her return from New York, where she has invariably compared herself unfavorably to the other interns, her self-esteem is further damaged by a rejection from a writing program which she had hoped to attend. By heightening her confusion about her identity and her future, this relatively minor setback comes to assume disproportionate importance for her and is a key factor in precipitating the downward spiral into the nadir of her suicide attempt.

Esther's depression can be traced to a concatenation of factors that extend from her present conflicted position back into her childhood. Her father's death is a severe trauma, aggravated by unresolved mourning. In a mistaken endeavor to protect the nine-year-old, her mother had forbidden her to attend the funeral. Since her father had died in the hospital, "the graveyard and even his death had always seemed unreal to me" (135). It is as though her mother had virtually sought to deny the death by excluding Esther from the scene and keeping up the fiction of a happy family. Esther's loss of her crucial male support figure at an early age may account in part for her difficulties in maintaining appropriate relationships with men as she grows up. In addition, her mother's domineering rationalism as the only sensible, acceptable approach to living forecloses the free expression of feeling so that Esther is in effect emotionally deprived. The music and dancing lessons and sailing camp are no substitute for the missing loving warmth. When Esther fantasizes about throwing herself at the feet of some Boston priest with the plea "O Father, help me" (135), the appeal is implicitly addressed to the departed natural father as well as to a spiritual one. She visits the graveyard but it "disappointed" her, and she becomes "very depressed" because among the multitude of graves "I couldn't find my father anywhere" (136). So even her concrete quest for her lost father ends in a frustrated failure.

The death of her father is the event that touches and forms Esther most decisively. It is probably one of the sources of her fascination with death in every guise throughout her narrative. The opening sentence, "It was a queer, sultry summer, the summer they electrocuted the Rosenbergs," announces a theme that will recur in many variations. The Rosenbergs' violent death, discussed by the interns with a kind of lurid pleasure (81-82), is one of a series of unnatural deaths or near deaths that Esther records. She sees newspaper headlines: "SUICIDE SAVED FROM 7-STORY LEDGE" (111) and "STARLET SUCCUMBS AFTER 68-HOUR COMA" (119). The inmates of the first mental hospital she visits as an outpatient strike her as "shop dummies, painted to resemble people and propped up in attitudes counterfeiting life" (116). Even many of the flowers in the maternity ward where she volunteers have to be discarded, in her opinion, because they are dying. She lays them out in a deep white basin that "felt as cold as a tomb," and reflects, "This must be how they laid the bodies away in the hospital morgue" (132).

Esther's perception of death as surrounding her is a projection of her own obsession. Along with the roles she tries on, she experiments with possible different ways of killing herself. The Japanese practice of disembowelment is not an option since "my trouble was I hated the sight of blood" (113). Nevertheless, "for practice" (121) she lets a razor blade drop onto her leg and thinks of getting into the tub to complete the process, but realizing that her mother will soon be home, she bandages the cut, puts away her Gillette blades, and catches the bus into the city. Next she explores the mechanics of hanging herself; however, here "the trouble was, our house had the wrong kind of ceilings" (129), low, smoothly plastered, without a light fixture or a wooden beam. She has no more success with drowning, popping up like a cork after every dive. The straight-faced, seemingly detached, almost distanced tone of Esther's descriptions of her suicide research invests them with an ironically comic tinge even as they underscore her desperation and numbness.

Esther's suicide research and nearly successful attempt with sleeping pills take place after her first round of psychotherapy with Dr. Gordon. He is a psychiatrist in private practice whom she sees initially in his office and then once in his clinic where she is given electroconvulsive treatment. She is referred to him by her family doctor, a gentle woman who is her aunt's sister-in-law, after exhibiting all the classic symptoms of major depression: intractable insomnia, neglect of personal hygiene, apathy, inability to concentrate, fixation on thoughts of death.

Esther has three meetings with Dr. Gordon, to whom she is taken by her mother. Her resistance to him from the outset is rooted in his association in her mind with her mother. So his waiting room already arouses fears in her. Its dreary beige colors, its plants that strike her as vaguely threatening, the confinement caused by the lack of windows, and the air-conditioning that makes her shiver: all this alienates her. Yet the decor, which includes Dr. Gordon's certificates from various medical schools, is likely designed to be calming and reassuring. That it has the opposite effect on Esther may be an objectification of her disturbed state of mind, which converts everything into negatives.

At this point it is essential to take into account the narrative disposition of *The Bell Jar* which conforms to the predominant format of narratives of psychotherapy as a first-person narration interspersed with dialogic scenes, although always from the viewpoint of the narrating persona. As a result, both the therapists who treat Esther are, like her mother, focalized exclusively through her eyes, specifically through the bleak, darkening vision of a deeply depressed person. Under these circumstances the potential for distortion based on her subjective responses is considerably magnified. To what extent then does the first-person narration of *The Bell Jar* lead to a one-sided, biased account of psychotherapy? Is Dr. Gordon excessively demonized just as the other therapist may be unduly glorified?

Esther's resistance to Dr. Gordon is mobilized before he has said a word when she notices that he is twiddling and tapping a silver pencil, a mannerism that continues to annoy her. Her irritability could be another manifestation of her depression. By the beginning of their second meeting the pencil has turned into "a slim, silver bullet" (110), an emblem of the aggression toward her that she postulates on his part. A pencil held by a man could also have phallic connotations alarming to Esther. The silver pencil is accompanied by a photograph on his desk in a silver frame, positioned so as to be visible to both him and her. It is a photograph of an ideal family, "a beautiful dark-haired woman, . . . smiling out over the heads of two blond children" (105). Esther interprets this as a categorical signal: "Doctor Gordon was trying to show me right away that he was married to some glamorous woman and I'd better not get any funny ideas" (105). Again, the reader suspects a misreading on Esther's part; physicians' family pictures generally intend to send the message of stability and kindliness. Esther's response to the photograph, which makes her "furious" (106), seems rather to confirm an imbalance on her part. It also corroborates the wisdom of Wolberg's advice about the importance of the therapeutic setting[2] and of the therapist's posture.

Esther's negative transference is instantaneous: "I hated him the minute I walked in through the door" (105). Like many patients, she had projected magical expectations onto the therapist: "I had imagined a kind, ugly, intuitive man looking up and saying 'Ah!' in an encouraging way, as if he could see something I couldn't, and then I would find words to tell him how I was so scared, as if I were being stuffed farther and farther into a black, airless sack with no way out" (105). Overstated and slightly comical though her wish image is, her instincts are sound in her desire for a therapist who will enable her to "find words." Dr. Gordon is unable to exert such a therapeutic effect on Esther because he is self-centered rather than patient-oriented. She registers him as "conceited," with features "so perfect he was almost pretty, and with eyelashes so long and thick that they looked artificial. Black plastic reeds fringing two green, glacial pools" (105). The adjectives "artificial," "plastic," and "glacial," irrespective of their appositeness to Dr. Gordon, are clear expressions of her rejection of him.

Dr. Gordon makes a grave tactical error by beginning with a reference to her mother: "Your mother tells me you are upset" (105). His invitation to her to open up, "Suppose you try and tell me what you think is wrong" (106), sounds a fairly innocuous gambit. But Esther's reaction is extreme: "I turned the words over suspiciously. . . . What did I *think* was wrong? That made it sound as though nothing were *really* wrong. I only *thought* it was wrong" (106). Her negative transference leads her to question and to spurn, with mordant animosity, whatever he says or does. Her customary cleverness lets her realize quickly, "I could control the picture he had of me by hiding this and revealing that, all the while he thought he was so smart" (107). If the patient here creates an image of herself as more astute than the therapist, she does not grasp that she cheats herself of any possible benefits of the therapy by her manipulative dishonesty. To that extent Esther becomes coresponsible for the poor outcome. The close of this initial interview provides, in Dr. Gordon's own speech, extraneous support to Esther's view of him. His ineptitude and insensitivity become inescapable when he begins to free associate to the name of her college: "I remember your college well. I was up there, during the war. They had a WAC station, didn't they? Or was it WAVES?" (107). As an attempt by Dr.Gordon to establish contact with Esther, this is wholly inappropriate, indeed out of order professionally through the intrusion of his personal life. He is remiss too in not attempting to apply any of the prescribed techniques for handling a refractory patient who comes to therapy with little or no motivation.[3] On the contrary, his false joviality exacerbates Esther's depression by making her retreat even further into herself. He does not understand what every intelligent medical student learns: "that how a doctor behaved was at least as important as what he knew."[4] By the end of their first encounter, Esther's impression of him has come to seem justified, though possibly exaggerated.[5]

The second, much briefer interview is a heightened repetition of the first. Again, the silver pencil is twirled, again Esther notices that Dr. Gordon seems "so slow to understand" and "unimpressed by what she says" (110). This time, as if to provoke him, she shows him scraps of her peculiar handwriting which lead him to prescribe shock treatments at his private hospital on the city's outskirts. Such hasty recourse to electroconvulsive therapy is in consonance with the report of a Massachusetts task force that some psychiatrists were "so enthusiastic about shock treatment that they recommended it for almost all patients, believing, with only personal clinical experience to support their opinions, in the relative omnipotence of ECT."[6] At this point, too, Dr. Gordon handles his patient badly, walking "out of his office without another word" (111) to confer with her mother. His lack of respect for her as a person and his reduction of her to an object further lowers her self-esteem. The failure of the interaction is epitomized in the reiterated absence of any meaningful verbalization.

The shock treatment is likewise administered without a single word from doctor to patient. It is left to a nurse to give Esther some reassurance: "'Don't worry,' the nurse grinned down at me. 'Their first time everybody's scared to death'" (117). This contravenes the recent assertion that ECT "counted merely as one psychiatric treatment among many and had no particular profile";[7] patients' fears are deemed "unusual" (221) until the opposition of the antipsychiatry movement of the 1970s generated hostility. In Esther's case, fear is immediate: the electric shock, graphically evoked as taking hold of her "like the end of the world" (117), makes her wonder "what terrible thing it was I had done" (118). She experiences it as a punishment for an unknown guilt, and Dr. Gordon does not take the trouble to talk it through with her. The session ends on a repetition of their first meeting:

"Which college did you say you went to?"
    I said what college it was.
    "Ah!" Dr. Gordon's face lighted with a slow, almost tropical smile. "They had a WAC station up there, didn't they, during the war?" (118)

In the face of this egocentric callousness Esther declares emphatically, "I'm through with that Doctor Gordon" (119). Her contempt and loathing are summarized in the "that"; he is identified as her enemy. His words and behavior, initially open to interpretations other than the narrator's, cumulatively bear out her judgment of him. Whether Dr. Gordon's parodistic version of therapy actually contributes to Esther's suicide attempt is hard to determine, although her experiences with him would certainly have made her lose faith in psychiatry's capacity to help her. He is a destructive force in her life as she reaches the conclusion that she is "incurable" (130).

It seems at first curious that less space is given to Dr. Nolan, the constructive therapist who has a restorative impact on Esther after her suicide attempt than to Dr. Gordon. Esther becomes Dr. Nolan's patient at a private hospital with grounds and a golf-club like a country club. She is transferred there from a dishearteningly impersonal and confused public institution at the behest of the philanthropist Philomena Guinea, who had endowed the scholarship Esther held at college and who wants her to have the optimal care. Esther is utterly taken aback to discover that her doctor is a woman: "I didn't think they had woman psychiatrists. This woman was a cross between Myrna Loy and my mother. She wore a white blouse and a full skirt gathered at the waist by a wide leather belt, and stylish, crescent-shaped spectacles" (153). Combining the glamor of a filmstar with the nurturing capacity of a good mother, Dr. Nolan is able to act as the vital instrument of Esther's recovery by providing her with an alternative role model. As a self-assured, dignified professional woman, Dr. Nolan affords Esther a glimpse of a female path other than marriage, shorthand, typing, or being a waitress. This second psychiatrist's gender is therefore crucial in her influence on Esther, for it facilitates the fulfillment of one of the therapist's potential functions as a behavioral model.[8]

Dr. Nolan's approach is the diametric opposite to Dr. Gordon's. From the outset she grants her patient respect, for instance by seeking her permission to smoke at their first interview. Esther is thus given the right to a certain degree of autonomy and self-determination even in her then abject condition. Dr. Nolan's posture of leaning back in an arm-chair and smoking creates a relaxed atmosphere. Although initially wary of speaking about Dr. Gordon in the belief that "the doctors must all be in it together" (155), Esther is reassured by Dr. Nolan's candor toward her. Her positive transference to Dr. Nolan is confirmed by the psychiatrist's calm acceptance of Esther's sudden blurting out that she hates her mother. This releasing confession is the only instance in the narrative where this undertalker voluntarily voices an overt statement on the source of her distress. Dr. Nolan proves to be tactful, ready to listen to her patient, aware of her as an individual, and supportive of a brittle ego. Within a short time Esther comes to see this therapist as an ally and friend in her struggle to find herself.

But her trust is sorely tested when she finds herself scheduled for further electroconvulsive therapy: "It wasn't the shock treatment that struck me, so much as the bare-faced treachery of Doctor Nolan. I liked Doctor Nolan, I loved her, I had given her my trust on a platter and told her everything, and she had promised faithfully to warn me ahead of time if ever I had to have another shock treatment" (173). It is important to note here that Dr. Nolan's prescribed treatment is no other than Dr. Gordon's; in this respect, in the area that Kipling called "east of Suez," which coincides in this novel with major depression, "the best is like the worst." However, where Dr. Nolan differs essentially from Dr. Gordon is in the administration of the dreaded procedure. She steers Esther through this crisis by an open explanation of her reasons for not telling her sooner and by gestures that reinforce Esther's sense that she really cares about her. She is, for instance, there to speak to her softly as she regains consciousness: "I woke out of a deep, drenched sleep, and the first thing I saw was Dr. Nolan's face swimming in front of me and saying, 'Esther, Esther'" (176). She wins Esther's confidence by the attentive listening and sincere responses absent in her interactions with Dr. Gordon. What really distinguishes the constructive from the destructive therapist is the quality of the talk between patient and psychiatrist. Although Dr. Nolan is relatively sparing with words, compared to Dr. Gordon's loquaciousness, she is wholly attuned to her patient. Her stance induces the reciprocal trust that is at the core of the therapist's remedial power.

To impress on the patient the importance of her active involvement in the therapy and to foster a genuine alliance, Dr. Nolan tells her that its length "depends . . . on you and me" (176). The emphasis is on cooperation, on the necessity for shared responsibility. Instead of the authoritarian, directive manner Dr. Gordon favors, Dr. Nolan encourages her patient increasingly to take control of her own life. For this reason she appears to play a less prominent part than he does. Her restraint has to be seen as an expression of her excellence as a therapist who puts the needs of her patient's personality before her own. She conducts the reeducative process with a blend of empathy and humor that prompts Esther to change her assumptions about her future. She experiences an exhilarating sense of liberation when she acquires, on Dr. Nolan's referral, a birth control device. Armed with this protection, she is ready "to practice" her "new, normal personality" (184) on Irwin, a mathematics professor. While her deflowering ends ludicrously with massive bleed-

ing that requires emergency room attention, nevertheless Esther is trying out an adult, independent act on her own. Dr. Nolan's constructive
presence is shown once more in the closing pages of *The Bell Jar* as Esther
prepares to meet the committee considering her discharge. "Don't be
scared, . . . I'll be there," Dr. Nolan reassures her, and just before she
enters the room, "Doctor Nolan appeared from nowhere and touched
me on the shoulder" (199). Her sudden appearance at Esther's side suggests the almost magical element that has crept into their relationship.
As Esther moves out into the world, she knows that she is not quite
alone, that she has a wise, professionally successful mother substitute
discreetly in the background. Dr. Nolan gives her the support she needs
without stifling her, as her own mother and Dr. Gordon had done.

The crassness of the antithesis between Dr. Gordon and Dr. Nolan
is a weakness in an otherwise subtle novel. The image of the two therapists as ogre and fairy godmother respectively seems too schematic as
well as hyperbolic. It must, however, be read within the context of the
narrative's disposition as a first-person account: these are Esther's perceptions of her two therapists, and she is inclined to a certain adolescent
exaggeration, emotionally and verbally. Her negative transference results in a vilification, while the positive produces idealization. The ogre
perpetuates, indeed intensifies, Esther's enclosed silence by not bother-
ing to listen to her. The fairy godmother, on the other hand, releases her
voice by recognizing the worth and validity of what she has to say. Dr.
Nolan's handling of Esther as a responsible adult propels her toward
that position.

The Bell Jar is open-ended, closing at the moment when Esther steps
into the committee room to be evaluated for possible release. But the
direction is positive, for this is a very different young woman from the
one who had made a list of all the things she could not do. Readers'
knowledge of Plath's suicide undercuts the hopefulness of the novel's
ending; it is hard, indeed almost impossible, to bracket out the autobiographical completely at this particular point. Nonetheless, the potential
promise in Esther's future should not on that account be underestimated.
Although the narrative is predominantly reminiscent in its mode of confiding self-exploration, one striking flash-forward occurs right near the
beginning when Esther mentions having "cut the plastic starfish off the
sunglasses case for the baby to play with" (3). Evidently she has a child
and presumably has got married. Even more auspicious in light of Esther's
ambition to be a writer is the imaginativeness of the prose in *The Bell Jar*.

From the eerie, ominous opening evocation of New York with its "goggle-eyed headlines staring up at me on every street corner and the fusty, peanut-smelling mouth of every subway" (1), the novel is studded with memorable phrases that brilliantly capture Esther's moods and apprehensions. The pin curls on her mother's head at night are seen as "glittering like a row of little bayonets" (100), an emblem of the threat she represents to Esther. Similarly Dr. Gordon makes her feel "as if I were being stuffed further and further into a black airless sack with no way out" (105), a metaphor that conveys how he exacerbates her condition by its passive construction ("being stuffed into") and the intensification from the at least transparent bell jar to the "black airless sack," the locus of death.

The scenes of psychotherapy are central to *The Bell Jar* in showing how therapy can either impede or foster the patient's development. After her encounters with Dr. Gordon, Esther makes her most serious suicide attempt; after her therapy with Dr. Nolan, she is prepared, albeit gingerly, to venture out into the world beyond the institution.

10

Petrified Feeling

Robertson Davies's *The Manticore*

The world is a comedy to those that think, a tragedy to
those that feel.

—Horace Walpole

A manticore is a fabulous beast with the head of a man, the body of a
lion, and the tail of a dragon or a scorpion. The combination suggests
intellectual power, physical strength, and the capacity for a damaging
sting from the tail. In Davies's novel the creature is identified in the
interpretation of a dream told by the analysand, David Staunton, to his
therapist, Dr. Haller. David has seen himself with a man's face and a
lion's body that ended in a kind of spike or barb. Dr. Haller comments
that this is not a bad picture of him as a lawyer in court: "Head of a man,
brave and dangerous as a lion, capable of wounding with barbs? But not
a whole man, or a whole lion, or a merely barbed opponent. The Unconscious chooses its symbolism with breath-taking virtuosity" (179). What
in David's unconscious leads him to choose the manticore as the symbol
for himself?

This key passage occurs near the center of *The Manticore*, toward the
middle of the Jungian analysis David, a Canadian lawyer, is undergoing.
However, its deeper implications become apparent only gradually as the
complex story of the patient's life unfolds. Indeed, the full extent of that
story spills over into the two other novels of the Deptford trilogy of
which *The Manticore* is the second; the first is *Fifth Business* (1970), and
the third *The World of Wonders* (1975). The three tales cover much the
same ground, told from differing perspectives. The narrator of *Fifth
Business* is Dunstan Ramsey, a historian schoolmaster and close friend

of the Staunton family. In *The Manticore* the telling voice is that of David, the only son of Boy Staunton, who had risen from modest origins in Deptford to immense wealth and a position of enormous influence on the economic and political scene in Canada. In *The World of Wonders* the recorder is again Dunstan, although the main figure is Magnus Eisengrim, a famous illusionist who had begun life as Paul Dempster in Deptford. While each work in the trilogy is more or less self-contained, the three overlap and dovetail in a cumulative effect. Their focal unifying mystery is the shocking death of Boy Staunton under bizarre circumstances when his car plunges into Toronto harbor.

The stress occasioned by his father's death, which he considers a murder, is the immediate precipitating impetus for David's decision to go to the Jung Institute in Zurich. At a theatrical performance in Toronto by a kind of soothsayer David has shouted out, "Who killed Boy Staunton?" (4), thereby causing a furore. This incident has made him realize the extent to which he had lost control of himself. His generalized nervousness and proclivity to drink, although he refuses to admit his drinking to be excessive, also play a part in the step he takes. Yet it is made clear from the outset how surprising a move this is for David, how out of character because, as he explains to the director of the Jung Institute, "I had told myself and other people countless times I would never submit to—talking to a psychiatrist, ostensibly seeking help, but without any confidence that he could give it. I have never believed these people can do anything for an intelligent man he can't do for himself. I have known many people who have leaned on psychiatrists, and every one of them was a leaner by nature, who would have leaned on a priest if he had lived in an age of faith, or leaned on a teacup-reader or even an astrologer if he had not had enough money to afford the higher hokum" (5). His ingrained skepticism is connected to his conviction of his own intellectual perspicacity and emotional strength—the man and the lion aspects of the manticore. He ponders about his hostility "toward a course of action I had undertaken of my own free will" (8), a phrase that makes readers suspect he is under greater duress than he is ready to concede, given his contempt for psychiatry. He chooses Zurich over New York because it is "a long way from Toronto" (10) and therefore more likely to assure the secrecy so very important to him to save face. That he has nevertheless come bespeaks his desperation, his recognition that he has reached a point in his life at age forty when he can no longer resolve the problems besetting him on his own by rationalism and endurance alone.

Or, as his therapist puts it to him, "your decision to come here was a cry for help" (103).

David's slow, grudging acceptance of the value of psychiatry, not to say his conversion to it, is a subtext of *The Manticore*. Outwardly the novel appears to be a detective thriller centered on the question David articulates in the theater, "Who killed Boy Staunton?" That puzzle is never entirely resolved, certainly not in this middle of the three narratives. Davies cleverly engineers a shift of interest from the death itself onto the intricate network of relationships among the people surrounding the senior Staunton and affected by his often high-handed behavior. The people grouped around him include Dunstan Ramsey, the Dempsters, and most notably his immediate family: his two wives, his son, and his daughter. In each part of the Deptford trilogy the spotlight is concentrated on a specific figure; in *The Manticore* it is on David, on the exploration of "a dark corner" (136) of himself. So like many narratives of psychotherapy, this novel is cast as a psychiatric thriller: what ails this person? how has he landed in the impasse that calls for therapy? and how can he be helped to remediate his situation? The issue has an added edge in *The Manticore*, for David, like Alexander Portnoy, Tubby Passmore, and Marie Cardinal's protagonist, is a highly successful, indeed outstanding trial lawyer who has won fame for his unrelenting, acerbic probing of witnesses in court, exhibiting the manticore's barb or spike. But his public self-confidence and fluency are in striking contrast to his impoverished personal life, which is characterized by the longstanding repression of essential facets of his personality that eventually drives him to seek psychiatric help. A stellar talker in public by avocation, David is in his private life an undertalker.

The Manticore differs from the other narratives of psychotherapy so far discussed through its adherence to Jungian doctrines, which are freely invoked by the therapist. Thinking, Feeling, Sensation, and Intuition are posited as the fourfold means of perception (101). When David speaks of his long attachment to Felix, his teddy-bear, the toy animal is cast as "the Friend" (137), while he himself in this scenario fulfills the role of "The Orphan of the Storm: the Battered Baby" (136). David learns to acknowledge the appearance of his "Shadow" (153), encounters his "Anima" (182) in various guises, and is taught that the "saturnine lawyer-wizard who snatches people out of the jaws of destruction" is his "Persona" (251). Among the archetypes that "represent and body forth patterns toward which human behaviour seems disposed" Magnus

Eisengrim signifies "the Magus, or the Wizard, or the Guru" (229). These reiterated allusions to the Jungian system serve too the function of foregrounding the ongoing therapeutic process in the same way as the rituals of greeting and leave-taking do in *Les Mots pour le dire*. The Jungian therapist in *The Manticore* also resembles the Freudian in the French narrative in having two doors to the office, one for arriving and the other for departing patients so that the utmost privacy is upheld.

David's multiple misapprehensions about psychotherapy are disclosed almost comically in his reactions to his initial interview with the therapist to whom he has been assigned. There is, to his surprise, no couch. The arrangement of the chairs is such as to make the situation seem "more social than professional" (10). Above all, "it was a sharp jolt to find that Dr. J. von Haller was a woman" (10). In speaking of psychiatrists David had always used the masculine pronoun on the automatic assumption that he would be seen by a man. Even as he affirms his lack of prejudice against women in general and in the practice of somatic medicine, he fears that no woman would be able to understand what is wrong with him because of the gender difference. In facing this disconcerting dilemma David instinctively resorts to the tactics of a lawyer assessing an unexpected witness. He samples her as though she were some strange specimen, noting her fine face, beautiful brown eyes, big but not coarse features, large mouth with nice white "but not American-white" teeth, pleasant low voice, not quite impeccable in its command of colloquial English, unremarkable clothes, neither fashionable nor dowdy, best described as "classic" (11). In short, she is more than adequate though not perfect, neither repulsive nor provocatively attractive. Correctly, as it turns out, he guesses her to be thirty-eight, just slightly younger than he. Maintaining a proven tactic of the legal profession, he decides to "keep quiet and let the client do the talking," which results, however, in "a very stilted conversation" (11). David thus implements his suspicious resistance to psychiatry largely by passivity and undertalking, but he still finds himself "losing ground": "This was humiliating. I am a fine cross-examiner and yet here I was, caught off balance time and again by this woman doctor" (14). The terms he uses here as well as his summation of the meeting as "a dogfight, a grappling for advantage" (18), indicate that he conceives their interaction as a battle. He does recount a recent dream, though for an inappropriate reason: "this was costing me money. I might as well have the full show, whatever it might be" (15). Dr. Haller disarms him by her frank confrontation of his ambivalence, suggesting bluntly though not tactlessly: "Wouldn't it simplify things if you skipped the preliminary flight and continued? I am sure you are much too reasonable to have expected this kind of treatment to be painless. It is always difficult in the beginning for everyone" (14). So she calls his bluff by reducing his stance to a norm while at the same time tempering her comment with the mild flattery of acknowledging the effect of his intelligence and wealth. She is abetted by strong motivation on his side, for his reluctance is neutralized in part by curiosity about himself and more potently by his overwhelming need for help. When he leaves at the end of the hour, he is full of conflicting feelings: "very angry" at "being put on the spot," "furious with myself and Dr. von Haller. But in a quiet corner of my mind I was not displeased that I should be seeing her again" (19). The primary barrier of resistance has been overcome. Her position is further reinforced by the shaking of his hand, which both of them notice, as he reaches for his hat; that tremor points to a worse degree of alcoholism than he had been willing to concede.

In this opening interview Dr. Haller's voice is often heard in direct speech although the perspective is that of David, the first-person narrator. This basic pattern is followed throughout the three sections of *The Manticore*. The first, "Why I Went to Zurich" (3-74), and the last, "My Sorgenfrei Diary" (265-310), are considerably shorter than the central part, "David against the Trolls" (75-264). Its contents are explained in a prefatory headnote italicized and in parentheses to mark its metafictional status, as it were: "*(This is my Zürich Notebook, containing notes and summaries used by me in presenting my case to Dr. von Haller; also memoranda of her opinions and interpretations as I made them after my hours with her. Without being a verbatim report, this is the essence of what passed between us)* (75). David here chooses legal terms ("memoranda of her opinions," "verbatim report") just as Dr. Haller does in asking whether he would consider "writing a brief" of his case (72). This translation of his analysis into the language of his profession is a clever strategy on her part for making the process more familiar and more acceptable to him. Dr. Haller cites a poem by Ibsen:

> To live is to battle with trolls
> In the vaults of heart and brain.
> To write: that is to sit
> In judgement over one's self. (73)

As in Svevo's *Confessions of Zeno* and Lodge's *Therapy*, self-exploration by means of writing becomes a central vehicle of the psychotherapy.
In this instance it is a device for restoring to David a measure of the
control that is so extremely important to him. It also induces self-de-
tachment as the writer contemplates himself as the active figure from
the distance of the desk. Whereas the titles of the other two sections
comprise a first-person element ("I" and "My" respectively), in the middle
part David refers to himself by his name as though he were an other.
However, his occasional interruptions of his own narrative are reminders of its role as a tool of the analysis: *"(Here I found I was weeping and
could not go on)"* (92); *"(It was not easy work, this dredging up what could be
recovered of my childish past and displaying it before another person)"* (98).
Such asides represent ways of "digesting," that is, of giving a literary
portrayal of the psychotherapeutic process.

This combination of first-person narration with written memoir is
one of several distinctive features of the novel's narrational disposition.
The intercalation of conversations into all the sections both problematizes
the narrative organization and endows it with vividness. Exchanges with
Dr. Haller are often recorded as dramatic dialogues framed simply by
the two speakers' names. In addition to this kind of talk in the present
time of the therapy, David's writing is punctuated by flashbacks not only
to scenes of his past but also, at crucial moments, to colloquy between
the participants in the events. Those episodes are remembered talk, filtered through David's perceptions at that point and his recall years later.
The question of his reliability, or bias, inevitably arises, particularly in
the murkiest areas of his family's history. What is more, the most alarming conjectures come from David's sister Caroline, who seems to be more
astute in worldly affairs than he, but who may have a lurid imagination
too. It is she who asserts, "I have every reason to believe that you are the
son of Dunstan Ramsey" (128); she also believes that the family retainer,
Netty, in love with their father, "killed Mummy" (129) by opening her
bedroom window to the extreme of a Canadian winter during a phase of
convalescence. Whatever their actual validity, such hypotheses have clearly
aggravated David's disturbed state of mind and contributed to the panic-
stricken disarray into which he falls after his father's death. Were both
his mother and his father murdered? The question remains open in *The
Manticore*; its factuality is immaterial, only its impact on David matters.
His mixture of remembered and present pain is forcefully intertwined in

the hybrid form devised by Davies for the representation of this colorful narrative of psychotherapy.

The revelation of his childhood and his family situation makes it plain that David is suffering from more than stress consequent to his father's violent death or even from "nerves" (20) as he claims. His preliminary physical examination reports depleted general health, underweight, some neuritic pain, and occasional marked tremor of the hands.

Both his talking and his writing site the crux of David's problems in his conflict with his father, which goes far beyond a merely generational tension. The opening statement of his Zurich notebook, "It is not easy to be the son of a very rich man," could, as he himself comments, "stand as an epigraph for the whole case" (75). For the situation carries a burden of privilege as well as of expectations that weigh heavily on David. Although he lives in the midst of great wealth, he does so without any sense of either possessing or deserving it. He is kept so short of cash that his school fellows regard him as mean. His father's restriction of his allowance is part of a calculated campaign to teach him to manage money wisely, and more broadly, "to make a man of me" (76). As a result he is constantly preoccupied with "some new method of scrimping or cheeseparing" (76) and in debt to his sister who, as a girl, does not have to be taught such harsh lessons. Her relative affluence puts her in a position to dominate him from an early age. Since David believes that his father loves him very much, he never questions the sagacity of the theory on which he is brought up. Thus his father's posture instills into David a consciousness of his own innate inferiority; he feels that he badly needs "character," "manhood," "the ability to stand on my own feet" (78). He has to become "worthy" (78) of his father's love and trust, in other words, he has to win it instead of having it bestowed as a birthright. Arguably, despite his signal eminence in his profession, he always sees himself as falling short of the ideal his father held for him. To withhold pocket money also connotes symbolically to deprive of love. So the thwarted expression of good feelings between father and son can be seen as a major source of David's impoverished personal life in adulthood and of his metaphoric undertalking in the realm of the affective.

Nor does his mother have the capacity to nurture this aspect of her son's personality. A great beauty without much education, she is out of her depth as the wife of a very rich man. David recalls her as "Poor Mother!" (107), toward whom he felt guilty because he should have loved and supported her more. But under his father's "spell" (107), he could not love anyone who disappointed the head of the family. As he grew older, he adds ruefully, he came to realize that "I was a disappointment myself" (107). Thus his guilt toward his mother is conjoined to a low self-esteem. His fervent dislike of his stepmother for the vulgar hypocrisy with which she ensnares his father is "one more serious thing" (254) left unspoken and unresolved between father and son. Any warmth he might have got from Netty, whom his sister nicknames "the Demon Queen" (82), was limited by her strictness. Now his housekeeper, she still regards herself as his "keeper" (82). An equally ambivalent posture is characteristic of his Grandfather Staunton, who does speak more to the boy during the summers he spends with him in the country, showing him various quaint old medical instruments from his collection, but also exhibits a streak of sadism not unlike Boy Staunton's. No wonder that at boarding school during the war, when his father is mostly away, Dunstan Ramsey becomes "a much bigger figure" in his life (117). An old friend of his father's from their youth in Deptford, he has understanding of David's circumstances, and extends to him the kindness and compassion he had never been given at home. Another of his educators and mentors, Father Knopwood, a homosexual, is also remembered "with lasting affection" (147). In preparing David for his confirmation, he begins to open up to him the complex area of sexuality with a blend of idealism and flexibility.

David's first love is the lively Judith Wolff, whom he meets when she has a leading role in the musical at his sister's school. He woos her as best he can with the most roses he can afford. But although he feels physical desire for her, as he tells Dr. Haller, he is rarely alone with her because she is the carefully protected only child of an intellectual German-Jewish family. Through Judy he is introduced to "a new sort of world" (158) of a sophisticated international culture beyond the ken of his own environment. For a year this love "fed his life" and "expanded my spirit" before it is "destroyed by an act of kindness which was in effect an act of shattering cruelty" (158) when Judy is packed off to Europe to complete her education and to remove her from the danger of an unsuitable match.

David's sexual initiation is orchestrated by his father when he takes the seventeen-year-old to Montreal to have dinner with Myrrha Martindale, an old friend of his, a former singer in Broadway musical comedies, allegedly witty, expert in wine and food, and so forth. David naively takes the dinner to be "educational in the very best sense" (189).

On the pretext of another appointment his father leaves David with Myrrha, who skillfully seduces him. At the time David appears to experience no resentment against his father. However, in the subsequent twenty-three years he has had no further sexual encounters. Judy has become Mrs. Julius Meyer, wife of an admired chemistry professor, mother of three clever children, and an important member of the committee of the Jewish hospital.

It is Judy's father who cites a Burns poem to David as gentle means to dismiss him:

> I waive the question of the sin
> The hazard of concealing;
> But, och, it hardens a' within,
> And petrifies the feeling. (199)

Such a petrification of feeling as a result of concealment and repression is what has shaped David over the years. While his sister is "a very advanced Feeling Type" (132), he has had to learn to check feeling as a potential danger to himself. The pattern is set in his relationship to his father where natural, expansive responses are suppressed in the face of a distanced severity. Yet even at seventeen he still had "a belated bout of hero-worship" for his father (186), who had attained even greater prestige and power through his war service. His misprision of his father is illustrated by his misunderstanding of the term "swordsman" applied to him; in the belief that "swordsmen were people of natural distinction" (187), he is proud to be the son of one of them. He is humiliated to discover that far from denoting a gallant person of superior behavior and temperament, as he had assumed, the word means a self-seeking, womanizing manipulator. If David proves a disappointment to his father, the reverse holds too. His disillusionment is heightened by further grotesque revelations when genealogical research uncovers the family's descent from a common barmaid, who had fled to Canada with her illegitimate child, not from the aristocratic origins his father had boastfully implied. To counter the emotional abuse, the meanness, the edifice of lies, David has developed a protective carapace that serves well to shield him from hurt but that also immures and isolates him by stifling the normal flow of feelings. His unfortunate debut in love with Judith gives added impetus to his endeavor to harden himself by deadening feeling. His drinking serves the same purpose: "to blunt the edge of that heavy axe that seems always to be chopping away at the roots of my being" (56). But contrary to Walpole's aphorism that the world is a comedy to those that think and a tragedy to those that feel, David's existence is made tragic by the absence of feeling. And when a strong feeling does intrude, as on his father's death, it is destructive because he has become conditioned to eliminating feeling, not to coping with it and incorporating it into his life. The manticore, the symbolical image his subconscious has chosen to characterize him, lacks an organ of feeling.

In place of the petrified feeling, David has, in terms of the Jungian schema, enthroned Thinking. The practice of law consists of the application of logical rationalism to the exclusion of emotion. He has opted for this field partly as a result of witnessing a gratuitous act of shameless vandalism at summer camp, despoliation perpetrated by adolescents of his own social level for the sheer joy of it. So in his choice of profession as in his personal profile David is motivated primarily by opposition. Repeatedly his path is determined by the urge to react to negativities in his environment rather than to take assertive steps on his own. His sexual abstinence falls into the same category. While David's decision to become a lawyer has an idealistic aspect too in his desire "to be a master of my own craft," and "a great craft" (214), it stems mainly from antagonism to his father, as he confesses to Dr. Haller: "I was determined not to try to be like him, not to permit myself any thought of rivaling him but to try to find some realm where I could show that I was worthy of him" (212). This is still the voice of the child pressed to prove his worth. Dr. Haller responds by deeming him "a fanatic" and explaining that fanaticism is "overcompensation for doubt" (212). His professional brilliance is also a form of overcompensation for petrified feeling.

David extends his legalistic thinking to the conduct of his own life in a sustained fantasy:

> I imagine a court, you see, all perfectly real and correct in every detail. I am the Judge, on the Bench. And I am the prosecuting lawyer, who presents whatever it is in the worst possible light— but within the rules of pleading. That means I may not express a purely personal opinion about the rights or wrongs of the case. But I am also the defence lawyer, and I put the best case I can for whatever is under examination—but again I mayn't be personal and load the pleading. I can even call myself on the witness-box and examine and cross-examine myself. And in the

end Mr. Justice Staunton must make up his mind and give a decision. And there is no appeal from that decision. (63)

This is the incarnation of the supremacy of thinking over David's actions, the prohibition on "personal opinion," let alone preferential feelings. When the prisoner Staunton is found guilty of creating a public disturbance in a Toronto theater, Mr. Justice Staunton sentences him to seek psychiatric help at once. Within the fantasy scenario David is therefore capable of sound self-assessment, including the recognition that he has reached the end of his own resources, the point where most patients reach out for expert help. Although the predominance of thinking clearly has its drawbacks as a guiding principle, it also has advantages. In a daring image hardly complimentary to psychiatry, David compares himself to an eighteenth-century soldier confronting a battlefield amputation. His alternatives would be to "die of gangrene or die of the surgeon's knife. My choice in this instance was to go mad unattended or to go mad under the best auspices" (66).

In designating herself as "the Prisoner's Friend" (75) Dr. Haller tacitly enters into David's fantasy and at the same time assimilates it to the Jungian system in which the friend is an archetypal figure. Since the Jungian Friend can prove either benign or hostile, the term is particularly apposite to the rapport between analyst and analysand. In *The Manticore* this relationship is depicted as predominantly positive; its vicissitudes devolve from fluctuations in David's subjective perception of Dr. Haller. After he overcomes his initial surprise and resistance, their talk rapidly becomes quite open and genial. In the opening sessions she asks him to speak of his "trouble now" (23). As he tells his tale, he compares himself to "Scheherazade unfolding one of her never-ending, telescopic tales to King Schahriar" (31), but he realizes too that frankness brings "enormous relief" (43). When he divulges his fantasy of self-indictment and judgment, Dr. Haller is encouraging: "Very frank. We are getting on much better already. You have begun to insult me. I think I may be able to do something for you, Prisoner Staunton" (66). The tone is at once serious and jovial. She urges him to "give up the luxury of easy despair" (66), to turn a corner in his life so as not to smash into a brick wall. She also dispels his fear, common among patients seeking psychiatric help, about going mad by describing his current state of mind with the low-key word "unsatisfactory" (68), which does not suggest any pathology. Indeed, she never makes any medical diagnosis of him, though she deems him "not a whole man" on account of his repudiation of feeling. In this, as in her entire stance toward David, Dr. Haller shows exemplary tact, practicing what she preaches: "respect on both sides" (67). Where he expects her treatment to consist of "bullying and lectures" (69), she reassures him: "I am not going to *do* anything to you. I am going to try to help you in the process of becoming yourself" (69). The emphasis is on the cooperative nature of the enterprise in which her function will be that of "an interested spectator" (73). This is an astute self-presentation, especially appealing to a patient such as David to whom control is of central importance. Dr. Haller begins the process of reeducation by enlightening him on the delicate mechanisms of psychotherapy. In proposing that he write a brief about his case, she grants him control of the narration while she herself maintains control of the therapy.

In this Jungian analysis the quantity of the therapist's input is considerable, in contrast to the Freudians' almost notorious reserve. Dr. Haller herself informs David that he will hear her express many opinions, whereas, for instance, Cardinal's "petit bonhomme" hardly utters a word. In keeping with her active participation Dr. Haller is endowed with a palpable corporeality—facial features, a style of clothing—absent in the calculated anonymity of the Freudian analyst. Her forthcoming manner seems more likely to succeed with a hesitant, reticent undertalker like David, while the self-starters such as Portnoy, Zeno, and Tubby Passmore need none of the encouragement David requires and is given by Dr. Haller. She is very much a verbal presence, even in the notebook section, through the intercalated dramatic dialogues in which she discusses with him candidly and directly the matter he has recalled. Always her role is essentially a corrective one as, for example, when she points out how Caroline has sown a variety of debilitating doubts in his mind, foremost about his paternity and his mother's death. Not the model that Dr. Nolan is to Esther in *The Bell Jar*, Dr. Haller is nonetheless a teacher who amends David's lawyerly faith in the unbroken sequentiality of Reason, Understanding, Opinion, and Conjecture by impressing on him that understanding and experiencing are not interchangeable: "Feeling is the point. Any theologian understands martyrdom, but only the martyr experiences the fire" (101).

David comes to experience feeling through his positive transference to Dr. Haller. This is hinted early on when he admits to himself, "I looked forward to my next hour with her in a state of mind I could not clarify, but which was not wholly disagreeable" (44). As his view of psychiatry undergoes a fundamental modification, he wonders tentatively, "had it something to do with her being a woman?" (43-44). Just as for Esther in *The Bell Jar* the coincidence of gender between patient and therapist is decisive, so in *The Manticore* it is the differentiation that is vital in enabling David to develop a feeling that takes him toward normal sexuality. When Dr. Haller speaks openly to him about his avoidance of feeling, he becomes "angry enough to abandon the whole thing, pay off Dr. Haller, and go out on a monumental toot" (103). The anger is clearly an indication of the painfulness of the issue she has raised and of David's unwillingness to confront it. Gradually he becomes aware of the successive changes in his attitude toward her: from dismay at being treated by a woman, to indifference, to distaste as he suspects (or fears) "a covert antipathy toward me" (171). The major surprise, which brings him no pleasure however, is his discovery that he is in love with her. He behaves absurdly in this situation, like a lovelorn adolescent, going for walks near her house, lurking around in hopes of seeing her, speculating whether she has a husband, a family, or is perhaps a lesbian. When he finally confesses to her, having dressed with unusual care and announced that he had something important to say, she takes it with utmost calm: "Better be completely frank: it is part of the course of the analysis, you understand. A very pleasant part. But still well within professional limits" (174). Despite her matter-of-fact coolness, David's spontaneous feeling for Dr. Haller represents a crucial breakthrough in releasing him from his petrification.

As the therapy progresses, David comes to a better understanding of both the process and of himself. Dr. Haller's initial explanation of her job as "to listen to people say things they very badly want to tell but are afraid nobody else will understand" (13) is echoed in David's later reference to the difficulty of saying things "even to someone who listens professionally to what is usually unspeakable" (252). Apart from this firmer intellectual grasp (and a concomitant higher opinion of psychiatry) David achieves improvement in several telling areas: he drinks less, he sleeps better, his general health is invigorated, and he becomes altogether a "much pleasanter, easier person" (261), less aggressive-defensive. For instance, "those humiliating sessions in Mr. Justice Staunton's court" (264) disappear completely as David attains a self-acceptance that obviates the necessity for self-incrimination, self-recrimination, and self-punishment. He is, in his words, "a psychic convalescent" (267).

This is the stage he has reached when his sessions with Dr. Haller are interrupted by the Christmas holiday. Whether he will continue the therapy is left open; if he wishes to arrange further appointments, he is to let her know in the week between Christmas and New Year. In considering termination David inquires what happens to other people and is told, "They finish their work, or that part of it that can be done here, with a markedly improved understanding of themselves, and that means of much that goes beyond the self. They are in better command of their abilities" (261). David presumes this involves greater happiness, but Dr. Haller is careful to make no such promises. However, she envisages the possibility of "further work" which "would aim at showing you *what* you are" whereas "the work you have been doing during the past year has told you *who* you are" (262). Therapy, if not necessarily interminable, is certainly not finite.

The concluding section of *The Manticore*, "My Sorgenfrei Diary," does not foster the supposition that David will resume therapy in the new year. Sorgenfrei is the name of a strange mansion where he spends the holiday with Dunstan Ramsey, Magnus Eisengrim, and his eccentric friend Liesl, the mansion's owner. Since "sorgenfrei" means free of worry or anxiety, the implication is that David has found at least respite, at best perhaps healing. But the ending of *The Manticore* is rather contrived, beginning with the chance meeting with Dunstan in a bookstore in St. Gallen. Coincidence escalates when it turns out that Liesl knows Jo Haller well. She urges David to undertake further self-exploration on his own: "Jo has put you on your path; do you need her to take you on a tour of your inner labyrinths? Why not go by yourself?" (292) instead of clinging "to Jo like a sailor clinging to a lifebelt" (296). Liesl tries to become Dr. Haller's successor in her attempts to direct David. The contrast between the two women's styles underscores the difference between the amateur and the expert therapist. Liesl uses overt persuasion in her efforts to influence David, including the casting of mild—and comical—aspersions on her rival: "Jo is like a boiled egg—a wonder, a miracle, very easy to take—but even with a good sprinkling of salt she is invalid food" (292). Dr. Haller never adopts such crass, indeed primitive strategies; although she is quite outspoken, she does not become directive, seeking rather to steer her patient toward the development of the capacity to make his own decisions. Yet while David finds Liesl a "maddening woman" (297), she exerts a curious power over him: "Liesl has the ability to an extraordinary extent to worm things out of me. My temperament and professional training make me a man to whom things are told; some-

how she makes me into a teller" (291). Talking is "a trial and a triumph"
to him; for the first time he is able to be "comparatively objective" (279)
about his past and his family. In the perilous exploration of a cave, on
which Liesl takes him, he undergoes an experience of near death and
rebirth. This represents the enactment of and possibly substitute for the
"kind of rebirth" (296) that further therapy might provide, according to
Liesl.

The ending of *The Manticore* is, like that of many narratives of psychotherapy, open. The focus moves away from the actual scenes of therapy
that are at the core of the first two parts with the introduction of a whole
new set of characters who connect this novel to its predecessor and its
successor in the Deptford trilogy. It could be argued that the "Sorgenfrei
Diary" section allows for the assessment of the outcome of David's therapy
as he begins to function in a different environment. There can be no
doubt about the success of Dr. Haller's treatment: David is now able to
speak more freely about himself and to relate better to others. It may
even be that Liesl, despite her decided ugliness, has sparked a streak of
feeling in him. If Dr. Haller acted as a "lifebelt" to David at a time when
he was on the verge of going under, she has also taught him to swim and
to navigate the waters of life.

PART III

DUETS

Duets are those narratives of psychotherapy where both patient and therapist have written an account of their transactions so that two distinctive voices are heard coming from different directions. Such duality is particularly interesting for the insights it may give into not only the patient's responses and transference to the therapist but also the latter's tactics of treatment and countertransference. To what extent do the two partners in psychotherapy experience the process in congruence, or are there significant discrepancies between their perceptions?

In the occasion and disposition of duets there is a wider range of format than in the more customary single voice narratives. The closest integration occurs in *Every Day Gets a Little Closer* (1974) by Irvin Yalom and Ginny Elkin when patient and therapist agree at the outset each to produce a report of every session immediately after it has taken place.[1] More commonly the duet arises retrospectively, often after the closure of the therapy. For example, Fayek Nakhla and Grace Jackson decided to compile *Picking Up the Pieces* (1993) by drawing on his notes and her diaries together with their respective memories of their interaction.[2] Ludwig Binswanger, too, includes lengthy citations from his patient's diaries, letters, and poems in his "Case of Ellen West" so that posthumously her voice has assumed an active, momentous force expressing a self-perception largely at variance with her therapist's views. Finally, there may be no overt cooperation between the duettists, merely parallel renditions when patient and therapist write independently as did Joanne Greenberg in her novel *I Never Promised You a Rose Garden* (1964) and Frieda Fromm-Reichmann in her articles published between the late 1930s and the 1950s collected in *Psychoanalysis and Psychotherapy* (1959).

Yet the unmistakable cross-references between these two writers clearly amount to a duet.

Duets are highly important for an understanding of the chemistry of healing because they afford a double take on the process of psychotherapy. The subjectivity of the predominant first-person mode of narration is opened up in the duet to an at least partial corrective. The doubling uncovers disparities in perception and thus alerts readers to bias or distortion. Which account is to be invested with the greater credibility? Does the therapist's professional authority validate his or her version? Is the patient therefore subjugated to medicalized power? Are these therapeutic encounters, as Liesl assures David in *The Manticore*, "duets between the analyst and the analysand, and you will never be able to sing louder or higher than your analyst" (292)? If this indeed were the usual situation, a central purpose of psychotherapy, namely the strengthening of the patient's ego into self-confidence, would be defeated. To what extent do the recorded duets show the therapist's preponderance or a fruitful cooperation?

11

More than Just Talk

Irvin D. Yalom and Ginny Elkin's
Every Day Gets a Little Closer

> Oh that my words were now written! oh that they were
> printed in a book!
>
> —Job

The subtitle of this unique narrative, "A Twice-Told Therapy," is much more apposite than its puzzling main title, which was chosen by the patient for personal, sentimental reasons.[1] For the therapy is literally twice told as patient and therapist each write an independent rendering of their apprehension of every session right after it has taken place. So the process of psychotherapy is recorded here literally as a "symbiotic drama" (x) and as an immediate eyewitness experience. The narration is simultaneous with the therapy, not retrospective from a temporal distance, as in *Les Mots, The Bell Jar,* or *The Pumpkin Eater.* Because its format is similar to that of journal entries, *Every Day* does not include either direct conversation or scenic enactment of the patient's memories, the usual literary means to "digest"[2] the numerous hours of a psychotherapy. Here the weekly interaction between doctor and patient firmly holds center stage as the core of the book; it also proves to be the crux of the therapy.

The method of the twice-telling is specifically devised as the singularly appropriate mode for this particular patient, Ginny, a twenty-three year-old woman who had recently moved to California on being accepted into a one-year creative writing program. Referred to Yalom by the woman therapist she had seen for a time in New York, Ginny has "major difficulties in living" (xii). During his initial interview with her, Yalom has reservations about treating her individually because of his disquiet at the depth of her admiration for him. For eighteen months she attends a therapy group codirected by him, but makes no progress, even with the addition midway of twice-weekly private sessions with another psychiatrist at the clinic. Finally in fall 1970 Yalom decides to take her on himself since "Ginny's great faith in me colluded with my rescuer fantasy to convince me that only I could save her" (xvii). The therapy is therefore preceded by a history of failure and animated by irrational motivations on both sides. Between fall 1970 and summer 1972 Ginny has sixty hours of therapy with Dr. Yalom.

The idea of translating just talk into writing is "a bold procedural ploy" (xvii), that aims to circumvent Ginny's admitted "monster shyness" (xix) and break the total writing block that besets her, further robbing her of positive self-regard. In lieu of payment which, jobless, she cannot afford, Ginny is "to write an honest summary of each session, containing not only her reactions to what transpired, but also a depiction of the subterranean life of the hour, a note from underground" (xvii-xviii). At the suggestion of his wife, a literary critic, Yalom also writes "an impressionistic nonclinical note" (xviii) following each meeting. Every six months their respective write-ups, meanwhile stored by the secretary, are to be exchanged. While conceding that the procedure might be "artificial" or even "contrived," Yalom is "intrigued by a potentially powerful exercise in self-disclosure" (xviii) in hopes that it would induce talk in a patient unable to reveal herself face-to-face as well as counter her veneration for him by making her realize his fallibility.

The two-year therapy is divided into six chronological segments: "The First Fall," "A Long Spring," "Summer," "A Passing Winter," "A Final Spring," and "Every Day Gets a Little Closer." The regular alternation of reports, each pair devoted to the same single session, is visually presented in the distinctive typography for the two writers. Occasional gaps occur in the sequence: once near the beginning when Ginny confesses that she does not have her piece, had delayed writing it for five days, has not yet typed it, and may have mislaid it. This default suggests resistance on her part. Later, tapes and notes for three meetings are lost in the office. Toward the end four contributions are included from Karl, Ginny's boyfriend, after he participates in sessions. The write-ups are embedded in an elaborate frame, beginning with three forewords: a brief one from the editor, Marilyn Yalom; a much longer one from Yalom, who sketches the clinical picture at his first meeting with Ginny; and last, a vivid evocation by her of her past as an A student in high school but "a human sundial" (xix) whose "permanent logo" (xx) was her grin. Corresponding to this prefatory matter are two afterwords: a lengthy, professionally reflective one by Yalom and a shorter review by Ginny of what the therapy has meant to her. The origins of *Every Day* cast the therapist as the experiment's instigator and impelling force; however, the final word is left to the patient. So although the physician commands medical authority, the disposition of the narrative creates near parity between the two writers.

Ginny's problems, personal and professional, surface as her habitual undertalking. She is afflicted, according to Yalom, "with a disease of hyper-consciousness" that has made her "too much a part of the audience, too little a member of the cast" (109). Most clinicians, he ventures, would deem Ginny "schizoid" or "borderline" because of "her ego boundary blurring, her autism, her dream life, the inaccessibility to affect" (xiv). It is striking how much less gravely she perceives her self although she experiences almost daily the impediment in her relationships, particularly to men, caused by her lack of assertiveness and her persistent immaturity. Yet she shows an astute awareness of her own behavior, describing herself as "too dependent" (81) or "just putty" (124), habitually "putting things off" (82) so as to suspend her active life, reverting instead to a childlike retreat from decisions or responsibilities that is symbolized in her hallmark grin, an evasion of deeper affect. She is torn by contradictions: even as she castigates "the 'poor me' of the reports" (86), she confesses to both nurturing that inadequate self and cringing when she finds herself seen "as a lump" (85). Her insecurity and passivity are most damaging in her dealings with her boyfriend whose attachment she craves so much that she tolerates his inconsiderate conduct without being able to express her own wishes, even in minor domestic matters, for fear of losing him. After the end of the creative writing program she drifts aimlessly through a series of trivial jobs.

Unlike most other narrators of their psychotherapy Ginny does not have to make fundamentally new discoveries about herself. Her previous therapist had already told her that she was "stuck" (xx); her calm acceptance of this verdict is confirmation of her emotional stagnation. Yalom's aim is to dislodge her from this rut by suggesting and encouraging changes in her attitude, beginning with greater self-assertion toward Karl. He urges her to express her feelings openly, to voice the anger and resentment she regularly suppresses, to talk spontaneously, to convey to Karl her sexual likes and dislikes. Implementing his view that "psychotherapy is a dress rehearsal" (219), he has her practice what to say through role-playing. For long she does indeed seem to be stuck in "the same familiar dreary mire" (126) so that Yalom ruefully refers to psychotherapy as "cyclotherapy" (164, 174) in its endlessly revolving repetitiveness. But eventually she does grow into increased confidence in her self. The forced grin fades as she becomes "more like a woman and less like a girl" (243). Her distancing from the old self-pitying "poor me" is evident in her witty, humorous spoof of a report, "The Misfit," written by "Ms Fits" (167-68). She has the courage finally to move to another state, break with Karl, find a more satisfying job, and embark on a more promising relationship with another man. In the happy outcome of this successful therapy *Every Day* has almost the aura of a fairytale.

While Ginny's problems in living are the overt matter of this course of therapy, its true center of gravity lies in the strong transferential and countertransferential rapport between patient and therapist. This crucial facet of psychotherapy can be far more brought into the open in duets than in solos where only one side is told. When both participants independently record their respective responses to each other, the complicatedness of their interaction comes to light. In urging Ginny to deal with "the subterranean life of the hour, a note from the underground" (xviii), Yalom makes an intertextual reference to Dostoyevsky's *Notes from Underground,* the emotionally charged first-person revelation of the psyche of a mid-nineteenth-century Russian incarnation of a "poor me." The underground substratum of *Every Day,* and in some sense its most riveting aspect, is the impact on both patient and therapist of the relationship between them. It is this that shapes the symbiotic drama of psychotherapy.

That drama has in the patient's experience a decided element of hero worship. Ginny declares unabashedly, "That first interview with him, my soul became infatuated" (xxi). "Infatuated" is a strong word, denoting the primordially extravagant nature of her feelings. Her description of the frame of mind in which she met Yalom suggests that she was unconsciously predisposed to find in him the savior figure she craved. She mentions that her expectations, an important factor for her, were "great" because he had been recommended by her New York therapist so that there is, as it were, a grafting of a ready-made transference. In a "vulnerable and warm" mood, she immediately senses that she can "talk straight," cry, ask for help and not be ashamed. Genuine though this belief no doubt is at that time, it is disproven by later events, for when she does have the opportunity to talk straight to him, she has enormous difficulty in overcoming her inhibitions. Her intense need to win his approval acts, ironically, as a deterrent to a self-disclosure unflattering to the image she wants to project. Her transference, therefore, has a negative as well as a positive potential, as is evident in the group situation where the cotherapist notes her "tortured transference to Dr. Yalom which withstood all interpretive effort . . . everything she did in the group was considered in the light of his approval or disapproval" (xvi). The oddity of her infatuation emerges too from her comment, "He was Jewish—and that day I was too" (xxi), which expresses her desire for a togetherness amounting to a fantasy identification. Yet she rightly judges him not to be "a Santa Claus psychiatrist type" (xxi), a slightly comical phrase, especially incongruous in juxtaposition to the notation of his Jewishness. With an insight that transcends her infatuation she realizes that he will not be content to send her on her way with facile Band-Aid clichés of comfort.

As the therapy gets underway, Ginny's reticence and her fears are so dominant that for long she cannot directly address the transference. There is a marked difference in this respect between her foreword, written retrospectively after the conclusion of the therapy, and her reports, especially in the earlier phases. The discrepancy shows just how much progress she did make in her ability to express feelings; in the reports she seems to be playing a game of hide-and-seek with herself as well as with Yalom. After four months she acknowledges, "I still haven't really spoken to you as though you are as near as you are"; instead, "my talking is kind of like me alone in a rain barrel" (46). The image evokes desolation, an aching isolation in an echo chamber. In the early stages of the therapy Ginny's transference can be deduced more from Yalom's observations and his probing than from her own words. She is "very on guard" (28) as soon as he wants to explore her feelings toward him. In reply to his questioning, for instance, she admits, on the verge of tears, that she wondered how she had allowed him "to become such an important part of her life" (48). One oblique way to defuse the dangers innate to her intense transference is to cast Yalom in a quasi-parental role. At one point she sees herself as coming to "buzz for an hour with someone like my father who knows I'd be all right if I just wrote," but she instantly grants that this "was an impersonation of myself" whom she calls with a nice self-irony

"Mrs. Slothman" (97). She tries to invoke the "huge generation gap" to make him "become like a parent" (139)—hardly a convincing argument in view of the relatively small age difference between the forty-year-old therapist and the twenty-five-year-old patient, although it might well seem greater to her because he is already well established professionally and she is still in search of her self. She returns to the parental theme when she contemplates the effect of "having an audience with you, Papa Yalom" (153). The note of irony implicit in the phraseology is again quite marked: "having an audience" is a formal arrangement, a ritualized meeting with a monarch or, more commonly, the pope. The alliterative linkage of "Papa" to pope suggests a subconscious tactic for disarming an intuited threat by means of either domestication ("Papa") or sublimation (pope). This blunting of the transference into something innocuous, even innocent is perceived by Yalom when he describes himself as "a priest-pardoner" (73) in her eyes.

Ginny's conversion of the transference into a father-daughter or priest-penitent relationship is a means to evade the threat lurking barely beneath the surface. The threat stems from the sexual current driving the transference that is particularly intimidating to a young woman who has considerable sexual difficulties with her boyfriend. Yet from the opening phase of the therapy Ginny thinks about Yalom in physical terms, about parts of his body. Characteristically, she does not confess to such thoughts of her own accord; Yalom draws them out of her and notes them in one of his reports. Her open curiosity about the pretty young woman with whom she sees him in San Francisco indicates her jealousy as she adds how happy he seems with his wife. The issue of sexuality first comes closer to utterance through the discussion of the exchanged write-ups, although once more it is up to Yalom to articulate the implications of her behavior: "She made quite an issue of the fact that she had no time to consume them [his reports] carefully because she couldn't possibly read them around Karl as they were so incriminating. She made me feel as if we were conspirators in a political plot or lovers having an affair which had to be totally concealed from Karl" (80). The word "lovers" stands out conspicuously as an undisguised naming of the kind of association that Ginny clearly desired in thinking about his physique. On a parallel occasion later Yalom remarks "that it sounded like a novel where the heroine frantically thrusts love letters out of sight at the approaching steps of her husband" (148).

The association in her mind—and the competition—between her

boyfriend and her therapist becomes an increasingly frequent theme in
Every Day. Her lament about her inability to show her feelings toward
either of them alerts Yalom to her perception of them as the "two men"
in her life (111). In this same session the cast on his leg owing to a knee
injury and the consequent rearrangement of his office heightens his
consciousness of "a definite sexual undercurrent in everything she said"
(111). The "sexual strings between us" (112) are at once confirmed by
her dream of a psychiatrist and a weird girl who is schizophrenic and
does "funny things with her hands"; the psychiatrist likes her very much
and prescribes birth control pills for her. Ginny also produces blatant
fantasies about Yalom taking her away to a cabin in the woods, where he
takes care of her, feeds her, and sends his assistant (i.e., a cover for him)
for "a sexual romp" (225). But the underlying link between boyfriend
and therapist lies as much in her fear of losing them both as in her
attraction to them. Again it is Yalom who voices the dynamics of this
triangle: "When she talked about her relationship to Karl, how uptight
she felt and how unable she was to tell him she was feeling badly, I
began thinking of the parallels between Karl and me. Whenever Ginny
feels she had done the wrong thing with Karl, she fears he will throw her
out, and the same with me" (101). Ginny takes a significant step forward
when she becomes able to write—and to speak—of these key concerns:
"I brought up the topics of conversation—my inability to talk with Karl
about serious things, for example. This is part of my one-dimensional
nature, and I think the way I behave with him is the way I do with you.
So to know how Karl feels—how do you feel? (I should have asked) and
how long will you both last?" (116). She is induced to confront this fear
when Yalom invites, almost dares her to ask something directly, and she
finally says, "How long will you continue to see me, continue to let me
come and babble?" (121). A termination date is eventually set by mutual
consent. Ginny's acceptance of an end to the therapy enables her by a
metonymic extension to make her later decision to break with Karl, "to
inhabit myself," as she puts it, instead of living by "osmosis" (239). In
using the powerful transference first to nurture Ginny and then in wean-
ing her from it to make her more independent, Yalom is indeed her "true
friend" (182). That insight at the end of the first session also attended by
Karl shows Ginny still conflating boyfriend and therapist, but now recognizing which is her truer friend. The transference thus fulfills its therapeutic function of boosting Ginny's sense of her self-worth by showing
her in Yalom's write-ups his "interest in and regard for her" (79). His

"bold procedural ploy" (xvii) of exchanging reports therefore serves the dual purpose of loosening the patient's writing block and of changing her self-image.

The "dramas on the other stage," which Yalom calls "the ultimate and terrible secret of the psychotherapist" (132), are openly played out in *Every Day* in Yalom's responses to Ginny in a way that is wholly beyond the reach of the solo rendition of psychotherapy. As a trained psychiatrist Yalom is fully conversant with the normal phenomenon of countertransference, although he is more troubled by it in this case than usual. The "other actor in this drama" (230) very properly subjects his own position to the same scrutiny "through a magnifying glass" (102) that he recommends to Ginny: "To what extent did my own unconscious or barely conscious needs dictate my perception of Ginny and my behavior toward her?" (230). He is often devastatingly honest about his own motivation: "I *want* to appear wise and omnipotent. It is important that attractive women fall in love with me" (231), or the parenthetical self-criticism: "(Will I never stop needing applause?)" (181). He repeatedly acknowledges his wish to "rescue" her and his faith that he will be able to do so. He needs to be "the miracle worker" (231) with the capacity "to transform her, to succeed where others had failed" (230), yet paradoxically treating her also entails a painful self-confrontation because "she was the writer I always wanted to become" (231).[3] If transference is at once the riskiest and the most effective aspect of psychotherapy, countertransference turns out to be equally fraught with problems. The therapist has to maintain a difficult balance between benign commitment to and overinvestment in the relationship, for continuing detachment is crucial to good clinical judgment. In a striking formulation Yalom refers to the interplay of transference and countertransference as "this crazy business of titrated love" (203). Because it is such a crazy business Yalom is, especially at the outset, very explicitly aware of its hazards: "I must keep this in focus—the Almighty God 'Countertransference'—the more I worship it the less I give to Ginny. What I must not do is try to fill her sense of inner void with my own Pygmalion expectations" (13). In helping his patient to strengthen her ego, the therapist must take care not to let the gratification of his pride interfere with her development.

The evidence of Yalom's rapidly unfolding countertransference is abundant. One decisive factor is the intellectual and professional challenge Ginny poses precisely because Yalom knows from the opening interview "that she was seriously troubled and that therapy would be long and chancy" (xiv). His refusal at first to treat her individually on account of her preexisting excessive admiration for him can be taken as an indication of his resistance to a precarious enterprise. The eighteen months of stagnation in group therapy only intensify the challenge to Yalom's therapeutic powers. For this reason he is particularly conscious of the necessity of keeping his "Pygmalion expectations" in check even as he sets out to prove, not least to himself, his exceptional abilities.

In the course of the sixty hours of their meetings Yalom's responses to Ginny are subject to shifts, mainly determined by the quality of their interaction. Sometimes after a dull or unproductive session he exhibits disappointment and/or discouragement; at other times he is elated at the progress being made. Even his image of her appearance fluctuates; whereas in the group he had seen her as "rather homely," he is suddenly struck by "how pretty" she looks in profile when their chairs are at a ninety degree angle (17). This corrects his initial impression, "Not pretty, no matter how one arranged the parts," which is in turn immediately amended by "Yet curiously appealing" (xi). On the whole Yalom comes to see her in an increasingly favorable light, partly as a result of her own greater attention to her grooming and dress that accompany the rise in her self-esteem. Her gradually more "buxom" (222) physique together with healthy signs of some resistance to therapy remove one early dilemma in the countertransference. So long as Yalom perceives her as "a fragile flower" (8, 48), he withholds some of his comments lest they should leave her "crushed and defenseless" (48); on the other hand, as he warns himself, "I must not let her 'fragile flower' pose control me to the point of impotent gentleness" (8). Once Ginny learns, from reading his write-ups, that he has "positive feelings toward her" (79), in fact "like[s] her very much" (9), he can allow himself to put more pressure on her in the effort to open up her anger.

In "this shameless transference, countertransference, minuet" (154), the most perplexing strand for Yalom as for Ginny is that which touches on sexual or amorous impulses. Why else would this "minuet," a highly decorous dance, be qualified as "shameless"? Yalom introduces a suggestive word too when he writes of "the embrace of therapy" (221). He wrestles with severe self-doubts: "I worked hard and I helped her to get at some things, although I wonder if I wasn't just trying to impress her, trying to make her fall in love with me. Good Lord! Will I never be free of that? No it's still there, I have to keep an eye on it—the third eye, the third ear. What do I want her to love me for? It's not sexual—Ginny doesn't stir sexual feelings in me—no, that's not completely true" (11). He rationalizes the conflict by envisaging himself as "seriously interested in Ginny as a person, . . . and having only a mild flirtation with Ginny, the writer," but this contention is undermined by its opening, "I hope the truth really is" (43), which raises doubts about its trustworthiness. At one session they are both "silly and bilaterally coquettish" (93); at another, when she looks "very pleasing," "well groomed, with an attractive blouse and a long skirt," and "the chairs have been placed rather close together by the cleaning man," he feels "cozy sitting next to her" in sharp contrast to his unease the previous day with another patient when he had moved his chair away (161-62). After she finally stops grinning, "I felt decidedly different about her" (133). Indeed, to reassure her about her weight gain and her associated anxiety that she will end up like her mother, he not only "insisted that she actually looked better" but also "found myself being somewhat seductive to her" (133). The reflexive "found myself" implies an involuntary act, as if he were surprised at his own behavior. To round out the episode, in a kind of self-justification, he adds in a rather stilted manner, "It's interesting to note that when she left my office, a friend who came in to chat for a moment commented on the 'attractive girl' who had just walked out" (133). Soon thereafter another colleague, who has read some of his reports, says, "You know I think you're a little bit in love with Ginny" (138). And when she comes with Karl, he feels "little pangs of jealousy" (179).

In his afterword Yalom reconsiders and assesses his countertransference. Despite his initial caveats to himself about "Pygmalion expectations," he concedes at the end, "I was Pygmalion, she my Galatea" (230). He specifies his feelings when they were together with careful differentiation: "('snug' and 'cozy' are just the right words—not clearly sexual but by no means ethereal)" (223). He resorts to another phrase with distinctive sexual connotations when he asks, with unwonted tentativeness in a rhetorical question: "Would it be going too far to say that our affair has been consummated in this shared work?" (232). His conclusion is an affirmation of countertransference as a positive impetus to this therapy:

Countertransference was always present, like a gauzed veil through which I attempted to see Ginny. To the best of my ability I tugged at it, I stared through it, I refused, as best I could, to allow it to obstruct our work. I know that I did not always suc-

ceed, nor am I convinced that the total subjugation of my irrational side, needs and wishes would have promoted therapy; in a
bewildering fashion countertransference supplied much of the
energy and humanity which made our venture a successful one.
(232-33)

So the dualism of this "Twice-Told Therapy" holds interest for its disclosure of the efforts and struggles on the therapist's side in a difficult
case when the therapist must take risks in order to achieve a good result.

   Another kind of duality, that of role-playing, further complicates
the interaction between therapist and patient, occurring at both a conscious and a subconscious level. Yalom purposefully engages Ginny in
role-playing as a method of getting her to learn a new pattern of self-
assertiveness. But when he plays the part of Karl, he not only superim-
poses it on his function as therapist endeavoring to coach, indeed to
provoke Ginny to respond in a different manner; he also inadvertently
fosters her emotional coalescence of the two men in her life. The boundaries of pretense and reality here become blurred. Alongside this overt
role-playing, both figures in this symbiotic drama perform the parts they
consider to be expected of them. Ginny, who had taken acting lessons in
New York and had thought of becoming a professional actress because
of her considerable talent, admits that she "acted in his office, deliberatly
subduing my spirit to coincide with the therapy hour" (240-41). For
Yalom, who actually styles himself "the other actor in this drama," a
certain stance and its accoutrements are a way to project his professional
persona: "In my office I hide behind my title, my interpretations, my
Freudian beard, penetrating gaze and posture of ultimate helpfulness; in
this book behind my explanations, my thesaurus, my reportorial and
belletristic efforts" (230). The presence of role-playing intensifies the
ambiguities of transference and countertransference; the titrated love,
like the entire relationship, is revealed to be at once genuine and calculated, "authentic" but "antiseptically packaged" (223). The essentially
equivocal nature of the "therapeutic epoxy" (225) is one of the central
paradoxes of psychotherapy: "We mean much to one another, yet we are
characters in a dress rehearsal. We care deeply for each other, yet we
disappear when the hour is up" (223). The image of the dress rehearsal
summarizes Yalom's conception of psychotherapy as a prelude to and a
preparation for the realities of existence. The therapist's office is a safe
stage on which to experiment with and acquire sounder attitudes and

behaviors. According to this view, a certain amount of role-playing is intrinsic to psychotherapy, even though it indirectly heightens the tensions of the transference/countertransference "embrace."

But the fundamental disparity in the roles assigned to therapist and patient in this drama do not prevent them from perceiving their sessions primarily in very parallel moods. That is, perhaps, the greatest surprise in the duet of *Every Day*. Despite the "obvious discrepancies in perspective" (222), the affective momentum of each write-up is generally in close consonance with its pairing. Whether a session has gone well or badly does not diminish the similarity of the two writers' impressions. In one discussion of their exchanged reports Ginny notes "the pendulum effect" in the alternation of good and bad meetings (150). Both are fully aware of these vicissitudes in the course of the therapy; several times both express unease or dissatisfaction or downright disappointment. Once both are uncharacteristically evasive, sensing the shadow of something vital that is not faced: this is the hour that Yalom designates as "very important, puzzling" (83), when Ginny is "incredibly resistive" (84), while her report, as if in echo, opens with "You're right. I don't want to write this" (85). Rarely, and more often at the outset than later, are they at cross-purposes. Once an encounter when Ginny knows herself to be "very on guard" (29) is deemed by Yalom as "fluid and close," with Ginny "willing to stretch herself" (25). The previous session points to the source of such dissent as stemming less from misapprehension than from a conflict of underlying philosophies: "You prompt me into analyzing sensations, whereas I just want to have them," Ginny complains (24). Interestingly, the only radical variance comes after a break of a month over Christmas when Ginny sees her old self as "already a fossil" (129) while Yalom feels "helpless and irritable" (126), caught in "cyclotherapy" (127) because he does not see the incipient change she believes to have been occurring. However, these exceptions stand out conspicuously from the largely consistent concurrence of the write-ups.

This congruence is the more remarkable since neither writer loses sight of the basic "inequality" (62) of the relationship. Ginny invariably refers to him as Dr. Yalom whereas he calls her by her first name. She acknowledges the doctor as "the master of ceremonies" (122), a phrase that once more suggests the performance of a ritual. In a sporting analogy, she again sees him in charge when she comments, "I probably wait for you to start the ball rolling" (129). It is indeed Yalom who usually initiates talk and who is obliged to push, prompt, and press her whenever she falters, as she not infrequently does, falling back all too readily into her customary inertia. So Ginny's undertalking forces him into a compensatory overtalking in his incessant quest to stimulate her into the spontaneity held in check by her hyperconsciousness. His task with a patient who silences herself is arduous. Yet although his active interventions are the antithetical opposite to the withdrawn reserve of the classical psychoanalyst, the ultimate goal is the same: to bring the patient to confront her self-defeating tendencies by persuading her to open up through verbalization.

Hindered in free talk by her inhibitions, Ginny finds a substitute outlet in the pseudoprivacy of writing. More than for Zeno in Svevo's novel, Tubby in Lodge's *Therapy*, or David in *The Manticore*, writing is for Ginny the crucial instrument for her psychotherapy insofar as the obligation of the weekly write-ups forces her to a degree of reflection on herself that she normally eschews. By functioning as a kind of mirror held up to the sessions by both participants, the writing comes to form a meta-level to the therapeutic process as well as its potent adjuvant. Indeed, the writing becomes the central vehicle for the psychotherapy just as the reports themselves are the substance of *Every Day*. In a curious displacement it is the writing about the talk rather than just talk itself that has the therapeutic effect.

But in contrast to their concordant experiencing of the sessions, the two writers exhibit quite divergent modes of expression. Even visually Yalom's long, solid paragraphs set off Ginny's much shorter, lapidary layout. While intended as "impressionistic, nonclinical" notes (xviii), his accounts nevertheless devolve in part from the tradition of the case report. He tends to begin with an evaluative assessment of the tone of the entire session, often in a brief phrase, though from a subjective point of view. Ginny protests against his being "too intellectual sometimes" (103). Certainly his intellectual mastery drives him to seek out firm ground and to proceed analytically, yet he also shows a decided aptitude for improvisation, especially as he comes increasingly to terms with Ginny's nonconformity and her resistances. Still, the facade of control and self-assurance that he must uphold vis-a-vis his patient is moderated by bursts of doubt and frank self-criticism. At times he is distracted by the pressure of other obligations or the intrusion of his own residual private weaknesses. After exchanging write-ups with her, he feels "personally embarrassed" because "some of my observations seemed sophomorish and my language ungainly in comparison to hers" (79). This is an extraordinarily outspoken and harsh judgment on himself. His writing in fact undergoes a perceptible evolution over the two years of Ginny's therapy; the exercise in self-expression proves releasing for him too. The most notable development is his growing recourse to metaphor as against the initial preference for similes. Thus early on Ginny is said to be "drawn to emptiness like a magnet" (4), and "dealing with the ideational content of her anxiety spell was like walking on quicksand" (7). Later Yalom envisages himself on a "therapeutic ledge," "facing an absolutely smooth stone cliff with only the tiniest chink in it of a foothold" (121), and finally no longer experiencing "her as lying on a taut sheet of anxiety" (209). Clearly, this experiment in a twice-told therapy depends for its success as a literary artifact on the therapist's as well as the patient's gift for words.

From reading Ginny's reports it quickly becomes evident why she had been offered a place in a creative writing program. She has an originality, indeed an audacity with words that belies her "monster shyness" in personal encounters. "I can't come to a conclusion with *words* out loud. I never have," she laments (83). On the other hand, writing is her natural medium, it is "automatic" (55); facing paper she has the brio and spontaneity she lacks toward people: "I've always written fast. I write by the rhythm method—just sounds and rhymes, no intellectual thoughts, no thinking" (210). While she is here characterizing her approach to her work as a novelist, the description applies equally to her write-ups, for as she emphasizes, "I don't even think in them" (54). As a result they are quirky, erratic, episodic, oscillating between the associative and the disarticulated. Instead of Yalom's penchant for opening with an inclusive overview, Ginny favors abrupt, idiosyncratic starts whose implications emerge only gradually as she elaborates on her theme: "Something might happen if I were more natural looking. So I left my glasses on. Something might not happen though" (13); "The thing about a migraine is you can't have anything ruffle your balance" (27); "If I were accused of a crime I would be my own best witness" (43); "I think I was trying to entertain you" (36). This wording shows too Ginny's choice of a quasi-letter form as if her reports were addressed to "you," Dr. Yalom. The repeated "you" suggests a wish to communicate with him by putting into writing things she cannot say. The sense of intimacy is fostered also by her system of writing: she writes first by hand and then types up her account, whereas Yalom mentions dictating his notes, a more business-like, impersonal mode. As she rightly discerns, "yours is a diary and mine's just a phone conversation where I'm always conscious that I am connected to you" (75). The term "conversation" is startling from a person who has such difficulty in direct talk, even though the qualifying "phone" removes the element of face to face meeting. The phrase underscores the function of the write-ups as not merely a complement to the sessions but as an important forum for the therapeutic working through.

From the foreword onward, the vigor and forcefulness of Ginny's writing are apparent, particularly in its profusion of metaphors. When she once reads a short piece of hers aloud to Yalom, he finds it "a touching little vignette which sparkled with bright metaphors" (161). But the sporadic criticism she directs at her writing—"(A murky line!)" (213)—encompasses also "all the bad metaphors" she uses "to cover up real statements" (46). She makes a similar attack on herself when she asserts, "I really think I must still be burrowed in the cave, like Plato's cave, since I write and think only with analogies. Everything is like something else. Even this write-up is so veiled" (44). Such disparagement is another manifestation of her low self-esteem. For the metaphors, far from covering up or veiling, obliquely and vividly voice her sense of her own inadequacy: "all I've been is the top part of the flower, and never crawled under the dirt and exposed roots" (28); "a warehouse of echoes" (32); "my unchanging self—a butterfly under glass" (96); "something inside me throws a blanket over my head" (100); "a punchbag of vapor" (128); "no more discipline than a piece of gum" (141); "I sunk my anchor again in the muck" (157). Her depreciation of the distinctive metaphoricity of her writing, an aspect of her overall self-contempt, blinds her to the power she wields. Yalom, however, following one of their six-monthly exchange of write-ups, immediately recognizes her strength: "One thing that was evident to me was that in one sense the tables are turned—Ginny often sees me as having the upper hand and yet when we look at the use of language, it is quite clear that my language is clumsy and unimaginative as compared to hers" (72-73). The near parity between therapist and patient in *Every Day* springs not only from the alternating disposition of the narrative but also from the distribution of power. Her literary virtuosity matches his inventiveness as a therapist.

What then is gained by the twice-telling of this therapy in a close duet? Every narrative of psychotherapy gives a glimpse behind the door closed on the privacy of the session. But here as nowhere else the profoundly symbiotic nature of the therapeutic enterprise emerges with an almost startling clarity. It is not so much the formation of a therapeutic alliance that is at issue in *Every Day* as its modification. Ginny's initial obsessive fixation on Yalom is gradually tempered into a healthier state of trust. The exchanged write-ups play a paramount part in convincing Ginny of Yalom's genuine liking and regard for her, and so implement change by persuading her that she does not lack worth, as she believes. In the reciprocal struggles and stresses with transference and counter-transference the emotional intricacy of the interaction is illuminated with an unparalleled intensity.

This duet affords rare understanding of other aspects of the psycho-therapeutic relationship too. The disturbing impact of what appear to be mere technicalities becomes very plain: breaks in continuity because of public holidays, or Yalom's travels, or the canceling of an appointment because he has colleagues in town, or the imperatives of Ginny's employment. Occasional lateness is much more a problem to her than to him. He even takes a positive view of her arriving fifteen minutes late (having taken a bus that could not possibly have got her there on time) as promising "flickerings of rebellion" (88). On the other hand, Ginny is deeply disturbed when he is five minutes late: "I started to get angry, because I wanted to see you, didn't want to be sent home. And I fantasized that you had left for lunch partially forgetting me, and later leaving word for me to come back tomorrow. And I said (knowing I shouldn't be angry since you were doing me the favor and not vice versa) to forget it, that I would just come the next week. See I'm getting emotions but they're all evolving from fantasies or turning into fantasies" (63). The vehemence of her reaction testifies to her insecurity and her acute fear of abandonment. But Yalom too feels "somewhat guilty during the meeting" (68) if he has been late. The inflated significance of minor lapses in their contract indicates the extent of the underlying ego investment on both sides.

Above all, perhaps, the twice-telling of the narrative exposes the extraordinary delicacy of the therapist's function. Throughout Yalom expresses his concern about the appropriateness of his words: is he too reluctant to speak openly because of her "fragile flower" (48) appearance? or is he being too "authoritarian" (94), thereby enhancing her dependency and sending a message of submission to him? or is he too "pushing" (119)? He worries that her passivity is making him too directive. He takes partial responsibility for an unprofitable hour because he has been "very distracted" (141) by what had happened in a previous session. The dullest hour follows "a bad night's sleep" (170). And he is incessantly aware of the paradoxical pull of closeness and detachment, and of the "psychotherapeutic Catch-22: Do what I suggest, but do it for yourself" (227). In his afterword Yalom expounds more systematically many of these troubling facets of psychotherapy, but they derive a striking immediacy from his weekly interactions with Ginny as dilemmas of the moment rather than generalized reflections. The simultaneity of therapist's and patient's renditions as well as the contemporaneous translation of talk into writing is unprecedented before *Every Day*.

12

Containing the Break

Fayek Nakhla and Grace Jackson's
Picking Up the Pieces

I took her to pieces; sifted her, and separated her failings. I
studied 'em.
— William Congreve, *The Way of the World*

The "pieces" in the title of this twofold, collaborative account of "a psychoanalytic journey," as it is described in its subtitle, are to be read at
once literally and metaphorically. On the physical plane, pieces refers to
the shards of glass and paper that the patient scatters during her destructive and self-destructive phase. Figuratively, the pieces to be picked
up denote the reconstruction of her identity and her life after her spectacular breakdown. In a third meaning, perhaps slightly more remote,
pieces could be taken to signify the repeated stitching up of the cuts she
inflicts on herself at her nadir. This multifaceted title is apposite to a
complex, melded account of the dissolution and reconstitution of a personality as experienced by the therapist and the patient.

Published in 1993, nearly twenty years after *Every Day Gets a Little
Closer, Picking Up the Pieces* is the nearest approximation to another close
duet between the two participants in a psychotherapy. While it bears
certain resemblances to its predecessor, the differences in both form and
content prevail. The two-and-a-half-year time span covered in *Picking
Up the Pieces* is an almost parallel duration to that in *Every Day;* however, this is only part of a sixteen-year treatment. Likewise, the two narrators coalesce, though not in the regular alternation of Yalom's and
Ginny's write-ups. A more important divergence is the retrospective cre-

ation of *Picking Up the Pieces,* begun in 1988, to recount the phase that had occurred between October 1973 and December 1976. Based on the therapist's notes and the patient's memories and diaries, it was written cooperatively in contrast to the independent, dovetailed reports in *Every Day.* The respective patients, too, are heterogeneous, although both were exceptionally good students until they graduated from college. Both have problems in fashioning their self. But Grace is far more severely disturbed than Ginny; a schizoid, borderline personality, she undergoes two hospitalizations and is a serious threat to herself. On the other hand, she is similar to Ginny in responding well to an "unorthodox form of practice" (135). And Nakhla, although aware of "the controversial nature" (132) of his approach, engages in considerably less self-scrutiny than Yalom, turning outward instead for confirmation.

One of the major obstacles to psychotherapy that Grace presents from the outset is her undertalking. In his prologue Dr. Nakhla recalls his impression of her as "timid and detached," "soft-spoken" (7), and "reluctant to discuss her problems" so that "I found myself taking the initiative" (8). Here precisely the same reflexive verb appears as in *Every Day* with a taciturn patient forcing the therapist into (over)talk. At their next meeting Grace "was silent. This silence was to continue for eighteen months" (8). Grace also recalls the doctor's mixture of exasperation and encouragement in the opening stages of their interaction when she cites his lament: "I talk too much; out of proportion. I am supposed to listen. I ask questions that you hardly answer—I don't care what you talk about. I am not trying for any specific thing. I just want you to talk" (26-27). Grace's struggle to verbalize her feelings is a recurrent motif throughout *Picking Up the Pieces.* With a previous therapist too there had been long silences: "I told her how I can't talk when there is any sort of pressure: at school, or here, with her" (17). However, again like Ginny, she does write, having kept a diary since early adolescence. Begun in imitation of one of her teachers, it soon became "more complex and introspective" so that "I could exist only if I was written down" (12). Writing is for Grace a substitute not only for talking but in a wider sense for the reality of living.

Her undertalking is addressed partly in her first section, "A Perfect Child," which follows immediately on the doctor's prologue and explains her family background. As the eldest child she had always felt the responsibility to be good and helpful: "Easy" and "Perfect" (10) were her nicknames, and being good also entailed being happy and wanting "everything to be neat and smooth" (10). Proud to be praised, she becomes the victim of her own youthful success through the necessity to uphold the high standards she has set herself. The origins of some of her subsequent problems can therefore be traced back to her childhood. One of the conventions of this apparently "happy family" was that "No one talked about things beneath the surface" (10). Clearly, Grace's entrenched undertalking is rooted in this conditioning. Connected to this accustomed repression as another insidious effect of the persona she had fashioned in childhood is the importance of "keeping up the appearances" (11). This forms a further prominent theme in *Picking Up the Pieces*. Even though unable to talk about herself, "no matter how disturbed or chaotic I might be inside I would always be able to keep up appearances outside; it was what I had been doing for all of my life" (33). Nakhla comments on "the fact that she continued to function smoothly in her day-to-day life" (65), holding down a job through periods of serious disarray. Her long habit of self-containment enables her to conceal her sick self from her physician and even to some extent from herself.

So Grace's undertalking and her emphasis on keeping up appearances are the means to which she resorts to stave off a breakdown. She manages to maintain what Nakhla terms "a false self" (21) during the two years she spends in London after college with her close friend Susan. Doing a variety of odd jobs, pretending to be practicing to be a writer, she is wholly devoid of direction and increasingly dependent on Susan who acts as her "connection to the alive world of people, events, activity—not only my connection but my viewpoint, my bond" (14-15). They had come to London "to find ourselves" (14), though they set about it in different ways, Susan going out into the world while Grace turns in on herself. To counteract Grace's "repression of emotions" (16) Susan, who was by then seeing an analyst, urges Grace too to go into therapy.

In consulting a psychiatrist Grace for the first time departs from her family's creed, which disapproved of such a step as a sign of weakness, an admission that "you couldn't solve your own problems" (16). She rationalizes her decision to go to Dr. P. "not as seeking help but as a way to 'know' myself" (16). Obviously her defense mechanisms are strong, for the last thing she really wants is to face what lies behind the appearances. Her weekly sessions for eight months center on her relationship to Susan and to her younger sister Eleanor, who is cast as the Medusa, "the monster" (17) in Grace's life. Credibly, Dr. P. points out to her that she and Susan "support each other's unreality" (19). Grace's rapport with

Dr. P. is not elaborated, perhaps itself a symptom of her ingrained reticence. The most vital insight from this short therapy is Grace's realization that she is able to give only her "own distorted version of the truth" (19). All our versions of truth are, of course, distorted insofar as they are "versions," that is, intrinsically subjective perceptions, which may be corrected or amended by the therapist. Since we have only Grace's narration of this London psychotherapy, it is impossible to tell whether she intuits at this early stage just how distorted her version is. Nevertheless, her London therapist seems to have initiated a small breach in her systematic self-containment.

Recommended, like Ginny, by Dr. P. to a colleague of hers in New York, Grace reacts to the change quite differently. In retrospect, her image of her former therapist (whom she had resented at the time for sitting there "unmoved" [19]) is nostalgically idealized: "With Dr. P. I had felt some sort of connection and sympathy" (24). After two months she writes to her: "I have been going to see Dr. Nakhla and mostly we have been talking (or not talking) about why I cannot talk to him" (25). Her transference to him undergoes many vicissitudes. At first he strikes her as "strange [and] distant" (24); despite his earnest attempts to find something to talk about, she cannot respond. In fact, she projects her own distance onto him, finding fault with his "sterile, impersonal, formal" office (24), which she now contrasts unfavorably with the light room in Dr. P.'s house with its view of treetops. The transition from one therapist to another is compromised by Grace's flagrant negativity: "He talks and talks, to me, at me; on the edge of the chair, looking at nothing" (27). This passage provides perhaps a clue to the source of her resistance: she evidently feels terribly threatened by his persistent talk, conceding for the first time, "Maybe I will break down, break out, lose control" (27), that is, stop keeping up the appearance of being alright except for her silence. Her muteness now begins to emerge for what it is: a protective strategy to maintain a semblance of control and to postpone her collapse. She continues to ascribe her own oppositional detachment to the therapist: "He asks questions but I feel he isn't interested in the answers. The feeling that I don't matter to him, that he is doing a job, as boring to him as my job is to me, pretending a sort of interest as I do with commas" (27). Even the "mean little hour" of the session becomes "another grasping at a pretense for existence" (27), that is, just another way of keeping up the appearance. "I almost never talked about my actual life," she adds (27).

What does Grace mean by her "actual life"? To all appearances, she grants, she has a life: a job at which she was good, involvement in the office, and friends there and outside. But there is for her no connection between her daily activities and what she calls "reality" (27); her diary states, "I cannot talk about my life: there is nothing to tell. I went to work; Neil came to dinner, Lynne came to dinner. I made paella with the fish Eyre gave me; I washed the dishes. . . . There is no consistency, no wholeness; only fragments" (28). That last word already adumbrates the pieces into which she will break. In a letter to the doctor during his summer vacation in August 1974 when she had been seeing him for nearly a year, she bluntly avows, "I truly do not believe that I am real" (28). After Susan acquires a boyfriend, whom she eventually marries, Grace feels more and more isolated and "afraid of my own emptiness" (35), yet "still unable to talk to the doctor, even to tell him what was happening" (33). More acutely conscious than ever of her "lack of a self" (34), without the strength now required to contain the illness, she finds herself "breaking into pieces, . . . destructive and destroyed" (34). Living alone in an apartment, she begins to see the doctor's office as "the only safe place, where I could be contained and, at least for that hour, would not disappear" (35). The departure of Susan, who had indeed supported her unreality, suddenly drives her toward the therapist. He suggests hospital "as a place to cry, a rest" (35), a respite from her silent, solitary struggle. But the hospital, with its "quick-fix, band-aid approach" (38) in its diagnosis of depression and its antidepressant medication, creates only a false and temporary calm. Nevertheless it is "a container at a time when I needed to be contained, when perhaps the doctor also needed me to be contained" (38).[1]

Grace's first hospitalization is more consequential for Nakhla than for her in making him discern the depths of her disorder and in leading to a change of approach toward her. At the beginning he has less to say openly about his countertransference than Yalom. In the foreword, written by Joyce McDougall of the Paris Psychoanalytic Society with whom Nakhla discussed this troubling case, the emphasis is on his "distress and bewilderment" (xi) at listening to his patient's mute transmission of her suffering. Because he at first interprets her silence simply as resistance, he experiences a "sense of isolation and defensive detachment" (22) very parallel to hers. Interestingly, his narrative here reveals how right Grace was in her perception of his remoteness. But her depersonalization following Susan's removal jolts him "into an anxious state" (39). At this juncture the intertwining of the two tales proves most valuable by disclosing the disparity between the two writers' reaction to Grace's incipient break: the patient's passive indifference as she abdicates responsibility for her behavior is in counterpoint to the therapist's rising perturbation as he assumes greater responsibility.

His decision to change his approach precipitates a shift in their relationship. *Picking Up the Pieces,* even more than *Every Day,* shows the mutual responsiveness of doctor and patient, especially as they get to know each other better. So long as Nakhla perceives Grace as merely resisting or blocking the therapy through her silence he in turn is hampered by "stubbornness and anger" (22). Once he realizes her "psychotic decompensation" (39), he embarks on a deeply committed search for the best means to help her. A kind of domino effect takes place, for as Grace senses his growing acknowledgment of her neediness, she comes to rely on him as a bulwark against total dissolution, a container, and an access to reality. In her extremity Nakhla takes the unusual—and in classical psychoanalysis absolutely forbidden—step of physically holding her: "he takes my hand, puts his arm around me, hand on my head. Then I am there, he is there, real" (45). Since she feels in touch with herself only through him, she now becomes obsessively attached to him, watching for his car, seeing where he parks, and what street he takes to go home. His phone calls evenings and weekends are literally vital to her because "being connected to the doctor is being connected to myself" (73). The very intensity of this almost identificatory dependence fosters a conflicted love/hate transference. As she envisages herself as "a marionette on a string controlled by him" (50), but controlled, that is, contained, only by his presence, she resents his absence. He becomes "destroyer and savior" (50), "bad-demon and good-demon" (52); oriented wholly to him, she addresses him in her diary as "you" in the same way as Ginny does Yalom: "I hate you, but I know I don't hate you" (60). The vehement directness of her language conveys the violence of the passions that grip her.

Grace is incapable of such pronounced feelings about herself; mainly she experiences herself as a nonpresence, an emptiness. It is at this, her lowest, point that she hits on pain as a tool for apprehending reality. At first it is no more than a fantasy: "Like scraping your hand along a brick wall to see the blood; you see the blood, you know that you are real" (34). She begins to translate the fantasy into action when she shreds tissues in the doctor's office, throwing them over his clean suit. In her apartment and increasingly in vacant lots at deserted times of day she acts out her delusional equation of blood and reality, arriving at the doctor's "smashed and bloody" (51), or, as the injuries grow more serious, having to go to an emergency room for stitches. "I made myself an expert in bottles, the different kinds, thicknesses, shapes, colors; and different ways of breaking them; and the different vulnerabilities of parts of the body: where to get the most blood, the most pain" (51). Cutting denotes freedom to her, power over her own body so that "being in pieces [is] being in touch" (55). Above all, self-injury signifies an abandonment of her old stance of containment; now she externalizes her inner void by her wilfully self-assertive breaking. No longer is the surface intact and quiescent. Only by enacting its fragmentation can she make contact with her body. Even at the typewriter "nothing comes out. NOTHING" (53). Through the violence of shredding, breaking, self-inflicted harm she tries to communicate her suffering. In a climactic episode she shreds the whole Sunday *Times,* stuffing most of the pieces into a bag to throw away, but keeping "one bouquet" (47) she had made and giving it to the doctor in a pot. Obviously, she is figuratively presenting him with the broken pieces of her self in a container, a pot. According to classical Freudian theory, the pot as a symbol of the vagina could also carry sexual connotations, although the text does not hint at this possible interpretation. Taking the newspaper remnants out of the pot, even as she tears them into ever smaller pieces the doctor uses them to explain explicitly to her that they stand for the way she feels. She derives "a kind of hope"—her first faint glimmer of hope—from her ability to "destroy the unliving, self-containing part of myself" but also is dogged by "the fear that having once begun I will be unable to stop destroying" (47). Her fear of her destructive rage is heightened by her not knowing what it is she wants to destroy nor who it is that is doing the destroying. She imagines going into the doctor's office, "armed, to tear myself and him to shreds, to pieces" (56). Out of considerations of safety as well as to provide a respite for the doctor, and a rest from the tempestuousness of the therapy for the patient too, a second hospitalization (November to December 1975) is agreed upon. For Grace hospital is the ultimate form of containment, though at the cost of autonomy. "It's like nursery school or camp" (75), she remarks in an unintentionally ironic comment on the regression she has been going through.

The drama of this psychotherapy is even more closely symbiotic than that in *Every Day.* Nakhla's statement "We're in it together" (68) has to be read not only as an affirmation of his continuing commitment to his patient but also as an expression of his compelling involvement in this case. He admits his own perplexity at his fascination with it: "I don't know why I go on seeing you. The experience must mean something to me, though I couldn't say what" (68). These phrases are verbatim repetitions of his words as reproduced previously from Grace's diary, from which she cites in her account of those months of the therapy. The two voices are almost eerily interwoven as doctor and patient echo each other. Nakhla calls his report on this phase "A Basic Unity" on the theory that in a state of regression the patient experiences "a psychic undifferentiatedness" (65) between self and therapist. It seems at times as though he too were subject to the same phenomenon as he recalls his own mounting tension and anxiety in the face of Grace's overt breakdown. The symbiosis is powerfully abetted by the literary disposition of *Picking Up the Pieces,* which follows a less symmetrical pattern than *Every Day.* The introduction, prologue, and epilogue are all by the doctor so that he fulfills the function of a kind of container for the entire work. In the intermediate eight sections the two writers alternate in varying order. In sections 3 through 8, Grace's report precedes Nakhla's. However, section 1, "Grace's Story," is wholly hers, while section 2 comprises first a contribution by Nakhla and then two by her. Inversely, section 8 consists of two by him, followed by one from her. But within this outer arrangement a blending of the two voices occurs through the citations from Grace's diary by both patient and therapist and in the excerpts from her letters to him, which he incorporates into his reports with commentaries. So although the doctor is the controlling organizer of *Picking Up the Pieces,* the patient's voice breaks through insistently into his narrative as if it could not be contained. The choral simultaneity of the duet in *Every Day* is intensified in *Picking Up the Pieces* into a fugal counterpoint as the echoing sounds meld. The extraordinary psychological fusion between Grace and Nakhla is therefore embodied in the literary format they choose to explore their separate but inextricably linked struggles to contain the break.

But the therapist, too, is in need of some sort of reassuring containment in coping with an illness that turns out to be not just the depression diagnosed at the first hospitalization, manifesting itself instead in "a violent delusional state," as the title of the fourth section describes it. Nakhla takes great risks in handling the case in procedures that far exceed the mere unconventionality of Yalom's suggestion of exchangeable

write-ups. He actually transgresses the boundaries of professional etiquette in psychiatry by physically holding his patient. In addition, he
puts his patient's life and well-being into jeopardy by delaying the second hospitalization after she takes to injuring herself. While he certainly does not approve of her behavior, he partially condones it because
he believes that through the cutting she is beginning to come alive. He
cleans and bandages her wounds, accompanies her to the emergency
room whenever necessary, arranges for a plastic surgeon to carry out
repairs. One of the doctors who stitches her up asks her point-blank,
"Doesn't your doctor think you should be in the hospital?" (52). We have
to rely solely on Grace's account for this comment and also for her report of Nakhla's words: "He said: 'It is I who must take care of you, not
you taking care of yourself, holding yourself. Break the glass here, cut
yourself here; let me take care of you'" (52). His own memories of "those
frightening times" (67) exude far less self-confidence; indeed, he deems
it "almost impossible, . . . to describe or to reflect dispassionately on" his
"feelings and actions during that time" (67). His delineation of his dilemma is something of an apologia: "My responses were shifting and
contradictory—at times sounding like pleas or threats—and thus reflected the overwhelming strain and the bewildering effort to convey to
Grace the sense of my being there for her while at the same time step-
ping back, both separate and whole in myself, and leaving her with her
life and body in her own hands" (67-68). The balancing of these antipo-
dal demands and the burden they imply make the end of each session
and the period between sessions "as stressful for me as they were for
Grace," he asserts (68).

To read Grace's version of this phase is to feel added disquiet at
Nakhla's stance. For when she tries to articulate her urge to break and to
cut, she concludes from his reply that he "had not understood" (51). A
passage in her diary vividly chronicles the embattled tension between
them: "You sound like a schoolteacher, I say bitterly. That's terrible, you
cry. For once really surprised. A schoolteacher . . . but after all I am a
child" (60). Although he tells her that she is "somehow in control" (60),
their miscommunication arouses the suspicion that control eluded them
both during this crisis, which extended from April to November 1975.
More disturbing still, the patient appears at times to be taking advantage of her regression to browbeat and blackmail the doctor into sub-
mitting to her dependency needs. The doctor's quest for a self-protective
containment for himself has to be viewed in the context of the dangers

of his own position and of his patient's onslaughts on him as well as on herself.

Nakhla's search for the refuge of containment is masked as a professional issue. Trained as a psychoanalyst at the famous Tavistock Clinic in London, he turns to British and American psychiatric literature for guidance in the treatment of Grace. But it would be erroneous to conclude that in *Picking Up the Pieces* "this unusual experience [is] presented from the viewpoint of technical management" (xii), as Joyce McDougall maintains in her foreword. "Technical management" represents merely one aspect of Nakhla's work with Grace; arguably that is what she receives in the medications during her first hospitalization with poor results. Nakhla's assiduity in scouring articles and books on regression, transference neurosis and transference psychosis, countertransference, transitional objects, the separation-individuation process, and work with borderline personality is the manifestation of his profound desire to find ways to help Grace. In his contributions to *Picking Up the Pieces,* particularly in the latter half, he frequently reviews the papers he has been reading in his pursuit of precedents to this case and of successful modes of therapy. His foremost mentor is the iconoclastic British therapist, D.W. Winnicott who wrote extensively about human development and experimental psychotherapeutic approaches from the late 1940s to the early 1970s. A quotation from Winnicott's *Human Nature* is the epigraph to *Picking Up the Pieces:* "In psychology it must be said that the infant falls to pieces unless held together, and physical care is psychological care at these stages."

This is the principle underlying Nakhla's treatment of Grace. He draws on an eclectic mixture of methodologies, certainly not what is normally understood as psychoanalysis, although the term features in the book's title. Nakhla's primary model is Winnicott and some of his followers. By interpolating summaries of his readings into his narration of the course of Grace's illness, he assimilates her pathology to that of similar previous cases. Apart from its overt function in furnishing precedents, his references to the professional literature serve two further purposes. They counteract his own insecurity by placing his endeavors with Grace into the framework of an established albeit fluid tradition. They also distance her by grafting onto her technical descriptions such as "the schizoid's claustorphobic-agoraphobic dilemma" (92), "cocoon transference" (101), and "an encumbrance of psyche-soma" (118). In locating Grace in relation to psychiatric theories Nakhla contains her apparent idiosyncracy. She thereby grows less threatening to him but at the cost of also seeming more remote, almost generic, through affiliation to an antecedent group. The depersonalization she suffers from within in her breakdown is imposed on her from without by subsuming her under certain paradigms. Yet Nakhla does so without any attenuation of his continuing compassionate caring for her.

Nakhla's perusal of the literature, together with his inventiveness and his willingness to take risks, does prove fruitful as he manages to steer Grace toward recovery. Exactly how Grace's improvement is implemented is not wholly clear. Her "instinct to survival" fights the "destructive feelings" (99), and eventually fends them off with the help of the doctor's support. He uses the technique of regression, allowing her "to stay infantlike," to be "held infantlike" (83) as if she were finding a new good mother. Nakhla's mothering role is very clearly brought out in a quite bizarre incident: "she came to a session appearing distressed and sat on the edge of the couch, silent and cut off. I sat next to her and put my arm around her. She crawled into my body and several times forcefully thrust her head into me, letting out small shrieks. When she became quieter, I said to her that she had really wanted to get back inside me, into my womb, where she would again be one with me" (119). Grace implicitly connects these infantlike or embryonic drives to her incapacity for speech as if she were still at a preverbal stage: "I want to talk, and I cannot" (83). Her incipient wish to talk, even if she is as yet unable to realize it, is a significant advance on her self-enclosing silence at the outset. In a paradoxical antonym to her infantlike inarticulateness she begins to read Trollope and Dickens, "long nineteenth-century novels, which brought me into a completely different, safe world" (83). "Safe" is the key word. The feeling of safety is what the doctor can give her through holding, reassurance, and perhaps above all his faith in the possibility of improvement, his perseverance, his readiness to go on standing by her. Because she sees him as "safe," "I can say to him—I have learned to be able to say to him—I am pretending, I am not feeling. I am just talking. My words are meaningless" (83). In developmental terms her "meaningless" words correspond to a baby's babble. Through regression Grace is enabled to make a second, safer beginning to life. She becomes aware of the dangers of "being the 'good' child" (98), of always complying and thereby being suffocated as an individual. With that insight and the concomitant anger, Grace abruptly breaks away from both the regression and the dependence in order slowly to seek a separate, authentic self. The process is lengthy and difficult, but the dedication of *Picking Up the Pieces,* "For Grace's parents, her sisters, and her husband," allows us to surmise a satisfactory conclusion, although Grace, unlike Ginny, adds no afterthoughts about the therapy.

Grace's last section is about her diary, which is of central importance throughout. It is the mirror she holds up to herself during the time when she is unable to talk; as a register of her thoughts, moods, and self-imprisonment, it proves an invaluable source for the reconstruction of her illness and recovery. Early on, reading the solid, single-spaced pages with their narrow margins and no paragraph breaks, Nakhla is struck by "the deadness of what she wrote" (23). As Grace gradually comes more alive, her writing assumes a positive function as her sole pathway to reality other than through the doctor: "I'm only myself in front of the typewriter" (83), the self with genuine emotions, not the pretending persona of the "false calm" phase. Nakhla later reevaluates the diary, seeing it no longer as "a defensive mental activity of the false self" but "in relation to the creative and imaginative aspects of the self" (116). It is the diary, too, that precipitates the final major turning point in the therapy when the doctor visits Grace in her apartment to see the sixteen volumes. Again this is a transgression of the conventions of psychotherapy in which the segregation of the professional alliance from any social contact is a fundamental principle. Nakhla himself proposes the visit, which has several overlapping significations. First, his reading of her diaries brings her to reveal the self she had kept hidden before the break. That is the essence of the visit in Grace's eyes: "The coming together of doctor and diaries would be the coming together of two selves; it ought to be accomplished symbolically, but in my world that was impossible: it had to happen concretely (like cutting). I was lucky in his understanding of that" (125). Perhaps neither of them at the time grasps the further implications of his visit: the meeting with Grace outside his office, on her own territory, achieves the modulation of the doctor from a transferential or a transitional object into a real person, a part of her new world. In this sense Nakhla's visit is a crucial step, for which the diary provides the occasion.

The reading of the diary is instrumental in prompting Nakhla's suggestion that they jointly write *Picking Up the Pieces.* Begun in the final year of the treatment, it is, in his view, "an important and integral part of the therapy" (2). In contrast to Ginny's and Yalom's weekly write-ups concurrent with their ongoing sessions, Nakhla and Grace engage in an act of memory that takes them some fifteen years back. Although he worries that "reliving what she had been through would be upsetting and disturbing for Grace" (3), it proves to be much more difficult for him. For her, writing the book "seemed to be a psychic holding," a continuation on a metaphorical plane of "the years of physical holding" (6), whereas for him it brings an acute recrudescence of the anxiety he had undergone. But for him too the activity of recollection is therapeutic, for he has been successful in his treatment of Grace. The retrospective recreation of the therapy that the writing entails is therefore a powerful tool for closure for both of them. Moreover, the cooperation with the doctor elevates Grace from the role of infantlike patient to that of adult collaborator. She now shows eagerness for a cognitive comprehension of what had happened in the therapy, including its theoretical aspects. She even becomes Nakhla's helper by translating for him an article and a letter from Italian, a language she had been learning for a couple of years. This task in turn sparks her interest in Winnicott, whose *Playing and Reality* (1971) she then reads.

On readers too this section, "Writing the Book" (1-6), has a salutary effect. Its placement as the introduction to *Picking Up the Pieces* is the equivalent to a psychic holding for readers, acting as a safe container for the often alarming happenings that form the substance of this narrative of psychotherapy. If this organization reduces the suspense about the outcome, certainly in comparison to *Every Day*, it has its own advantages too. The revelation at the outset of the benign termination invests heightened interest in the means invoked to bring about the patient's recovery. As in *Every Day*, so in *Picking Up the Pieces,* the therapist's input affords a lively insight into the predicaments and challenges faced in any attempt at psychological healing. The combination of the two voices in duet lays open the intricate adjustments that both sides have constantly to make to each other in this most delicate relationship so replete with the potential for damage in the event of a failure of rightful understanding, or for good when patient and therapist alike have the flexibility to attain a congruent partnership.

The extraordinary degree of compatibility that Nakhla and Grace achieve does not undermine the continuing individuality of their voices even in the closest interaction. For, as the good mother, Nakhla nurtures Grace's separateness. Their respective modes of writing differ much more than Yalom's and Ginny's in *Every Day*. While they were each presenting their version of an immediately anterior encounter, Nakhla and Grace do their telling from vastly divergent perspectives. The doctor uses al-most exclusively the past tense, recalling distantly bygone transactions in a continuous sequence. Nonetheless, his sharing in the emotional drama of his meetings with Grace lends urgency to his memories. Grace, on the other hand, favors the present tense because her contributions draw heavily on her diary entries simultaneous with the ongoing therapy. Her total immersion in her current turmoil finds its outlet in an agitated instability. Syntactically she produces staccato, broken off phrases, rhe-torical questions, dashes, suspension points, in short, random, private jottings as against Nakhla's communicative prose. He is addressing an audience of projected readers, whereas she is free associating to vent the alternatives that race through her mind. But in the narrative portions that connect the passages from the diary and that were added at the time of the book's composition, her style, in the past tense, has rational cohe-siveness. Her two completely disparate types of phraseology allow read-ers to confront the Grace of the height of her illness and the Grace who has emerged from the therapy.

Both of Grace's modes of expression are characterized by the energy with which she manages to capture the pain of her suffering. Her im-ages are suggestive of her liminality: on a tightrope over an abyss, at the edge of a cliff, "enclosed in my block of ice" (83). The rawness of her distress hits hard:

> I must have the razor blades, for tonight or for tomorrow morn-ing or for tomorrow night when I go to see you. You haven't seen that, me with a razor blade. Plain and pure and direct and so simple. Reliving, acting out the experience. Why does it have to be acted out? And yet talking is obviously of no use. Or is like scratches, an indication, a mere glimpse or sight or signal of what I feel, scratching of surfaces.
>
> Reason enough to fall into a stuporlike sleep: to avoid having to kill myself. I don't want to be dead. But he is going to watch, the doctor, YOU, you are going to know better than words, bet-ter than light bulbs, better than pus-ridden wounds already in-flicted." (61)

The contrast between this sample of Grace's fragmented but vigor-ous writing and the opening of Nakhla's report immediately following illustrates the fundamental heterogeneity of their expression:

After Grace's discharge from her first hospitalization in March, there was a rapid and dramatic change in the treatment ambience. Her terrifying feelings of non-existence, which had been held tightly in check by her withdrawal and almost catatonic stillness and silence over the previous eighteen months, were at last in the open. She was visibly frightened; she found it difficult to remain seated in her chair and paced restlessly around the office. (61-61)

The doctor's manner tends toward intellectualization; by definition his role has to be that of detached clinical observer who keeps his head in the face of Grace's turbulence. The reasoning deliberation governing Nakhla's contributions is set off by her impulsive emotionalism. In his erudite assessments of the medical articles he reads his ratiocination is very apparent. His footnotes, clinical appendix, nine pages of references, and the author index all give the book a distinctly scholarly air (it was published by a university press). Through the doctor's predominance in these materials on the peripheries of *Picking Up the Pieces* and the patient's stronger presence in the middle, the volume enacts the containment it portrays.

13

The Elusive Patient and Her Ventriloquist Therapist

Ludwig Binswanger's "The Case of Ellen West"

The voice of one crying in the wilderness

—Isaiah 40:3

The voice of Ellen West, crying out from her wilderness, has attained considerable fame. She speaks out from Ludwig Binswanger's sequence of four long articles about her published in the *Schweizer Archiv für Neurologie und Psychiatrie* (*Swiss Journal for Neurology and Psychiatry*) in 1944-45. She reached a wide audience after their appearance in English in *Existence,* an exposition of the existentialist approach in psychiatry, edited by Rollo May in 1958. In the fall of that year at a conference held by the newly formed American Academy of Psychotherapists May organized a symposium to discuss the case; three psychiatrists, two psychologists, an anthropologist, and a social historian took part in the all-day session. This immediately suggests the interest this perplexing case aroused at the time. Since then scholarly articles have been written about Binswanger's handling of it,[1] and West has formed the subject of chapters in three books.[2] More surprisingly perhaps, in the past fifteen or so years West has begun to surface beyond the archives of psychiatry. Adrienne Rich published a poem in 1971, "For Ellen West: Mental Patient and Suicide," as did Frank Bidart, who wrote his honors thesis about Ellen West at Brandeis University in 1979, and included a lengthy poem about her in his 1990 collection *In the Western Night.* In 1983 Lisa

Britt made an audiovisual presentation, *Ellen West: Portrait of an Obses-sion*, and two years later a playlet, "The Triumph of Ellen West," by Dr. Salvador Minuchin was performed in New York as one of a cluster en-titled *Family Kaleidoscope*. She even moved into popular culture in 1991 in a song, "Ellen West," on a sound disc, *The Real Ramona*, made by the rock group Throwing Muses.

Yet although Ellen West still captures the imagination fifty years after Binswanger's articles, very little is known about her outside his account. Even the dates of her life, 1890-1924 are no more than an approximation. In marked contrast to the large amounts of information that have been uncovered about Freud's patient's,[3] the exclusive source for Ellen West is Binswanger's articles. None of her writings have been published; they are kept in the archives of the Bellevue Sanatorium, now deposited in Tübingen, and Binswanger's grandson, Dr. Dieter Binswanger, refuses researchers access to them.[4] The name is generally presumed to be a pseudonym (like Ginny Elkin and Grace Jackson) to protect the patient's privacy; this assumption is borne out by the parallel case of an Amalie East in Mendel's *Treating Schizophrenia*. All the sec-ondary work on Ellen West has therefore been dependent on Binswanger's report.

The biographical data in the case history are fairly perfunctory. Ellen is Jewish, non-Swiss, has two brothers, one four years older, who had once been in a psychiatric clinic for some weeks with a mental disorder including suicidal ideas, and a cheerful, well-adjusted younger brother. At age twenty-two she enters university with the intention of studying economics, but she drops out after a breakdown following an attach-ment to a student to whom she is for a while engaged. The fact that she met him again after the breakup of the engagement has been taken as evidence of her continuing love. At age twenty-eight she marries a cousin but has no children subsequent to a miscarriage. Her most pressing in-terest is in social work.

There are large lacunae in our knowledge, as Studer points out.[5] About her husband only his first name, Karl, is divulged, no age, profes-sion, character profile, let alone insight into the quality of the marriage. Similarly, the parents' age, their place of residence, her father's occupa-tion, the nature of the relationship between father and mother are not disclosed either. As a result of these glaring gaps, speculation has tended to proliferate. For instance, Studer surmises, "Die Eltern scheinen eine eigene Meinung der Tochter nicht zu tolerieren und scheuen wohl keine

Mittel, sich durchzusetzen. Dabei sind die Mittel vermutlich sehr subtil, so dass sich Ellen nicht dagegen wehren kann" (243; The parents seem not to tolerate an independent opinion on their daughter's part, and probably shun no means to get their way. Their means are likely very subtle so that Ellen cannot resist). As an example of the need "herauszulesen" (Studer, 237; to read out, that is, deduce), such argumentation is shaky as the high incidence of terms of conjecture ("scheinen," "wohl," "vermutlich") indicates. Ellen remains elusive.

A great deal more is known about the Swiss psychiatrist-philosopher Ludwig Binswanger (1881-1966). Born into a family distinguished over several generations for its physicians and notably its psychiatrists, he received his medical degree in 1907 in Zurich. There he also studied with Carl Jung and was a psychiatric intern under Eugen Bleuler. He did his residency in Germany at the Psychiatric Clinic for Nervous Diseases at Jena University under his uncle, Otto Binswanger, before becoming an associate of his father, Robert Binswanger, then director of the Bellevue Sanatorium in Kreuzlingen, Switzerland. In 1911 he succeeded his father (and grandfather) as medical director of this sanatorium, where he remained until his retirement in 1956. Bellevue was a famous institution to which problematic cases were referred from German-speaking areas. For instance, Bertha Pappenheim, Breuer and Freud's Anna O, became a patient there in July 1882. Like her, Ellen West went to Bellevue on the recommendation of her internist, staying six weeks from 14 January to 30 March 19—(Binswanger withholds the year).

At the Bellevue Binswanger developed his pioneering work in what he called "Daseinsanalyse," normally translated as "existential analysis," although its literal meaning is analysis of being. Its German name indicates its origins in Heidegger's concept of the analysis of existence, that is, of the dilemmas human beings face resulting from their being-in-the-world. While also in the wake of Freud, with whom he maintained friendly personal relations, Binswanger sought to expand psychoanalysis into a more comprehensive understanding of what actually was happening in the totality of patients' existence. Binswanger and his followers, because they saw knowledge as intrinsically empirical and phenomenological, had doubts about such unverifiable agents as libido or the devious processes of transference and countertransference. Binswanger was skeptical too of the notion of the unconscious, preferring to concentrate on the ascertainable manifestations of patients' view of their existence.

For this reason he insisted that "*phenomenological anthropology*" was the only designation properly suited to describe his endeavor.[6] He defined "a phenomenological view of life in the widest sense" as one that "aims at the grasping of the life-content of phenomena and not at their factual meaning within a precisely circumscribed object-area."[7] Without denying the value of natural sciences methodologies, he stressed the necessity of understanding patients' present meaning-context by attempting to reconstruct the universe of their inner experience. His approach is therefore essentially dynamic, devolving from the perception of human beings as constantly becoming and emerging rather than as collections of static substances or mechanisms or even patterns fashioned by their past. His belief in each person's totalizing world-design led Binswanger to deplore not only the separation of past and present but also, above all, "the theory of a dichotomy of world into subject and object."[8] Indeed, Rollo May insists that according to Binswanger "the cancer of all psychology up to now [was] the cancer of the doctrine of subject-object cleavage."[9]

The term "existentialist" in the name of his school of thought points to Binswanger's filiation from the philosophy of existentialism that was crystallizing into a powerful current at the time when Binswanger was writing his seminal treatise *Grundformen und Erkenntnis menschlichen Daseins* (*Basic Forms and Cognition of Human Existence*) which appeared in 1942. Binswanger shared the existentialists' conviction that the source of anxiety lies in the *condition humaine*, in existence itself. Although human beings cannot live apart from the world or exist in a world apart from themselves, Binswanger as a psychotherapist posited the necessity for transcendence as the path to an authentic existence. Transcendence involves an openness to continuing growth and change, an amendment of the person's way of relating on three interconnected levels: to oneself, to one's fellow human beings, and to the larger surroundings. For these three spheres Binswanger coined the terms *Eigenwelt, Mitwelt,* and *Umwelt,* which translate awkwardly into English as "own-world," "with-world," and "world-around."[10] The stasis consequent to refusal to grow and become underlies, according to him, the development of neurotic or psychotic traits.

It is in light of these tenets that Binswanger interprets the case of Ellen West. His intention is signaled in the subtitle, "An Anthropological-Clinical Study," which announces at the outset the antecedent system into which the patient is to be slotted. The priority of the philosophy over the patient's individuality is the salient characteristic of the method by which the case history is unfolded and for the resultant blinkered vision that occludes Binswanger's insight. He had already compiled his book on existential analysis in 1942 when he went back to the archives of the Bellevue Sanatorium to select an illustrative case. He describes it as "my first study planned as an example of existential analysis as applied to psychiatry."[11] The crucial word is "applied" insofar as it underscores the purpose of a paradigmatic exploration of a specific instance of previously outlined general principles.

Binswanger chose the case of Ellen West in preference to others for a special reason: "In this case I had at my disposal an unusual abundance of spontaneous and immediately comprehensible verbal manifestations such as self-descriptions, dream accounts, diary entries, poems, letters, autobiographical drafts."[12] Thus ease of access for the therapist to the patient's inner universe via her writings prompts Binswanger's choice of Ellen West as his exemplary case. In his explanatory article, "The Existential Analysis School of Thought," written immediately after "The Case of Ellen West" and published likewise in the *Schweizer Archiv für Neurologie und Psychiatrie,* Binswanger emphasizes how the "*structure of existence* as 'being-in-the-world' and 'beyond the world,'" far from representing vague life "concepts," consists of "phenomena to be interpreted largely as language phenomena."[13] This is clearly a continuity from the supremacy of free associative talk in psychoanalysis, although Binswanger is at pains to differentiate his interest in language from that of the psychoanalysts who focus "merely upon the historical content, upon references to an experienced or conjectured pattern of the inner life-history."[14] This critique does an injustice to psychoanalysis which shows a keen awareness of the playfulness of language and its role in verbalizing repressed material by means of oblique allusions. He goes on to enunciate the positive importance of language to his mode of analysis: "What attracts our attention in existential analysis is rather the content of language expressions and manifestations insofar as they point to the world-design or designs in which the speaker lives or has lived or, in one word, their world-content."[15]

Despite his rather demonstrative distancing from psychoanalysis on the role of language, Binswanger's mode of writing "The Case of Ellen West" is in one fundamental respect like Freud's approach to the presentation of his cases. Both follow the prototype of the detective investigation, with the patient's disturbance forming the equivalent to the crime as the point of departure. But whereas Freud looks backward temporally into the patient's early life in pursuit of the etiology of the current problems, Binswanger moves more in a laterally spatial direction into the patient's *Eigenwelt, Mitwelt,* and *Umwelt.* This divergence of thrust is a reflection of the underlying heterogeneity of their aims. Freud seeks to uncover the sources of the disorder; his predilection for comparing the psychoanalyst's work to that of the archaeologist unearthing layer after layer of buried material is an explicit pointer to his conception of his task. Binswanger, on the other hand, concentrates rather on the disorder's effects on the patient's rapport to self and to both the immediate and the peripheral environment. So in contrast to Freud's primary concern with individuals and his secondary interest in their surroundings to the extent that they had played a part in the maladjustment that is the presenting symptom or set of symptoms, Binswanger engages more with interpersonal dynamics. Both believe ultimately in the paramount importance of understanding as the instrument for healing, although Freud places the emphasis on self-understanding while Binswanger pursues understanding of the interplay between the self and the wider circumambient frame.

Binswanger's desire to encompass a holistic picture explains the format he uses in "The Case of Ellen West." It is segmented into four major sections, each dedicated to the scrutiny of the same materials from differing angles. The first, "Bericht," which is rendered as "Case History" but means literally "Report" (*Existence,* 237-67), is the story of Ellen's life, illness, and death. Binswanger's account is based on and fused with excerpts from her writings. The second, "Daseinsanalyse" ("Existential Analysis," *Existence,* 267-314), goes over the ground again, this time translated into the terminology of Binswanger's system. The third and by far the shortest part, "Daseinsanalyse und Psychanalyse" ("Existential Analysis and Psychoanalysis," *Existence,* 314-28), contrasts the existential-analytic conceptualization of the case with the psychoanalytic one. The final section, "Psychopathologische-klinische Analyse" ("Psychopathological-Clinical Analysis," *Existence,* 328-64), gropes for a differential diagnosis. The outcome of Binswanger's narrative strategy is, inevitably, a certain amount of repetition that becomes manifest, however, in a perspectivism somewhat like that in Faulkner's *Absalom, Absalom!* or the Japanese film *Rashomon,* where identical happenings appear under varying guises dependent on the subjective perceptions of the narrating persona. The parallel does not quite hold because the controlling

narrator in each of the sections of "Ellen West" is in fact Binswanger himself, although he assumes and incorporates others' voices and viewpoints
after the manner of a ventriloquist who seems to be producing sounds
distinguishable from his own but who is in reality regulating all the strains.

His ventriloquism is most apparent in the first section which contains frequent and at times lengthy citations from Ellen's letters, poems,
and the journal she had begun in late adolescence. Only in this opening
overview can "The Case of Ellen West" be deemed a duet, and even here
only in a limited sense, for it is the therapist who determines what the
patient is allowed to utter. The situation is in many ways entirely different from that in *Every Day* or *Picking Up the Pieces*. "The Case of Ellen
West" is recorded not just years after the attempted psychotherapy described in it but also after the patient's suicide. Still more to the point,
perhaps, Binswanger worked with this patient for a mere six weeks, hardly
long enough to get to know her at all well, even though she was hospitalized so that he would see her daily. The elapse of time, the patient's
death, and the brevity of Binswanger's care of her are factors in making
Ellen seem distant and puzzling. Her ghostly apparition in her writings
intensifies that effect through her presence in absence. Binswanger's procedure in analyzing a patient from written evidence has a near precedent
in Freud's analysis of Schreber ("Psycho-Analytic Notes upon an Autobiographical Account of a Case of Paranoia") which is based exclusively
on the subject's posthumously discovered testimony. Yet despite Freud's
identification of the forces impelling him into a delusional state, Schreber
remains a mysterious other. A similar semitransparency mists Ellen West
too. Since Binswanger always functions as the filter to her voice, she is
not an active partner in the therapy, as Ginny in *Every Day* and Grace in
Picking Up the Pieces are. This profound inequality of talk between the
partners makes "The Case of Ellen West" a very uneven duet. While
Binswanger in the second section offers his interpretation of her words,
she lacks the opportunity to respond so that she is turned into the object
of his enterprise. The circumstances under which the case is reported
therefore lay the foundation for the therapist's suzerainty. Binswanger's
enormous self-assurance, buttressed by his medical authority and his
ancestrally legitimated position as the institution's director, makes him a
dominating, possibly domineering patriarchal figure.

The denial to Ellen of a true hearing that is so prominent a feature
of Binswanger's account replicates her predicament in life as far as it can
be reconstructed from her journal. She rebels strenuously against the

established upper-middle-class social organization (of which he, too, is an incarnation), as she reaches early adulthood: "Ich bin 21 Jahre alt und soll schweigen und grinsen wie eine Puppe. Ich bin keine Puppe. Ich bin ein Mensch mit rotem Blut und bin eine Frau mit zuckendem Herz" ("I am twenty-one years old and am supposed to be silent and grin like a puppet. I am no puppet. I am a human being with red blood and a woman with a quivering heart"). She feels bound by the "eisernen Fesseln des Alltags: Die Fesseln der Konvention, die Fesseln des Besitzes und der Bequemlichkeit, die Fesseln der Dankbarkeit und Rücksicht, und am stärksten von allen die Fesseln der Liebe" ("iron chains of commonplace life: the chains of conventionality, the chains of propriety and comfort, the chains of gratitude and consideration, and, strongest of all, the chains of love"). Taking up her notebook again after a long break, she expresses keen regret "dass ich all die Kraft und Schaffenslust in ungehörte Worte statt in starke Taten übersetzen muss" ("that I must translate all this force and urge to action into unheard words instead of powerful deeds"). The silence imposed on a young woman of her social position by the ruling prescripts of propriety induces a frustration for which she can open "a safety valve" ("Sicherheitsventil")[16] only through her writing. This is the mood in which she composes "Uber den Beruf der Frau" ("On the Woman's Calling") which Binswanger mentions but does not cite.[17] This work's status is uncertain; described vaguely as a "Schrift" (literally, a written piece; translated as "a paper"),[18] it could be anything from a few fragmentary pages to a monograph. Significantly, it was written during a journey to Sicily, that is, at a remove from her home surroundings, a fact on which Bingswanger neglects to comment. His de facto censorship of her writing through his power to select and to suppress at will corresponds ironically to the curbing of her innermost desires during her lifetime.

Yet Ellen West does overcome that restriction through the writings she left; her words, far from remaining "unheard" as she feared, have through their eloquence become the "powerful deeds" she longed to perform. For like Ginny in *Every Day* and Grace in *Picking Up the Pieces*, Ellen is a much more impassioned writer than her therapist. Binswanger's sober, rather flat, medicalized discourse makes markedly less impression than her lively, energetic prose pulsating with feeling and studded with imagery. From this perspective the tables of power are turned in the patient's favor and to the therapist's detriment. The contrast is even greater than that between Dr. Nakhla and Grace Jackson in *Picking Up the Pieces* since the doctor in that case experienced considerable anxiety, whereas Binswanger remains imperturbable, seeing Ellen chiefly as a frustrating psychiatric enigma. The literary disposition of the opening section makes her excitement stand out still more against Binswanger's placidity: passages by her are intercalated into his narrative so that the difference in emotional temperature is put into high relief. Her mood fluctuations and her suffering become extremely vivid. Admittedly, the few snatches of her verse that are included tend to a halting awkwardness, aggravated by the flaccid translation:

> Ich möchte sterben, wie der Vogel stirbt,
> Der sich die Kehle sprengt in höchstem Jubel;
> Nicht leben, wie der Wurm der Erde lebt,
> Alt, hässlich werden, stumpf und dumm!
> Nein, einmal fühlen, wie die Kräfte zünden
> Und sich im eigenen Feuer wild verzehren.
> (I'd like to die just as the birdling does
> That splits its throat in highest jubilation;
> And not live as the worm on earth lives on,
> Becoming old, ugly, dull and dumb!
> No, feel for once how forces in me kindle,
> And wildly be consumed in my own fire.)[19]

Her prose, on the other hand, is characterized by an unfaltering energy, illuminated by a rich metaphoricity: "Noch empfinde ich die Schmach meiner Gefangenschaft. Wie modrig riecht dieses Kellerloch. Der Duft der Blumen kann den Geruch der Fäulnis nicht übertönen. Kein Wunder, habt ihr solch hässliche gelbe Seelen bekommen; ihr, die ihr aufgewachsen seid in dieser Luft. Ihr merkt schon gar nicht mehr, wie schwer das Atmen hier ist. Zwerglungen haben eure Seelen bekommen" ("I still feel the disgrace of my imprisonment. How musty is the smell of this cellar hole. The scent of the flowers cannot drown the stench of decay. No wonder you have got such ugly yellow souls, you who have grown up in this atmosphere. Already you have ceased to notice how hard it is to breathe here. Your souls have grown dwarf lungs").[20] Her most persistent images are variations on the theme of her sense of imprisonment: "Das Leben ist für mich zu einem Gefangenenlager geworden" ("Life has become a prison camp for me"); "Ich bin gefangen, gefangen in einem Netz, aus dem ich mich nicht befreien kann" ("I am in prison, caught in a net from which I cannot free myself"); "Ich bin in Sibirien; mein Herz ist eingefroren" ("I am in Siberia; my heart is ice-bound"); "Ich sitze in einer Glaskugel" ("I sit in a glass ball").[21]

The nature of this imprisonment modulates in the course of her life. At first it stems from the social pressures of propriety for a young woman of her class at her time. But this circumscription imposed on her from without gives way to a self-imprisonment which springs from inner drives that she cannot withstand. Ellen's diary entries show her becoming more and more enmeshed in the problem of her eating and her weight, which ranges from 84 lbs. to 150 lbs. Her eating is extremely idiosyncratic and erratic, oscillating between binging and starving. Binswanger reports that in one phase her daily intake consisted of several pounds of tomatoes and twenty oranges.[22] She has "*das fortwährende Verlangen nach Essen*" ("*the constant desire for food*"),[23] collects recipes, particularly for desserts and puddings, eschews pregnancy for fear of weight gain, and makes several suicide attempts. Yet when her weight is low, even though she becomes "immer lebensunfähiger" ("more and more debilitated"), retreating to bed in the afternoon, her mood is "eher heiter" ("rather cheerful").[24]

It is hard to conceive of a more classic case of anorexia nervosa than that revealed in Ellen's diaries. Her popularity in the past fifteen years or so undoubtedly stems from the recognition of the absolutely paradigmatic example of anorexia that she represents. Every one of the physical and psychological symptoms is mentioned including bulimic vomiting, the abuse of laxatives, amenorrhea, and what Binswanger calls "Fressgier" ("gluttony"), which is really an inverted obsession with the food that is being withheld. It is Ellen's increased appetite that leads Binswanger to conclude that her case is "gerade keine Anorexie" ("no anorexia at all").[25] He is led astray by the fact that there is no anorexia in the strictly limited meaning of a *loss* of appetite as well as by a defective understanding of the illness's insidious processes. The syndrome had been described as early as 1873 simultaneously by the French physician Charles Lasègue and by Queen Victoria's doctor, Sir William Gull (it was known for a while as Gull's Disease). Since it was for some hundred years considered a rare condition,[26] Binswanger has no awareness of it. He recognizes Ellen's disturbance as "an obsession" and directly poses the question, "Können wir nun die 'Angst vor dem Dickwerden' als Phobie bezeichnen?" ("Can we, then, designate the 'dread of becoming fat' as a phobia?").[27] His answer is an ambivalent "Ja und nein!" ("Yes and no!"), but after assessing the pros and cons, he decides, with an unconscious ironic pun, that the "no" has "grösseres Gewicht" ("greater weight").[28]

The argumentation whereby Binswanger arrives at his "no" shows how his whole approach to this case rests self-referentially on the system of existential analysis he had evolved: "Die Angst vor der eigenen Ungestalt ist keine eigentliche Phobie, sondern eine aus der Eigenart der Welt der Kranken, nämlich aus der Vorherrschaft der ätherischen Welt und deren Widerspruch gegen die Gruftwelt unmittelbar verständliche, intensive Angst vor der Bedrohung, ja dem Zusammen-bruch ihres existentiellen Ideals" ("The dread of her own un-*Gestalt* is not a true phobia but an intensive dread of the threat to, indeed the collapse of her existential ideal, immediately understandable from the peculiarity of the patient's world, namely from the predominance of the ethereal and its contradiction to the tomb-world").[29] Binswanger here returns to the terms of the interpretation he gives of Ellen's dilemma in the second section of his study. In the language of phenomenological-anthropological analysis, he conceives her as torn between the ethereal ideal, represented by the minimization of corporealty, and the tomb world, the imprisonment she abhors. In this scenario her refusal of milk at nine months denotes a significant "'Trennungsstrich' zwischen leiblicher Eigenwelt und Umwelt, ein 'Bruch' in der Einigung mit der Umwelt im Sinne einer grundsätzlichen Ablehnung der ersteren von der letzteren" ("'line of demarcation' between bodily *Eigenwelt* and *Umwelt*, a 'breach' in the uniting with the *Umwelt* in the sense that the former is set in opposition to the latter").[30] In attributing such life determining impor-tance to the infant's relationship to the breast Binswanger is following Freudian precepts, although he has transposed them into the language of existential analysis. At the same time he makes no bones about his skepticism in regard to psychoanalysis which he castigates as distorting the image of the human being through the narrowness of its conceptual framework. In Ellen's case, formal psychoanalysis, which she had tried twice, most recently just a few months before going to Bellevue, came up with an interpretation of her behavior as expressive of the hidden tensions in her subconscious: slimness means the higher intellectual type whereas plumpness stands for the bourgeois-Jewish way of life. The psy-choanalyst, who discerns distinctly hysterical traits in her, particu-larly in relation to men, posits an equation in her mind between eating, being fertilized, pregnancy, and getting fat.[31] Binswanger attacks such equations as reductive because they betoken a symbolizing act of deci-

pherment grounded in the focus on sexuality. Without rejecting psychoanalysis outright, Binswanger asserts that it can become genuine
"'Menschenkunde' nur im Lichte der gesamten Daseinskunde oder
Anthropologie" ("'humanology' only in the light of the total study of
existence or anthropology").[32]

Nonetheless, humanology's failure to produce a satisfactory diagnosis of Ellen's illness is a source of discomfort for Binswanger who devotes most of the fourth section of his study to an attempt to arrive at an
acceptable closure. There is a certain paradoxicality in his efforts to site
Ellen within the psychiatric spectrum even as he protests against the
tendency of clinical analysis to turn life history into solely illness history.
He continues to advocate the advantages of existential analysis for an
understanding of the way in which existence may be emptied "bis zum
blossen Lochsein" ("down to the mere being-in-a-hole") while clinical
analysis sees only "Gefährdung" ("damage") and "Störung" ("disturbance")
of an organism's function.[33] But notwithstanding such objections,
Binswanger stays within classificatory categories traditional to psychiatric diagnosis. He rules out depression because Ellen exhibits no sense of
guilt; he briefly considers the possibility of an endocrinological mal-
function; he reviews the problem of shame; under question marks he
raises the issues of anxiety equivalent, hysteria, addiction and existential
craving, compulsion, phobia, overvalent idea, delusional idea, and manic-
depressive psychosis.[34] With the backing of eminent further opinions
from Bleuler and Kraepelin, who are brought in as consultants while
Ellen is at Bellevue, Binswanger's final hypothesis of schizophrenia, based
on her sense of emptiness, is more or less agreed on, although Kraepelin
opts for melancholia.

This conflict of medical views shows each practitioner espousing his
own particular theory (Bleuler, for instance, is known for having coined
schizophrenia to replace the earlier dementia precox). All are in the last
resort more intent on affixing a recognizable label on Ellen than on
really achieving the understanding of her inner life for which Binswanger
pleads in the name of existential analysis. Concurring on their therapeutic impotence, three of the most distinguished psychiatrists of the time
give in to the patient's demand for discharge in the face of her will to
suicide. But however tempting it may be to scoff at this crass misdiagnosis, the unfamiliarity at that time with anorexia as a psychological disorder has to be borne in mind. Moreover, schizophrenia was then considered
not amenable to psychotherapy, and severe, persistent anorexia such as

Ellen had is even today resistant to treatment and sometimes fatal. Interestingly, recent opinions remain divided on the diagnosis: Chernin, from a feminist position, and Minuchin, on medico-psychiatric grounds, see Ellen as patently anorexic; Seinfeld regards her as a schizophrenic whose ideal of extreme thinness can be explicated in terms of the theory of the transformational object,[35] while Mendel, who admits that he "first believed her to be a clear example of someone with an eating disorder,"[36] finally subsumes her under schizophrenia because this disease, like hysteria, is an "imitator." Anyway, the possible misdiagnosis can at most be deemed a contributory factor in the negative outcome of the psychotherapy in this case.

How, then, to account for the singular failure of just talk in this instance? A patient's suicide is, after all, the ultimate default in psychiatry. From Binswanger's account it is legitimate to surmise that little talk actually took place. By the time Ellen arrived at Bellevue at age thirty-four, she had already been wrestling with the illness for at least fifteen years (even if Binswanger's conjecture is discounted that her rejection of sweet things in childhood is an early "Akt der Versagung" ["act of renunciation"]).[37] Psychologically she was drained to the point of complete demoralization, and physically the years of bizarre eating must also have taken their toll. At the intake interview on the day of her admission to Bellevue, "bricht die Patientin schon nach wenigen Worten in laut jammerndes Weinen aus, ist lange nicht zu beruhigen" ("after a few words the patient burst into loud wailing and cannot be calmed down for a long time").[38] She can give no more than a fragmentary and disjointed narrative of her illness history. The words "abgerissen" and "Bruchstücke" that Binswanger uses here refute Studer's supposition: "Ihm hat sie anscheinend bei der ausführlichen Anamnese viel erzählt" (Studer, "Ellen West," 245; at the detailed history-taking she apparently told him a great deal). Ellen sums up her unutterable weariness in her simile: "Jede Kleinigkeit komme ihr jetzt vor wie ein unübersteiglicher Berg" ("every trifle now seems to her like an insurmountable obstacle" [the translation loses the simile of an unclimbable mountain]). Even six weeks later she feels "ganz passiv als der Schauplatz, auf dem sich zwei feindliche Mächte zerfleischen" ("quite passive, the stage on which two hostile forces are mangling each other").[39]

The phrases just quoted are among the very scant words of Ellen's cited in Binswanger's record of her stay at Bellevue. Now it is he who keeps a diary with dated entries that note, however, more what Ellen does than what she says: how she sleeps, how she behaves at meals, and whether she participates in the sanatorium's recreational activities such as lectures or concerts. In the attachment she forms to an elegant, extremely thin fellow patient Binswanger sees a striking homoerotic component. Four of her dreams are briefly recounted by the therapist, all perceived as about food or death, but none is analyzed "aus psychotherapeutischen Gründen" ("for psychotherapeutic reasons"). No rationale is given for this decision, which seems a missed opportunity to probe the patient's overriding preoccupations. Perhaps Binswanger considers Ellen too labile to stand such probing at that juncture. Her thoughts of suicide come ever more into the forefront: she feels "wie eine Leiche unter Menschen" ("like a corpse among people").[40] Studer rightly raises the question (245) whether Ellen ever talked openly to anyone: to her mother? to the nanny who stayed with her as a mother figure? to her husband? to women friends (of whom we hear nothing)? Did anyone ever tell her, Studer asks, "dass sie Grund hat, sich zu wehren" (230; that she had the right to stand up for herself), that her drive for a more meaningful existence was, from a feminist viewpoint, wholly justifiable, although in this ambition Ellen was ahead of her time.

Such scant talk as did take place between Ellen and Binswanger had no healing impact. Several overlapping factors appear to have interacted, some extraneous, some internal, to impede talk. The short duration of Binswanger's interaction with Ellen has already been mentioned; six weeks are insufficient to establish a strong therapeutic alliance, especially at an advanced stage of an illness and after several ineffectual interventions, which very likely sapped any confidence she might have had in psychiatry. Since the function of psychotherapy is precisely to work through and beyond such resistances, the deeper issue centers on the patient's and the therapist's inaccessibility to each other and hence to trusting talk. But the problem is not to be envisaged in terms of blame, let alone guilt. An incompatibility—and conversely a compatibility—may occur in psychotherapy on irrational grounds. With Ellen West and Binswanger, however, there was arguably a discernible cause for the communicative shortfall, and, ironically, it had the same source on both sides.

They were alike in being, each in her or his own way so enmeshed in a self-constructed system that, by the time they met, they lacked the flexibility and openness to others necessary to the success of just talk. Ellen had become a total hostage to her obsessive-compulsive illness; she was fully aware of her bondage, which she expressed in her frequent metaphors of imprisonment. To the end of her life she remained capable of an amazing clarity of self-perception. She acknowledges that she is "in die Knechtschaft einer unheimlichen Macht geraten" ("enslaved to an uncanny power"),[41] "gefangen in mir selbst" ("a prisoner within myself"), "umzingelt" ("surrounded"),[42] "verhext" ("bewitched"). She cannot go on because she is unable to break this spell. In existentialist-analytical terms, her *entire world-picture ["Weltbild"] is disarranged ["verschoben"].*[43] Nothing is left but the urge to escape from this intolerable impasse.

Binswanger's situation was more complex since he was not in the grip of a delusional mental disorder. On the other hand, he, too, was in a sense entrapped, or at least engrossed: in the theory of existential analysis that he was expounding. Sandwiched between his treatise *Basic Forms and Cognition of Human Existence* (1942) and his expository article "The Existential Analysis School of Thought" (1946), "The Case of Ellen West" (1944-45) is less an investigation of a specific case for its own sake than an exploration of the phenomenological-anthropological approach. Binswanger proceeds in a manner diametrically opposite to Freud's in according priority to the theory of existential analysis and then moving inductively to the case history, which serves as an occasion to illustrate the methodology. By contrast, Freud, practicing in his early days as a neurologist and faced with refractory cases that did not yield to the standard repertoire of treatments at that time, begins to try then somewhat unconventional therapies such as hypnosis, suggestion, laying on of hands, and so forth. From the relative degree of response that each of these experiments elicits he gradually evolves deductively the principle of free association as the cornerstone of psychoanalysis. The steps in his professional growth and particularly how much he learnt from his patients becomes apparent in his *Studies on Hysteria.*[44] Freud is essentially pragmatic, whereas Binswanger is intent on the illustration of preconceived ideas. So the analysis of Ellen West is an "exemplification"[45] of a priori formulated tenets rather than an open-minded clinical study.

Another way of envisaging the difficulty is in the terms put forward by Carl Rogers in his article "Ellen West—and Loneliness." Starting from the discussion of the case at the 1958 symposium of the American Academy of Psychotherapists, he strongly advocates "a client-centered, person-centered approach to a human being in distress" (209). He argues that the ways in which Ellen was treated "could not possibly help her— ... would, in fact, certainly worsen her psychological health" (209).

Rogers does not reject existential analysis as such; indeed, he sees in Ellen West the development of modern man's basic isolation to a tragic point. Precisely because of her profound loneliness, she might have improved "had she had the opportunity to participate in person-centered therapy" (217). The "person-to-person therapeutic relationship" (217) that Rogers recommends is not provided by Binswanger. While Rogers is never explicitly critical of Binswanger's handling of the case, his closing remarks have negative implications: "To make an object of a person has been helpful in treating physical ills; it has not been successful in treating psychological ills" (219).

There is a terrible irony in the implicit charge that Binswanger makes "an object" of Ellen West because it is not "der seelisch *kranke* Mensch sondern *der Mensch*" ("mentally *ill* man, but *man as such*")[46] who is to be understood in existential analysis in order to achieve a better grasp of the life history as a series of modifications of the total structure of the patient's being-in-the-world. Yet Binswanger does not probe the *Mitwelt* and *Umwelt* of Ellen's relationships within her family and her marriage. Nor does he heed or address many other major facets of her as a human being: her struggle for an independent identity, her search for an appropriate place in the world, reflected in her changes of occupation, her marriage to a cousin, that is, within the family circle, after a broken first engagement, her rebellion against her bourgeois environment, her commitment to social work, the improvement in her condition when she is away from her family, her intelligence, her perspicacity, and not least her frustration. The significance of these elements, which lead into the very heart of Ellen's universe, is not examined. A particularly intriguing aspect of this lacuna is Ellen's "Uber den Beruf der Frau" ("On the Woman's Calling"), which Binswanger mentions just once without any elucidation. What were her views on woman's calling? Given the defiance in many of her other opinions, it is likely that her presumed feminism would smack of anarchy in a country so conservative that it granted the vote to women in Federal elections only in 1971. Writing from a feminist perspective, Studer is highly critical of Binswanger's "autoritäre Einstufungen" (249; authoritarian categorizations). Instead of coming to grasp Ellen's meaning-context in all its plenitude—and conflictedness—beyond the area of her illness, as existential analysis aims to do, Binswanger reduces her to the schemata dictated by his theories. And "the reduction must be recognized *as a reduction* and not treated as an *overall view of the human being.*"[47]

To dispute Binswanger's entire method because of its shortfall in this instance would be another form of reductionism. The inadequate cognizance of anorexia at the time certainly also played some part in the failure of communication. The therapeutic alliance did not come into being. The effectiveness of just talk depends on cooperation between a willing speaker and an alert listener. Neither precondition was fulfilled in this case: the patient preferred to confide to her journals, and the therapist was prejudiced by his philosophy. In some ways there is a tragic congruence between them.

14

Collecting and Disposing of Garbage

Frieda Fromm-Reichmann's *Psychoanalysis and Psychotherapy* and Joanne Greenberg's *I Never Promised You a Rose Garden*

> Garbage in, garbage out.
> A colloquial phrase in data processing
> for incorrect input which will
> inevitably produce faulty output.

"Psychotherapy with schizophrenics is hard and exacting work for both patients and therapists," Frieda Fromm-Reichmann declared in her Academic Lecture read at the hundred and tenth annual meeting of the American Psychiatric Association in May 1954.[1] This proposition is reiterated several times in *I Never Promised You a Rose Garden* as the doctor tells her patient, "with your very hard work here and with a doctor's working hard, I think you can get better" (24); "this science where the two of us work together" (94); "We will work hard together, and we will understand" (96). Always the emphasis is on the need for cooperation, for both patient's and therapist's willingness and capacity to work hard together. The conception of psychotherapy as essentially a duet is thus central to Fromm-Reichmann's theoretical articles and to *I Never Promised You.*

Yet this duet differs from the three previous ones in being intertextual, not intratextual. The therapist and the patient wrote about the same case separately and at discrete times: the papers collected in *Psychoanalysis and Psychotherapy* were originally published between 1939 and 1957, whereas the novel appeared in 1964. According to Joanne Greenberg, she and Fromm-Reichmann planned to coauthor a book on schizophrenia, but the psychiatrist's untimely death in 1957 made this impossible.[2] Their writings are, however, linked by cross-references: the portrait of "Dr. Fried" in *I Never Promised You* is closely modeled on Fromm-Reichmann, who in turn cites episodes narrated in the novel in several of her papers where the behavior of Deborah, the novel's central character, is immediately recognizable.[3] The therapist's scholarly papers and the patient's fiction are complementary, casting light on each other reciprocally from two distinct perspectives. The novel is, of course, far better known, having been a national bestseller; it is generally read independently of Fromm-Reichmann's papers, but both texts can be better understood if they are conjoined into a duet.

Who were the two authors? Frieda Fromm-Reichmann was born in 1889 in Karlsruhe, Germany, and graduated in medicine in 1914, then a still relatively daring step for a woman. As a result of her care of brain-injured soldiers during World War I she was drawn to psychiatry and psychotherapy. She worked in several psychiatric clinics, including Emil Kraepelin's in Munich. The great turning point in her professional career was her discovery of Freud's writings, which clarified many aspects of the doctor-patient relationship that had puzzled her, particularly the phenomenon of transference and countertransference. After completing her psychoanalytic training Fromm-Reichmann practiced in Heidelberg, where she established a private sanatorium for the psychoanalytic treatment of schizophrenics, and with Erich Fromm, to whom she was briefly married, founded a psychoanalytic training institute. With the rise of Nazism in Germany, Fromm-Reichmann fled first to Alsace-Lorraine just across the Franco-German frontier so that she could continue the analyses of some of her German patients. Then following a temporary stay in Palestine, she immigrated to the United States. From 1935 onward at the Chesnut Lodge sanatorium in Rockville, Maryland, she found a congenial forum for her experimental therapy with psychotics, with whom she was able to achieve surprisingly good outcomes. Her ingenuity was stimulated by her friendship with Henry Stack Sullivan, who shared her interest in schizophrenia which he conceptualized as an unsuccessful reaction to anxiety.

Fromm-Reichmann's cumbersome name is abbreviated in *I Never*

Promised You to simply "Dr. Fried," which has been interpreted as denoting that the patient "is freed by the analyst's insights and compassion."[4] "Fried" also invokes the German word *Friede* (peace), suggesting that her therapy relieves the patient's turmoil. But Deborah also gives her the nickname "Furii, or Fire-Touch" to summarize "the fearsome power" (*INPY*, 102) exerted by this physically diminutive and personally intense therapist who was at once so empathetic and so demanding. With her fire-touch she metaphorically cauterizes the diseased parts of Deborah's mind.

The patient's name, Deborah Blau, is also multilayered. It is a transparent cover for the author's purported real name, Hannah Green, under which *I Never Promised You* was first published. The German "Blau" (blue) is an obvious equivalent for Green. However, Hannah Green itself turned out to be a pseudonym for Joanne Greenberg. The triple name signals not only the usual authorial desire to protect her own and her family's privacy but also a double distancing from the sick self. That sick split self was an adolescent who had regressed into a secret fantasy realm with an esoteric language, yet who was intermittently accessible to the real world into which Dr. Fried coaxes, pushes, and cajoles her back.

The main lines of Deborah's family history, as recounted in the novel by her mother (33-38) and gradually by herself, are known to parallel Greenberg's own story. Deborah comes from a family of East European Jewish immigrants who had struggled to get established in the United States and who want to give their (grand)daughter the best of everything despite their continuing economic vicissitudes. But her grandfather's lavish indulgence and her parents' efforts to assimilate and to climb the social ladder cannot protect her from the damaging effects of ostracism at school and at summer camp as an expression of antisemitism: "In the camp a riding instructor mentioned acidly that Hitler was doing one good thing at least, and that was getting rid of the 'garbage people'" (*INPY*, 49). The young girl internalizes such discriminatory remarks to form the core of an extremely negative self-image full of self-incrimination. Her natural jealousy of her sister, five years her junior, is, for instance, converted into the belief that she had tried to throw her out of the window. She feels guilt too about a tumor of the urinary tract that causes her to wet the bed until she has surgery at age five. In short, she conceives herself as noxious to others by mere contact: "garbage." She counters her potential harmfulness by retreat from the world: if the world has rejected her, she responds by rejecting it through her withdrawal into a psychosis which she develops, at least initially, as a protective defense mechanism.

Since Deborah, in her self-destructive illness, envisages herself not merely as a garbage person but also as one who collects and harbors garbage, her therapist's function is to induce the patient to dispose of that garbage. Toward the end of the therapy Deborah actually affectionately calls Dr. Fried "you old mental garbage-collector" (*INPY*, 244), although it is she herself who has done the collection of the debris that the analyst has to strip and dispose of. It is lodged in Deborah's mind in the delusional fixed ideas diagnosed as schizophrenia.

In using psychotherapy in the form of talk with schizophrenics Fromm-Reichmann was highly innovative, bucking the then accepted fundamental divide between neurotics and psychotics. Freud considered only neurotics suitable for psychoanalysis; psychotics' basic irrationality was thought to render them unable to communicate and so to put them beyond the reach of verbal psychotherapy. Fromm-Reichmann is at pains to underscore at the opening of her paper on "Basic Problems in the Psychotherapy of Schizophrenia" that she uses "the term *psychoanalytically oriented psychotherapy* advisedly, and not simply *psychoanalysis*, because modifications of the classical psychoanalytic technique are necessary in the treatment of the psychotic person" (*P&P*, 210). For example, "the patient is asked neither to lie down nor to give free associations; both requests make no sense to him. He should feel free to sit, lie on the floor, walk around, use any available chair, lie or sit on the couch. Nothing matters except that the analyst permit the patient to feel comfortable and secure enough to give up his defensive narcissistic isolation" (*P&P*, 123).

Another significant modulation stems from the importance Fromm-Reichmann attaches to "non-verbal elements" because she appreciates "the degree of expressive skill with which the patient himself uses means of non-verbal communication" and emphasizes the need for the therapist's "specific sensitivity to the meaning of its use" (*P&P*, 201). "Implication or non-verbalized innuendoes" (*P&P*, 203) play a vital role in winning access to the schizophrenic, as Fromm-Reichmann demonstrates from her memory of a very suspicious, confused patient who became stuporous, mute, and resistive to food and excretion for a month following panic in psychotherapy: "In spite of this rather unpromising picture, I sat with him for an hour every day. The only sign of contact he gave to me or anyone was to indicate by gestures that he wanted me to stay; all that he said on two different days during this period was: 'Don't leave!'" (*P&P*, 122). Such nonverbal communication is prominent in *I Never Promised You:* when Dr. Fried begins "to jab out her cigarette butt with hard impatience" (44), she conveys to Deborah her anger at the way the five-year-old had been deceived by her surgeons. However, when the doctor touches Deborah's arm at the end of a session in a gesture intended to be friendly and reassuring, Deborah recoils "because of some obscure fear of touching" and feels as though her arm were being burned under the sweater sleeve. But Dr. Fried redresses the situation by her immediate and appropriate reaction: "'I'm sorry,' the doctor said, seeing Deborah's face go pale. 'I didn't mean to touch you before you were ready'" (*INPY,* 95). Later Deborah finds her doubts dispelled by the doctor's "familiar smile of greeting" (133).

In the articles she wrote from 1939 onward on the psychotherapy of schizophrenics Fromm-Reichmann addresses two paramount issues: whether psychotics are qualitatively different from neurotics, and whether they have the capacity for the transference relationship quintessential to all psychotherapy. On the differences between neurotics and psychotics she is somewhat guarded. In her last paper, which appeared posthumously in 1958, she categorically asserts, "I consider the differences between the psychotic and the neurotic—or the healthy, for that matter—to be much more differences of degree than of kind" (*P&P*, 210). In an earlier essay, "Psychotherapy of Schizophrenia" (1954), she seems to be arguing both ways. On the one hand, she concedes the disparity in the intensity of the neurotic's and the psychotic's respective dependency needs, hostile tendencies, and fantasies toward themselves and others. These characteristics of the psychotic generate a clash of powerful emotions that "becomes completely overwhelming. In other words, the quantitative difference between the schizophrenic's anxiety and similarly motivated tensions in people who have not been emotionally traumatized as early in life as the schizophrenic and who could therefore develop a stronger ego organization is so great that it acquires a totally different quality" (*P&P*, 198-99). It is precisely because, as she again acknowledges, "for all practical purposes, the difference in quantity . . . turns actually into one of quality" that the psychotherapy of schizophrenics is particularly "hard and exacting work" (*P&P*, 201, 207).

Nonetheless, Fromm-Reichmann insists in her 1939 paper "Transference Problems in Schizophrenics" that "*Schizophrenics are capable of*

developing workable relationships and transference reactions" (*P&P,* 126).
Such workability depends crucially, however, on the extent of the
therapist's understanding of the processes involved. Schizophrenics' extreme suspicion and distrust of people make it very difficult (and slow-
going) for them to accept the therapist as an ally. Once acceptance has
been accomplished, their dependence on the therapist is all the greater
as a concomitant of their underlying fears. Also, because their thinking
is magical, miscommunications are more frequent than with neurotics
whose oscillations between positive and negative transference are more
predictable. Consequently the therapist has to be prepared to tolerate
and to deal with surprising "stormy and dramatic changes from love to
hatred, from willingness to leave his delusional world to resistance and
renewed withdrawal" (*P&P,* 119). This pattern is repeatedly illustrated
in *I Never Promised You* as Deborah relapses temporarily into combat-
iveness, vituperation, self-mutilation, and hallucinations whenever she
has taken a step forward and so is afraid to forfeit the only world she has,
that of her delusions, in favor of the world of reality that Dr. Fried holds
out to her. Over and again the doctor impresses on the patient that the
choice to give up her fantasy realm is hers: "I think you will want to give
it up when you have the real world to replace it, but there is no pact with
me. I do not ask you to give up your gods for mine. When you are ready,
you will choose" (*INPY,* 191).

Through such gentle, respectful persuasion, as well as enormous
persistence,[5] Fromm-Reichmann pursues her aim of making patients
"co-worker[s]" (*P&P,* 190) in their therapy. She reaches out even though
she recognizes that "the schizophrenic patient and the therapist are people
living in different worlds and on different levels of personal development with different means of expressing and of orienting themselves"
(*P&P,* 120). Yet in her papers on the psychotherapy of schizophrenics
she uses the metaphor of a "bridge" to describe the therapist's pivotal
function: "In the light of his personal relationship with the analyst it
means that the therapist seduced the patient by giving him a bridge over
which he might possibly be led from the utter loneliness of his own
world to reality and human warmth" (*P&P,* 119); "In work with the psychotic, the psychiatrist is not only a participant-observer and a therapeutic agent, as he is in the treatment of the neurotic, but he is also to a
greater degree a representative of, and a bridge to, a better reality, the
experience of which had previously been denied to the patient" (*P&P,*
215). Because of these patients' deepseated insecurity and vulnerability,

the therapist bears particular responsibility in assuring that the bridge not prove "not reliable" (*P&P,* 119).

Although Fromm-Reichmann emphasizes therapists' obligations toward their psychotic patients despite discouraging setbacks, she never projects infallibility: "one cannot at times avoid failing one's schizophrenic patients" (*P&P,* 119), she openly admits. Schizophrenics' exaggerated reactions to minor incidents in the relationship with the therapist such as falling into a catatonic stupor at a change in the time of an appointment are explained as a repetition in the patient's mind of withdrawals of supporting forces in infancy. So the analyst's "defection" arouses severe anxiety at a "vital deprivation" (*P&P,* 119). Whether such an interpretation is valid or not depends on the predominant hypothesis about the genesis of the illness, which has varied greatly over the years (most recently, the possibility of a biochemical defect or deficiency has been posited). In the context of my study, the legitimacy of the competing claims is immaterial. What is striking throughout Fromm-Reichmann's writings is her absolute devotion to her patients and her sustained efforts to understand their bizarre behaviors both rationally and imaginatively. She does so as a preliminary to helping them. The ultimate therapeutic aim always takes precedence, even in her theoretical expositions: "While this whole question holds great theoretical interest, I believe now that its solution is not too important for therapeutic purposes" (*P&P,* 205). Unlike Binswanger, Fromm-Reichmann was not a system builder but a very practical, flexible clinician, "all there with the patient," her colleague Dr. Edith V. Weigert recalls in the memorial paper that forms the foreword to *Psychoanalysis and Psychotherapy* (viii). In contrast to Binswanger, who seeks to explore the case of Ellen West as an illustration of theories already crystallized, Fromm-Reichmann stands in the Freudian tradition of deducing generalizations from specific cases previously encountered in practice. So unmistakable references to episodes in the therapy of Deborah punctuate the articles published in the 1950s.[6]

Psychoanalysis and Psychotherapy thus acts as a frame to *I Never Promised You,* which in turn is an embodiment of Fromm-Reichmann's therapeutic principles. The two works harmonize into a duet as twin perspectives on the same turbulent course of therapy. The novel's title, which derives from the therapist's words to the patient, indicates the nature of the unison: "I never promised you a rose garden. I never promised you perfect justice . . . and I never promised you peace or happiness. My help is so that you can be free to fight for all these things. The only reality I offer is challenge, and being well is being free to accept it or not at whatever level you are capable" (*INPY*, 102-3). That "challenge" is the bond between the patient who collects garbage and the therapist who shows her how to dispose of it. Deborah needs to learn to acquire the will and the self-confidence to extricate herself from the hallucinatory world to which she has become captive and to have the courage to embrace a reality that is not a rose garden, while Dr. Fried has to devise the means to put her on this path and to give her the security to follow it through.

Unlike most narratives of psychotherapy, which use first-person narration, *I Never Promised You* is cast in the third person, although the focalization is predominantly through Deborah's eyes. It is she who experiences the routines—and the uproar—of life in a mental hospital, the hierarchy of its wards, the peculiarities of her fellow patients, and the idiosyncracies of the caregivers. This scenario, as ongoing in its repetitions and variations as that of a soap opera, is the backdrop to her therapy sessions with Dr. Fried, who lives in a house on the hospital grounds to which Deborah is at first escorted and then allowed to go on her own. The alternation between the intensive private scrutiny to which Deborah is subjected by Dr. Fried and the public hurly-burly of the ward structures the novel's rhythm. Transitions are often abrupt, temporality is attenuated, especially in the first half, and spatiality distorted in order to convey the disjointedness of the schizophrenic's perceptions. The short segments and quick cuts suggest a darting mind unable to concentrate or focus because of the distraction from its inner visions. Indeed, *I Never Promised You* has been praised as "one of the most psychologically sophisticated literary representations of mental illness."[7]

The pronounced preponderance of Deborah's viewpoint through much of the narration makes the sudden switches to an omniscient narrator conspicuous and disturbing. At the opening the third person narration is effective in evoking a mystery that arouses readers' curiosity: "They rode through the lush farm country in the middle of autumn, through quaint old towns whose streets showed the brilliant colors of turning trees. They said little. Of the three, the father was most visibly strained" (*INPY*, 9). Who are they? where are they going? why are they subdued? and why is the father so strained? However, once the situation has been clarified and readers have been initiated into Deborah's hallucinatory world, it proves more intriguing and absorbing than the intercalated returns to reality. Clearly, the snatches of the nurses' gossip, the junior doctors' discussion of a lecture Dr. Fried has given on Deborah's case, the conversations between her mother and her father and the interviews between them and Dr. Fried are intended as a foil to the confusion in Deborah's psyche. These vignettes act as reminders of the existence of a normal world beyond the confines of her illness. Yet the sporadic glimpses of the Blaus' family life and the insight into the thoughts of her parents or sister are intrusive because they divert from the central dramas of the battle within Deborah and between her and her therapist. Equally contrived are the cameos of Dr. Fried alone in her home between patients; lost in reverie while she waits for the coffee to perk and letting it boil over and spill from under the lid (*INPY,* 62), or longing to listen to her favorite Schumann records that have lain on the cabinet unopened for three weeks, and being interrupted once again by the ringing of the telephone. As attempts to humanize—and domesticate—Dr. Fried, these interludes are superfluous for she shows her humanity in her interactions with her patient and in her openness about the "many failures" she has had (*INPY,* 143). The choice of third person narration has the advantage of maintaining a measure of distance from Deborah's garbage collection. However, the expansion into omniscience is distracting to the point of seeming transgressive as a disruption of the paramount (that is, Deborah's) viewpoint. Just as the author's identity is hidden behind the fictional character, so the third person narration barely shrouds what is de facto a first-person perspective. The departures from this prevailing angle of vision strike readers as verging on inconsistencies.

This impression is reinforced by our primary interest in Deborah's illness and above all in following the uncertain process of her recovery. The psychotherapy sessions with Dr. Fried that punctuate the narrative are at the novel's core. As if to confirm the covert first-person perspective, these meetings are told almost exclusively as Deborah experiences them; only occasionally is the therapist's view incorporated. The most extensive such shift occurs near the beginning before much insight into Deborah's mind as Dr. Fried weighs up whether to take her on as a patient (17-19). Later interventions are briefer: "The doctor leaned forward in the chair, feeling Deborah's exhaustion at revealing the things which seemed to Deborah to most truly motivate her. A secret language concealing a still more secret one; a world veiling a hidden world; and symptoms guarding still deeper symptoms to which it was not yet time to go, and those in turn concealing a still, still deeper burning wish to live. She wanted to tell the stunned-looking girl in front of her that this sickness, which everyone shied from and was frightened of, was also an adjustment" (61); "Dr. Fried saw her patient turning and running, turning and running in her fear. Soon there would be no place to go and she would have to meet herself as she planned her own destruction. She looked at Deborah. At least the battle was being fought in earnest now. The old apathy was gone" (69); "Dr. Fried's thoughts drifted for a moment to an article she had written once discussing the question of how a doctor tells a recovering patient that her own newborn health must grapple with symptoms of madness in the world" (199). The effect of some revelation of the therapist's thoughts is to turn *I Never Promised You* into a duet. Therein lies the gain from the occasional shifts in perspective. In this respect the narrative technique of *I Never Promised You* contrasts with that of *The Bell Jar*, another third person narrative of psychotherapy where Dr. Nolan is always seen from the outside through Esther's eyes.

How then do the principles of psychotherapy laid out by Fromm-Reichmann in *Psychoanalysis and Psychotherapy* mesh with those portrayed in *I Never Promised You*? The relationship between the two is circular since the theories in *Psychoanalysis and Psychotherapy* were deduced from experiences with cases like Deborah's. In place of the sequentiality of Binswanger's selection of the case of Ellen West to illustrate tenets he had already put forward, here there is a temporal simultaneity as Fromm-Reichmann distills her concepts from groping—and wrestling—with her schizophrenic patients.

I Never Promised You interfaces with *Psychoanalysis and Psychotherapy* in showing Fromm-Reichmann's principles put into practice. With Deborah Dr. Fried uses the psychoanalytically oriented psychotherapy Fromm-Reichmann advocates. In its formal structure this is closer to contemporary styles of psychotherapy with patient and therapist sitting face to face and the therapist free to interject comments instead of being the largely silent, hidden listener behind the couch, as in classical psychoanalysis. But in content the psychotherapy in *I Never Promised You* is obviously dependent on Freudian psychoanalysis in its exploration of traumas in childhood and infancy as the source of current disturbances. For Deborah the recall of three discrete psychological injuries proves decisive: the brutality of the surgeons when she was five, notably their blatant lying, which radically undermined her trust in others; the repeated antisemitism that branded her one as one of the "garbage people"; and the birth of her younger sister whom the small child sees as an "intruder," an "ugly thing," a "red-faced puckered bundle of squall and stink," admired by a crowd of relatives for her "beauty and delicacy" (48). These, Dr. Fried explains to her, are "some of the ghosts of the past" still clutching at her in the present (95). The final and perhaps most crucial turning point in Deborah's recovery occurs when Dr. Fried proves to her that her memory of having tried to throw the baby out of the window "was only your guilt at wishing your sister dead" (201). While conceding that the hatred and the guilt were real enough, Dr. Fried conclusively convinces her that she was just not big enough to do the things she falsely remembers: "Our would-be murderess is no more than a jealous five-year old looking into the cradle of the interloper" (201). Deborah has fused her recollections of the bad happenings in her childhood, real or fantasized, into a very negative image of herself as contaminated and contaminating, and therefore to be isolated from the world.

In the liberalized version of psychoanalysis that Dr. Fried has evolved, she repeatedly and strenuously urges Deborah to talk, but she does so with utmost care. At their first meeting, after the courtesy of "Make yourself comfortable," the doctor says, "Is there anything you want to tell me" (23). That it is a question, not a command, is indicative of Dr. Fried's tact and caution in dealing with schizophrenics. The theme of telling, of trying to find words, sometimes being able to do so and at other times not is a central leitmotif of *I Never Promised You:* "Tell me about your life before this hospital" (43); "tell me what the rhythm is, of these upsets of yours" (58); "just tell me . . . tell both of us how" (134); "Try to tell me what this is" (140); "You must try to talk to me and tell me what is happening in your collided worlds" (175). The modifiers "try" and "just" soften the tone. Some of these exhortations are open-ended, some more specifically directed at an especially perplexing area, and often Dr. Fried backs the query with the nonthreatening apologia "perhaps I don't understand." Her endeavor to understand overlaps with her aim of guiding Deborah to self-understanding.

The counter term to "tell" is "mute." Deborah's half-hearted suicide attempt before her hospitalization is interpreted as a "call for help, the call of a mute and confused person" (39). Often Deborah is described as "lapsed into a mute, stunned silence" (44). With a substitute therapist during Dr. Fried's absence, "his humorless and automatic responses brought down the muteness like a night" (155). His "Tell me what you are thinking" (a crassly invasive formula Dr. Fried never uses) "seemed to come like a demand," falling "like a pickax" (154). Nonverbal messages determine Deborah's response to him too: she feels enveloped in a profound silence by the "brutally hard lines of his disapproving face" and "the austerity of his manner and the icy logic" (156), so that she experiences his questions as scalpels into her mind reminiscent of the surgeons' probes into her body. In her fear that Dr. Fried will not return, she foresees "there could be nothing but muteness" (156).

The variations in Deborah's capacity for intelligible self-expression are an important barometer of her progress. At first she is angrily resentful of the doctor's "prying," resistant to "the dragging forth of her history" with "retreats, camouflaging, and hiding" (47). The major vehicle for camouflaging and hiding is the secret language Deborah has devised, Yri, and its associated world, peopled by a large cast of figures. Initially these imagined characters were a refuge for Deborah from a terrifying reality, but gradually they in turn become more and more frightening and menacing as Deborah tries to free herself from their domination in order to be able to return to the normal world. Her creation of this secret realm, her withdrawal into it, and her resort to its peculiar language signify the hold the illness has on her. English, she tells Dr. Fried, "is for the world—for getting disappointed by and hated in. Yri is for saying what has to be said." Very astutely Dr. Fried replies, "I am perhaps a little jealous since you use your language to communicate with yourself and not with the world" (54). To speak Yri is for Deborah to remain locked in her private sphere of hallucination; to be able to speak English is to be released from it. Her efforts to emerge from the land of Yr are often conveyed by her mixed language: "when she spoke her words were the mangled Anglo-Yri-gibberish and there was only enough to try to answer a question or to hint at a need" (180); "As she struggled to translate, finding it almost impossible to span the light years of distance between herself and them, the confusion of tongues only alienated her further. She would become frightened whatever she said next could not be translated at all, and the formless sounds would make her feel even more frightened. Only with Furii was there any clarity" (181). That precious clarity demonstrates how Dr. Fried functions as the bridge between Yri and English, schizophrenia and health.

That Deborah does gradually come to trust and confide in Dr. Fried is convincing proof of the psychotic's capacity for a positive transference that Fromm-Reichmann asserted in *Psychoanalysis and Psychotherapy*. *I Never Promised You* reveals the resistance, doubts and fears that schizophrenics have about committing to such a relationship as an essential manifestation of their suspicious, withdrawn condition. The growth of Deborah's attachment to Dr. Fried is slow and hesitant, in marked contrast to Esther's immediate attraction to Dr. Nolan in *The Bell Jar* because she is a woman, looks rather glamorous, and shows respect for her patient. Dr. Fried is far from impressive in appearance: "a tiny, gray-haired, plump little woman" (22) whom Deborah at first sight comically takes to be the doctor's housekeeper. The transference develops only with many vicissitudes; after each advance Deborah recoils in terror of the retribution her Yri gods will extract for every step she takes back into the real world. So progress in speaking out alternates with regression into a self-defeating fury that is projected as the vengeful wrath of the Yri universe at Deborah's decreasing loyalty to it. In this succession of episodic ups and downs the novel's movement is a mirror image of its overall pattern. Deborah's story plays out the mythic model of descent and return, but while it follows that paradigm in its totality, its parts are reversals, that is, tentative returns that precipitate temporary re-descents.

Dr. Fried slowly wins Deborah's trust by her openness, her patience and persistence, and above all by her honesty. She has all the qualities most commendable in a therapist: tact, insight, empathy, and sensitivity. She is hopeful, supportive, gentle, and skillful in eliciting Deborah's version of her life history. But when necessary she can also be tough and blunt: "Another camouflage is to blame it all on someone else. It keeps you from having to face what they really did to you, and what you did to yourself and are still doing" (81). If "the figure of Dr. Fried remains highly idealized,"[8] that idealization itself has to be seen as an expression of Deborah's positive transference as well as of the novel's veiled first-person disposition. In the dedication of *I Never Promised You* "To My Mothers," Dr. Fried is cast as the second mother, better able to nurture the child in a healthy way than her biological mother had done.[9] The sense of idealization is fostered too by the contrast with some of the other doctors in the novel, particularly her substitute, Dr. Royson, whom Deborah criticizes with devastating shrewdness: "he wanted only to prove how right he was and how smart" (165). Dr. Fried, though generally right and almost invariably smart, is also willing to acknowledge her own shortcomings. Nor is she the only intelligent and sympathetic psychiatrist in *I Never Promised You*. Although Deborah brands the ward administrator, Dr. Halle, "Snake-tooth" (165), his words are "careful but not critical or hypocritical" (158), and in judging Deborah's escapade of staying out with a friend long beyond the permitted time, he shows as much liberality of spirit as Dr. Fried: "'You broke hospital rules—eight of them, I believe,' he said. 'Very reprehensible, your descriptions of your actions tally with each other's. It was fun, wasn't it? It was shared fun. That's rare here. I'm kind of proud of you. . . .' He rearranged his look toward discipline. 'I see no reason to change the status of your privileges. That's all'" (216). Rather than merely to dismiss the image of Dr. Fried as "highly idealized," it is fairer to see it in the context of the spectrum of physicians in *I Never Promised You;* among the bad, the indifferent, the good, and the superb, she is undoubtedly at the optimal end of the scale.

Dr. Fried surpasses her colleagues through her ability to foster security and hence trust in her psychotic patients. She succeeds in so doing not by special techniques of management but by the force of her own absolute authenticity. "You certainly don't go in for hyperbole" is Deborah's half-scathing, half-approving reply to Dr. Fried's formulation of what she is to fight for: "For nothing easy or sweet, . . . for your own challenge, for your own mistakes and the punishment for them, for your own definition of love and sanity—a good strong self with which to begin to live" (182). This statement reiterates the theme in the novel's title, that life is not a rose garden, and it is made with the same mixture of realism, directness, and truthfulness characteristic of Dr. Fried throughout. Her empathy, sensitivity, and gentleness do not mislead her into simply mollycoddling her patient, for the good therapist's task is to reeducate patients to be better able to face life on their own. So while she always provides supportive reassurance by emphasizing that "we will make it together" (182), she is also frank in specifying the effort that Deborah has to contribute. To underscore the cooperative aspect of the therapeutic endeavor is obliquely to show respect for the patient, since the covert message is that she is sufficiently hardy for the active participation demanded of her. Instead of being infantilized by narrow behavioral prescriptions, as in hospital rules, or being reduced to the status of an object to be handled, Deborah is credited by Dr. Fried's method with the inner strength to help herself, with the doctor at her side. Such empowerment of the patient as a consequence of the therapist's authenticity is a vital factor in her recovery.

In Deborah's case truthfulness is of cardinal importance, as Dr. Fried recognizes: "'Look here, my dear girl,' Furii said, and thumped the ash of her cigarette on the tray. 'I am your doctor and I see these years how allergic you are to lying, so I try not to tell lies'" (182). This illustrates

Dr. Fried's warmth ("My dear girl"), her perspicacity, her use of nonverbal communication (thumping the ash of her cigarette), and her outspo-
kenness. The issue of lies and deceptions is identified as at the very heart
of Deborah's illness. In early childhood the surgeon's lies to her about
the pain of the operation are the first major deception she suffers, and at
about the same age her candid view of her baby sister separates her from
her relatives' fatuous show of admiration for the infant's beauty. Her
family's convention of keeping up nice appearances whatever the reality
leads to a systematic masquerade. Listening to the account of Deborah
given by her mother, Dr. Fried immediately sees "a girl sick to death
with deception" (41). Even after her suicide attempt her father will not
acknowledge that she is sick: "Just unhappy!" he shouts (28), and for the
longest possible time the fiction is maintained that she is in a convalescent home, not a mental hospital. For Deborah it is actually a welcome
relief from all this hypocrisy to be demoted to the ward for the most
severely disturbed where there is "no more lying gentility" (141).

Dr. Fried's wholehearted commitment to truthfulness, even if it is
momentarily painful, is the opposite of and the antidote to the deception normative in Deborah's family. Through Dr. Fried's probity Deborah
comes to grasp her parents' evasive, indeed mendacious way of dealing
with problems, although she cannot at first utter it openly: "Deborah
knew that they must have taken the naked fact and buried it hurriedly
somewhere, like carrion. But she knew well how the stench of a buried
lie pursues the guilty, hanging in the air they breathe until everything
smells of it, rancid and corrupting" (82). It is the therapist who articulates the origins of Deborah's withdrawal into Yr: "The deceits of the
grown-up world, the great gap between Grandfather's pretensions and
the world you saw more clearly, the lies told by your own precocity, that
you were special, and the hard fact that you couldn't get to first base with
your contemporaries no matter how impressive your specialness was"
(94). When asked point-blank who she is now, she has to answer that
she doesn't know. Deborah's acknowledgment of the pervasiveness of
deceitfulness in her life marks the decisive turning point in the therapy:
"there was a seeming sound of good, strong truth, like the pop of a hard-
thrown ball into a catcher's glove. Connect. Deborah listened to the
sound and then began to tumble over her words" (94). This "rush of
words," "strong" words to replace the old "comforting lie" (95) initiates
Deborah's return to reality. The sessions become "hard-worked and honest" (153) as Deborah tries "to think of a truth to tell the doctor as a

present" (158). The truth that she gives herself as a present is the avowal that she too had been "a liar and a coward" (127) and that the Yr world she had constructed as an alternative to adult deceit had itself been a form of self-deception. Hers had been "the voice of a possession" (48), her image "a kind of hiding" (191); and coming to see this, she tells Dr. Fried, is "a good hurt" (191).

I Never Promised You ends on a modestly hopeful note for Deborah's future. Although she still has to undergo hospitalization for a transient relapse, she has managed to attend school, pass the high school equivalency diploma examination, live on her own, and take part in the choir at a local church. She is still separated from the normal round of life, but she has a "hunger for the new world," "the passionate hunger of a newborn worldling for her birthright" (221). She even begins realistically and with a certain healthy irony to consider the job possibilities open to her with the knowledge and skills at her disposal. Greenberg's own successful career as a writer, wife, and mother encourages readers' inclination to optimism about Deborah, in contrast to the shadow cast over Esther in *The Bell Jar* by our extraneous knowledge of Plath's suicide. The image of the volcano that pervades the first half of the novel as the emblem of the illness disappears from the second half. Once the anger has been recognized and understood, it plays itself out until it subsides. And as this happens, the "medieval gate" (29) behind which other people have been inaccessibly locked begins to yield to Deborah's desire to open the door.

Psychoanalysis and Psychotherapy and *I Never Promised You* are in many respects entirely heterogenous texts, each governed by the conventions of the genre to which they belong. Fromm-Reichmann's papers, soberly reportorial in tone, are devoted to the exposition of her theses. Addressed to a projected professional audience, they are closely argued and rational, though at times illuminated by metaphors such as that of the therapist as the patient's bridge to reality. Fromm-Reichmann consciously fights off the "temptation to dramatize" (*P&P,* 200) in the interests of scholarly seriousness. Greenberg on the other hand resorts throughout her novel to vivid dramatization in her preference for scenic representations with lively repartee. She appeals to readers' imagination in depicting Deborah's state of mind and inviting empathy with her. Despite this basic disparity, however, *Psychoanalysis and Psychotherapy* and *I Never Promised You* form an interlocutory duet. The tempestuous therapeutic relationship between Deborah and Dr. Fried in the novel has its cogni-

tive counterpart in Fromm-Reichmann's papers which in turn are indebted to materials drawn from this and similar cases. The dialogues
within the novel are put into a new light by the correlative intertextual
dialogue between the clinical discourse of *Psychoanalysis and Psychotherapy*
and the fictional mode of Greenberg's version.

15

The Chemistry of Healing

If life had a second edition, how I would correct the proofs.
—John Clare

If, as Socrates averred, the unexamined life is not worth living, what about the life examined in psychotherapy? The metaphor of correcting the proofs in a second edition, enunciated by the poet John Clare (1793-1864), who was himself mad, posits the possibility of amending misguided patterns of thought and behavior, of making another, improved start. Does psychotherapy foster such a positive change and enhancement of the patient's life? If so, what are the salient characteristics required on the part of both the therapist and the patient to bring this about? By what chemistry does just talk effect healing? The word "chemistry" here does not refer to biochemical modifications by drugs (none of the patients in these narratives takes any psychotropic medications); it denotes rather the ineffable nature of the transaction between two human beings, one of whom is professionally trained to give help, while the other is in need of such help. What factors are conducive to making that relationship work well in some instances and less so or not at all in others?

My conclusions cannot be other than tentative because the sample is small, the choice of cases literary not scientific, and the impact of psychotherapy, unlike that of a surgical intervention, is often not amenable to immediate or definitive proof. The attempt to assess its influence on a patient's life forces us to the recognition of its status as more than a narrowly medicalized set of encounters; it is instead an essentially humanistic endeavor.

The difficulty of any categorical evaluation quickly becomes apparent in considering the outcome of the twelve cases in the narratives I have analyzed. The outcomes are very variable, and not necessarily related to the severity of the initial disorder; indeed, two of the most disturbed, Grace in *Picking Up the Pieces* and Deborah in *I Never Promised You a Rose Garden*, turn out best. Only one is patently clear-cut: Ellen West's suicide is evidentially a negative conclusion to her long assortment of therapies. The rest of the patients can be aligned along a fairly open spectrum. Josephine in *The Ha-Ha*, for example, suffers a severe setback following Alasdair's amateurish and selfishly motivated attention, yet at the end she has the initiative to escape the institution; we are left to speculate, none too hopefully, on her future. Alexander Portnoy, according to the closing words of Roth's novel, is after his protracted monologue only just about to begin his formal analysis. The other ten instances all imply a more or less positive outcome, though not necessarily as a result of conventional therapeutic measures. Those most directly healed through their therapists include the narrator in Cardinal's *The Words to Say It* whose health, sanity, and marriage are saved, and who is launched on her new career as a writer; Deborah Blau in *I Never Promised You a Rose Garden* who has emerged from the hallucinatory realm of schizophrenia and demonstrates her ability to function in the normal world by living outside the institution and passing the high school equivalency diploma examination; Plath's Esther Greenwood in *The Bell Jar* who is also released from the mental hospital as capable of leading her life on her own; Grace Jackson in *Picking Up the Pieces* who desists from self-destructive behaviors, achieves autonomy in her first apartment and with a boyfriend; Ginny of *Every Day Gets a Little Closer* who has acquired the ego strength to cut loose from her tortured dependence on her partner, move to Illinois, find a decent job, and develop a new relationship; and David in *The Manticore* who feels no more need to continue therapy and is ready to venture into new experiences. Three figures attain significant improvement well after the end of their therapy: Mrs. Armitage in Mortimer's *The Pumpkin Eater* faces the reality of her role in and beyond her family and is willing to rebuild her foundering marriage; Zeno, too, in Svevo's *Confessions of Zeno* manages to amend his self-image fundamentally and so to revise his rapport to himself and to others; and Tubby in Lodge's *Therapy* becomes reconciled to the breakup of his marriage and renews his life by reviving his attachment to his first love. The reflections and paths of these three illustrate that the correlation between psychotherapy and healing is not as simple as is generally assumed, nor is the chemistry readily definable.

Clearly it is the quality of the rapport between therapist and patient that is at stake. The congruence—and the success—of the match cannot, however, be determined primarily by the rather obvious traits such as patience, tolerance, and persistence, listed in the manuals of technical management as necessary to both therapists and patients. As in love or hate, an elusive chemistry of sometimes conflicting emotions is implicated in the formation and maintenance of a truly healing alliance. It is precisely the imponderables in the relationship that often drive patients from one therapist to another in an instinctive quest for the optimal partnership. This corresponds on the human level to the common cycling through a succession of medications before the biochemically appropriate one is found. Significantly, in *The Bell Jar* Dr. Gordon and Dr. Nolan apply the same treatment of electroconvulsive shock to reverse Esther's intractable depression, the one with near disastrous consequences in the patient's attempted suicide, the other with signal success. The difference between the ogre and the fairy godmother lies, therefore, not in the medical means invoked but in the interpersonal chemistry.

There are no rules for good chemistry despite the sensible guidelines in the textbooks on the techniques of psychotherapy. The therapist's specific professional orientation is not decisive. A considerable range of psychotherapeutic approaches is represented in the narratives I have examined. Five of the therapists are Freudians, three of whom practice classical psychoanalysis while the other two use modified versions. One is an orthodox Jungian, one a cognitive behaviorist, two favor existentialist principles, and two can best be described as eclectic traditionalists. Each method elicits an accepting response from some patients and rejection by others. For instance, Ginny in *Every Day Gets a Little Closer* progresses well under Yalom's existentialist persuasion, whereas Ellen West remains completely untouched by Binswanger's similar beliefs. Only with Alasdair, the amateur therapist in *The Ha-Ha*, and Dr. Gordon, the mere technician in *The Bell Jar*, can the method used be directly linked to the outcome. By and large the therapist's orientation is relevant merely to the degree to which it evokes a positive resonance or a negative repudiation on the patient's part.

The question of gender is almost equally open. In the twelve narratives under discussion there happens to be a neat (unintentional) chiasmus with eight female and four male patients to four women and eight (or nine counting Dr. Gordon) male therapists. Statistically, it so happens that more women are treated for emotional disorders than men. On the other hand, psychiatry is a field that attracts women, and has done so since the early days of psychoanalysis when Freud supported the admission of women analysts, both lay and medically qualified. With the preponderance of female patients and male therapists in my sample, more women undergo therapy by men than vice versa. The reverse—male patient and female therapist—is shown only in *Therapy* and *The Manticore,* in the former in a comical mode and in the latter with gravity. Two women, Esther Greenwood in *The Bell Jar* and Deborah Blau in *I Never Promised You a Rose Garden* have women therapists.

To what extent does gender make a difference in psychotherapy? Are the women shown to be more naturally nurturing? Dr. Nolan in *The Bell Jar* provides Esther with the good mothering she had lacked, but even more crucially she affords her a role model as a competent, independent professional. Dr. Fried, too, in *I Never Promised You a Rose Garden* re-mothers her patient in a healthier manner. But so does Dr. Nakhla in *Picking Up the Pieces.* Indeed he shows greater tenderness than either Dr. Nolan or Dr. Fried, both of whom are quite astringent. The briskest of all the women therapists is Dr. Haller in *The Manticore;* when she becomes a love object to her male patient, she handles his outspoken declaration with utmost calm as an expected part of the transference. In fact, to fall in love with a woman is a central development necessary to David's therapy so that here the cross-gendering between patient and therapist is as important as the gender concurrence in *The Bell Jar.* In gender-inverted form, Ginny's transference love for her male therapist in *Every Day Gets a Little Closer* fulfills a somewhat parallel function. The most problematic of the women therapists is Dr. Marples in *Therapy;* while Tubby sees her as rather attractive, he is impervious to her as either a symbolic mother or a symbolic lover. The chemistry is simply missing, probably because Tubby is not used to taking women seriously. The narratives thus suggest a variety of possible roles for both female and male therapists vis-a-vis their patients, dependent not intrinsically on gender but on the patient's needs and the therapist's stance.

If neither therapists' orientation nor their gender is of paramount importance in most cases, what then are the qualities that induce a potent therapeutic alliance? The patience, tolerance, and persistence recommended in the textbooks are, of course, not to be underestimated. But Dr. Marples, who arguably possesses these desirable features, is decidedly ineffective. In this instance, the necessary receptivity is lacking on her patient's part. Instead of merely going through the motions, as Tubby does, patients as well as therapists must be wholeheartedly com-

mitted to making authentic and sustained efforts, intellectual and emotional, to confront the problems with the greatest honesty they can mus-
ter. The most deeply disturbed of these patients, Grace in *Picking Up the
Pieces* and Deborah in *I Never Promised You a Rose Garden,* sense their
therapists' genuine concern for them, and are jolted by the realization
that they *matter* to someone who holds out hope of healing to rouse
themselves to an analogous belief, which in turn leads to self-activity.
Perhaps this is the fundamental characteristic of the finest therapists:
the capacity to project their own hopeful faith in the patient's potential
for healing. To instill such a faith into a demoralized, despairing patient
demands more than a facile optimism expressed in cliched phrases of
encouragement. It means taking the patient seriously as an individual—
admittedly one of a series of similar cases, but nonetheless invested with
a particularity deserving of respect. A productive chemistry is initiated
by the patient's awareness of the therapist's true dedication to the joint
enterprise. The intensity of the therapist's listening together with the
unswerving gaze and the tenacity not to be distracted convey to the
patient substantive devotion rather than just a ritualistic professional
pose. It is the therapist's implicit attitude that conditions the patient's
response, irrespective of the details of the situation. Thus the therapist's
mandated position in classical psychoanalysis behind the couch out of
the patient's sight does not materially alter the patient's consciousness
of an alert listener, as Cardinal's *The Words to Say It* illustrates. The
therapist's compassionate investment in the patient inspires a concordant effort on the patient's side. This may be the closest approximation
to an insight into the chemistry of healing.

The impediments to such a chemistry are easier to formulate. The
pursuit of self-gratification, exemplified so crassly by Alasdair in *The
Ha-Ha,* is foremost among them. A doctrinaire need to be right and to
dictate to the patient is shown to be destructive of the relationship to the
doctor in Svevo's *Confessions of Zeno.* Binswanger's narcissistic assertion
of his system and his loss of hope for Ellen West are, literally, fatal to
her; it is surely no coincidence that she kills herself soon after she has
been written off by a council of three psychiatrists. Absence of reciprocal
respect undermines the talk between Dr. Marples and Tubby in *Therapy.*
The want of human sensitivity is Dr. Gordon's basic flaw. A certain narrowness and failure of imagination are limitations in Mrs. Armitage's
doctor in *The Pumpkin Eater;* nevertheless she feels the sincerity of his
desire to help her, even if he does not seem to know how, so that eventu-

ally and obliquely he plays some role in her move to a new course, a
second edition of her life. His tendency to rigidity contrasts with the
willingness of the most stellar therapists, such as Dr. Fried, Dr. Nakhla,
and Dr. Yalom, to explore unorthodox approaches because they are the
most fitting to specific patients. Their talent stems from their flexibility,
their readiness and capacity to extend themselves in order to understand
their patients.

How, then, are patients persuaded to strive for a second edition of
their lives? What signals from the therapist can arouse patients to the
self-activity of correcting their proofs? I am deliberately using the open
term "signals" rather than message because the therapist's influence may
be exercised, as I have already suggested, by the body language (and
compliment) of giving patients total attention and thus projecting hopefulness as much as by the voiced persuasion of words. The most dis-
traught and alienated patients may even not be able to heed ordinary
utterances, but they can be moved by an act. Frieda Fromm-Reichmann
tells us of just sitting for an hour at a time for weeks beside a schizophrenic who said only, "Don't leave." She had demonstrated her commitment; her willingness simply to give him time obviously had meaning
for him, for her gesture implied that she believed him to be not beyond
healing. In this way, the therapist's stance represents a vital subtext to
the talk that is the manifest core of psychotherapy.

That talk varies as widely among the therapists as among the patients. Like the patients, the therapists may be overtalkers or undertalkers,
although more than patients they are capable of a moderating self-control. The undertalking therapists are primarily those who practice classical psychoanalysis, which predicates scant intervention in their patients'
free associations. This is the scenario in Cardinal's *The Words to Say It*,
where the analyst has remarkably little to say compared to the torrent of
words released in her. Portnoy's monologue is an avalanche that does
not allow his analyst a word in edgeways until the very end; this silencing of his therapist can be seen as part of Portnoy's self-defeating tragi-
comedy. Tubby, too, overwhelms Dr. Marples by his exuberant
verbalization, while in Svevo's *Confessions of Zeno* the analyst is completely shut out, first through the happenstance of his absence, later
through the patient's vindictiveness. The literary disposition of both
Therapy and *The Confessions of Zeno* predisposes to the squelching of the
therapist as a byproduct of the patient's first-person narration. What is
more, these accounts are presented as being in writing which heightens

the measure of control over the other's voice. Elsewhere therapists are sparse talkers for differing reasons: Mrs. Armitage's psychiatrist in *The Pumpkin Eater* is inept at getting talk going largely because he appears to be on a wavelength so far removed from her domestic and maternal preoccupations (it is dust that worries her, she tells him). Dr. Nolan in *The Bell Jar* is also laconic, but she acts on Esther by example and bearing, for instance sitting down in a relaxed manner for an informal conversation which raises Esther's self-worth. So she instigates the chemistry of healing by being rather than saying.

Few of the therapists are overtalkers. Alasdair, the amateur in *The Ha-Ha* solely in pursuit of sexual gratification, is voluble in wooing Josephine in order to conceal his ulterior purpose. Dr. Gordon makes a pretense of engaging with his patient, but his vacuous patter merely exposes his incompetence, for he does not really listen to Esther. Binswanger suffocates Ellen West by appropriating her words and subordinating them to his agenda. By contrast, Yalom in *Every Day Gets a Little Closer* has to do a good deal of the talking, especially at first, so as to counter the block in writing—and speaking—that brought Ginny into therapy. His tactics are designed to jumpstart her, as indeed they do. A similar aim underlies the moderate talk of Dr. Haller in *The Manticore* and of Dr. Fried in *I Never Promised You a Rose Garden,* both of whom succeed in drawing their respective patients into a healing and revitalizing self-understanding. On the whole, the therapists' relative restraint—provided a sufficient modicum of support is forthcoming—tends to have the beneficial effect of impelling the patient forward into healthy self-activity.

For the therapist's function in the chemistry of healing is above all to act as a catalyst for the patient's advance toward that second edition of life. Psychotherapy, no matter how brilliant, cannot *bestow* healing; it requires the patient's active cooperation, input, and ultimately own initiative. The term "chemistry" is so apposite to characterize a good interaction between therapist and patient precisely because it denotes the combination of two substances to create a third—in this context, a renewed life. Yalom chooses the telling word "accoucheur" (birther) to describe his work; the image of facilitating a birth, or more accurately, a re-birth is the biological equivalent to putting out a second edition. From the patient's perspective, Cardinal resorts to the same idea in dedicating her book to the doctor who helped her to be born ("qui m'a aidé à naître"). As in the correction of proofs, so in psychotherapy patients have to be brought to take another view of themselves as a step in the process of eliminating or attenuating ingrained destructive habits of thought and of behavior, and replacing them with preferable ones.

The means that therapists use to achieve this end are open to variations dependent on the particular patient's needs and personality. The most direct form of psychotherapy is supportive, emphasizing the positive potential innate to the patient. Often support is the optimal mode for younger, diffident patients who suffer from low self-esteem. This type of approach is exemplified in the way in which Dr. Nolan in *The Bell Jar* sanctions Esther's dislike of her mother and bolsters her self-confidence by a confirming faith in her abilities which her social environment had till then systematically undermined. Dr. Fried faces a harder task in *I Never Promised You a Rose Garden* in shifting Deborah from the private hallucinatory realm into which she had fled back into normal communication in the commonplace world, but the therapist's persistence, insight, and devotion endow Deborah with the courage to deal with reality. Along similar lines, though in a much less severe crisis, Dr. Yalom nurtures Ginny's trust in her own judgment and in her capacity to write.

In all these instances support entails also a measure of reeducation to get patients to alter their self-image as a basis for changing their behavior. This corrective purpose is frequently central to psychotherapy. Deborah Blau has to be made to stop assuming blame—and guilt—for traumas that befell her early on. Cardinal's narrator must come to envisage her mother's conduct from a radically different angle. Grace Jackson in *Picking Up the Pieces* has to unlearn her rage at being cast as perfect or, alternatively, horrid so as to accept herself without self-hate or self-recrimination. David in *The Manticore* is driven by his father's violent death (suicide?) to embark on a painful reassessment of family dynamics and myths. None of these fundamental, harrowing corrections could be carried out by patients without a professional therapist's empathetic support and guidance.

But narratives of psychotherapy reveal, too, instances of healing where the therapist acts as a catalyst by irritation, so to speak, prompting the patient to self-healing in a kind of oppositional protest. This possibility is certainly never mooted in the textbooks of psychotherapy, yet it occurs in three of the narratives. The most striking case is that of Svevo's Zeno whose development is animated by suspicion and defiance of his analyst; his negative transference to Dr. S. is as potent a stimulus to change as is the positive transference of Cardinal's narrator to her analyst. Tubby in *Therapy* is far less adversarial to Dr. Marples, whom he quite likes, but he too discovers his own route to his second edition. However, in both these instances the therapist is still the catalyst because it is Dr. S. and Dr. Marples who start their patients on the writing that results in a life examined and corrected. It would, therefore, be unfair to maintain that the psychotherapy is irrelevant; it simply proves fruitful in a wholly unexpected manner. Likewise in *The Pumpkin Eater* Mrs. Armitage reaches a deeper self-understanding apparently without her psychiatrist after he has broken his leg skiing; yet despite the brevity of her formal therapy and her show of antagonism to him, he has stirred up a questioning that leads to her eventual self-healing. These characters' stories suggest that the chemistry of psychotherapy sometimes produces a strange reaction and an unanticipated outcome.

Like Zeno and Tubby, Ellen West, Ginny in *Every Day Gets a Little Closer,* Grace in *Picking Up the Pieces,* Esther in *The Bell Jar,* and Cardinal's narrator all take to writing. Most of their writing is directly autobiographical, including Esther's as she begins a story about an alter ego whose name resembles her own. Writing the self as a form of objectification appears as an extension of or possibly a substitute for the talk of psychotherapy. This imbrication of narration and psychotherapy is a reiteration of the belief in the healing power of verbalization. However, only Zeno and Tubby achieve a self-actuated healing through writing. Ellen West voices her frustration, anger, and desires but without much cathartic effect. To the other four writing provides partial self-knowledge; as a means of healing it can only complement, not replace, the supportive, corrective influence of a wise, compassionate professionally trained therapist, able to balance empathy and distance to a degree that is beyond the reach of individuals in relation to themselves. Just talk is a powerful agency of healing when the chemistry of the therapeutic alliance is rightly in place.

Notes

PREFACE

1. Gardiner, *The Wolf-Man*, 135-52.
2. Manning, *Undercurrents*, 31.
3. The various editions of the *Diagnostic and Statistical Manual* (*DSM*) will be identified by the roman numeral.
4. Wolberg, *Technique of Psychotherapy*, 40.
5. Berman, *Talking Cure*, 21.
6. Ellenberger, *Beyond the Unconscious*, 151.

1. TALKING OF MANY THINGS

1. Storr, *Art of Psychotherapy*, 13.
2. Ellenberger, *Discovery of the Unconscious*, 213.
3. Frank and Frank, *Persuasion and Healing*, 87-112.
4. Rosenberg, "Crisis in Psychiatric Legitimacy," 135.
5. Flyer in Chapel Hill, N.C., 29 March 1996.
6. See Ellenberger, *Discovery of the Unconscious*, for a history spanning from primitive shamanism to 1945.
7. Tatar, *Spellbound*, 5. For introductions to Mesmer, see Ellenberger, *Discovery of the Unconscious*, 57-69; Tatar, *Spellbound*, 3-25; and Miller, "Going Unconscious."
8. Zilboorg, *History of Medical Psychology*, 422-31.
9. Lunbeck, *Psychiatric Persuasion*, 177.
10. Hooker, *Physician and Patient*, 384.
11. Shorter, *From Paralysis to Fatigue*, 204-5, and *Short History of Psychiatry*, 122-23.
12. Oppenheim, *"Shattered Nerves,"* 139.
13. Shorter, *Short History of Psychiatry*, 139.
14. Laplanche and Pontalis, *Language of Psychoanalysis*, 373.
15. For a vehement attack on the worth of psychoanalysis, see Eysenck, *Fact and Fiction in Psychology*, especially 95-216. For a dispassionate summary of the doubts, see Wolberg, 7-8.
16. Wolberg, *Technique of Psychotherapy*, 7. See also 348-50 for a useful tabu-

lated differentiation between psychoanalysis (classical and non-Freudian), psychoanalytically oriented psychotherapy, and supportive and reeducative therapy.

17. Different terminologies have been used to characterize the main approaches: either by denotation of their methodology such as being behavioral, interpersonal, existential, developmental, cognitive, or more broadly as "evocative" or "directive" (Frank and Frank), or "supportive," "reeducative," "reconstructive" (Wolberg). The question of nosology is not relevant to this study because talk is common to them all.

18. I. Yalom, *Every Day Gets a Little Closer,* 218.

19. Ibid., 219.

20. Wolberg, *Technique of Psychotherapy,* 4.

21. Frank and Frank, *Healing and Persuasion,* 2.

22. Storr, *Art of Psychotherapy,* 8.

23. Havens, *Safe Place.*

24. Herman, *What Is Psychotherapy?* 6.

25. Ehrenwald, *History of Psychotherapy,* 221.

26. Reported in Taylor, "Attitude of the Medical Profession," 408.

27. Shorter, *From Paralysis to Fatigue,* 245.

28. Ellenberger, *Discovery of the Unconsious,* 285.

29. Ibid., 48.

30. I. Yalom, *Every Day Gets a Little Closer,* 227.

31. Herman, *Why Psychotherapy?* 40-41.

32. Laplanche and Pontalis, *Language of Psycho-Analysis,* 370.

33. For the successive changes from *Diagnostic and Statistical Manual-I* (usually appreviated to *DSM*)(1952) through *DSM-IV* (1994) see Shorter, *History of Psychiatry,* 299-305. Shorter asserts that the removal of neurosis and psychoneurosis from the most recent edition can be ascribed to the waning influence of psychoanalysts.

34. *American Psychiatric Glossary,* ed. Stone, 88.

35. *DSM-IV,* 5.

36. Byrd, *Visits to Bedlam,* 43.

37. Ellenberger, *Discovery of the Unconscious,* 245.

38. Frank and Frank, *Persuasion and Healing,* 155.

39. Kramer, *Listening to Prozac,* 1-21.

40. Kaysen, *Girl Interrupted,* 137.

41. See Kramer, *Listening to Prozac,* 47-64, for the history of antidepressants; also Sutherland, *Breakdown,* 209-17.

42. Vaughan, *Talking Cure.*

43. Foucault, *Mental Illness and Psychology,* 63.

44. Gilman, *Seeing the Insane,* 2.

45. Castel, Castel, and Lovell, *La Société psychiatrique avancée.* Less than twenty years after its publication, the praise for "le modèle américain" with the

free clinics and deinstitutionalization then characteristic of "Psychamérique" sounds ironic, to say the least.

46. Micale and Porter, *Discovering the History of Psychiatry*, 13.

47. Storr, *Art of Psychotherapy*, xiv.

48. Jamison, *Unquiet Mind*, 127.

49. Foucault, *Madness and Civilization*, 183.

50. Storr, *Art of Psychotherapy*, 25.

51. Ellenberger, *Discovery of the Unconscious*, 358 and 366. Janet's experiments are recorded in his papers: "Les Actes inconscients et le dédoublement de la personnalité,"and "Etude sur un cas d'amnésie antérograde."

52. Osler, *Counsels and Ideals*, 94.

53. Mitchell, *Diseases of the Nervous System*, 263-64.

54. Glenn, introduction to *Freud and His Patients*, 11.

55. Storr, *Art of Psychotherapy*, 16.

56. See Boxer, "Flogging Freud," for a survey of recent anti-Freud books.

2. FROM EYES TO EARS

1. Freud, *GW,* 1:227; *SE,* 2:160.

2. Guillain, *Charcot,* 121-25.

3. Ibid., ix.

4. "Hospice de la Salpêtrière: Réouverture des conférences cliniques de M. Charcot," *Prog. méd.* 8 (27 November 1880): 969-71 [970]; cited by Shorter, *From Paralysis to Fatigue,* 169.

5. Shorter, *From Paralysis to Fatigue,* 169.

6. Charcot, *L'Hystérie,* 49.

7. For an illustration, see Drinka, *Birth of Neurosis,* 127.

8. Charcot, *L'Hystérie,* 70.

9. Ibid., 95.

10. Drinka, *Birth of Neurosis,* 125.

11. Harrington, *Double Brain,* 172-73.

12. Charcot, *L'Hystérie,* 168, 181.

13. Gilman, *Seeing the Insane,* 164.

14. Long before photography, attempts had been made to capture the faces of madness in graphic forms. The painter J.-L.-A. Théodore Géricault (1791-1824) executed a series of ten portraits of mental patients between 1821 and 1824 for Dr. Etienne-Jean Georget while himself institutionalized under his care. Five of these have been lost; the surviving pictures of heads, notably *La Folle* (*The Madwoman*) and *Le Fou Assassin* (*The Mad Assassin,* also known as *A Kleptomaniac*), portrayed full face make a strong impression through their haunting depiction of emptiness, estrangement, and enclosure in a private world. Alexander Morrison's *Outlines of Lectures on Mental Disorders* (1825) included several plates with a discussion of the physiognomy of insanity. Such physiog-

nomic studies gained added impetus from the work of Johann Kaspar Lavater (1741-1801), who published *The Physiognomy of Mental Diseases* in 1838. In the same year, the treatise *Of Mental Diseases* by Jean-Etienne-Dominique Esquirol (1772-1840) carried illustrations too. The tradition of picturing the mentally disturbed and of trying to use pictures didactically had therefore been established before photography. The first textbook with illustrations, *Elemente der Psychiatrik* by Dietrich Georg Kieser, appeared in 1855 with the aim of enabling medical students to attain visual experience of the insane as part of their regular medical education without having to seek out one of the few institutions for harboring mental patients. John Connolly's series of essays on "The Physiognomy of Insanity" (1858) concentrated on the study of expression as a means of determining the fine line between the normal and the abnormal with the ultimate goal of devising an effective mode of restoring normality. These early efforts to document the physiognomy of the mentally disordered reached their apogee in 1857 in Benedictin Augustin Morel's *Traité des dégénérescences physiques, intellectuelles et morales de l'espèce humaine* (*Treatise on physical, intellectual, and moral degenerations in the human species*), to which was appended an "atlas" of twelve lithographic plates, reproductions of photographs.

15. Gilman, *Seeing the Insane,* 5.

16. For biographical information on Diamond, see Gilman, *Seeing the Insane,* 5-11.

17. Cited by Gilman, *Face of Madness,* 20.

18. Appignanesi and Forrester, *Freud's Women,* 65.

19. Showalter, *Female Malady,* 97.

20. See Rothfield, *Vital Signs,* 65, and Goldstein, *Console and Classify,* 35.

21. Foucault, *Madness and Civilization,* 68 ff.

22. Goldstein, *Console and Classify,* 379.

23. Falret, *Etudes cliniques,* 502.

24. Ehrenwald, *History of Psychotherapy,* 258-60.

25. Freud, "Charcot," 23.

26. Borch-Jacobsen, *Remembering Anna O,* 64.

27. In his account of Hansen's reception in Vienna Borch-Jacobsen speculates that Bertha Pappenheim, the real name of the patient presented by Freud's senior colleague Josef Breuer as Anna O, could have witnessed one of the performances, and/or would almost certainly have heard about them by word of mouth or read about them in the newspapers. He argues insistently but unconvincingly that her illness and treatment began at the end of 1880, and her symptoms "feature by feature, (intractable contractures, localized anesthesia, posthypnotic amnesia, positive and negative hallucinations, visual disturbances, aphasia, and so on) resembled those produced during Hansen's staged performances" (*Remembering Anna O,* 67).

28. Freud, *Uber Psychoanalyse, GW,* 8:7.

29. Freud, *Uber Psychoanalyse, GW,* 8:7. Whether Anna O was actually cured, as Breuer and Freud claimed at the time, or not is a moot point. The evidence is contradictory. It is true that she was twice thereafter confined to a sanatorium against her will: first in Inzensdorf near Vienna for exactly a year from 7 June 1881 to 7 June 1882, and barely a month later, on 12 July 1882, in the Bellevue sanatorium in Kreuzlingen, Switzerland, under Dr. Robert Binswanger. This second time she was suffering from severe facial neuralgia, which aggravated her addiction to the high doses of morphine that Breuer had prescribed for her in mid-March 1882 to alleviate pain following jaw surgery. During her first spell in a sanatorium Breuer was continuing his treatment, while during the second she presented symptoms directly attributable to a physical cause (the aftermath of jaw surgery) discrete from those of the initial illness. Eventually she did recover full health to become a prominent social worker. Borch-Jacobsen's denunciation of "the abysmal failure of the original 'talking cure,'" like his accusations of bad faith on Freud's part (*Remembering Anna O,* 26), his characterization of the transactions between Anna O and Breuer as "fraud" (28) or "a game" between "a gifted simulator" and "a rather gullible Viennese doctor" (92), is part of the recent revisionist momentum against Freud and psychoanalysis. The rhetoric of *Remembering Anna O,* in its abundant reliance on surmise, points to the tenuousness of Borch-Jacobsen's theory: "Obviously it doesn't take much for the thought to arise ..." (69); "Bertha Pappenheim got the point [of Carl Hansen's clairvoyance demonstrations in Vienna in 1880], it seems" (73); "It's a good bet that . . ." (81). Provocative and trendy though this book is in relation to the current "false memory" debate, it does not prove that Freud was engaging in a pretense that he knew to be hollow in exploring the kind of therapy depicted in the *Studies on Hysteria.* Why, after all, would he divert all his energy from neurology, where he had made a promising start, in a favor of a direction he already recognized as ineffective?

30. Freud, *GW,* 1:81-98; *SE,* 2:3-17.

31. Freud, *GW,* 1:85. Bold type in cited text.

32. Freud, *Uber Psychoanalyse, GW,* 8:7.

33. Freud, "Zur Atiology der Hysterie," *GW,* 1:439.

34. Freud, "Zur Psychotherapie der Hysterie," *GW,* 1:278.

35. Freud, "Charcot," 33.

36. Gilman, *Seeing the Insane,* 204.

37. Clare, for example, asserts that the series of four early cases "have little to do with psychoanalysis," and that Freud produced only six accounts of psychoanalytic treatment ("Freud's Cases," 274). The most thorough recent exposition has been given by Appignanesi and Forrester ("The First Patients," 63-116), but they focus biographically on disclosing the women's identities and relating their life stories to the case histories.

38. Freud, *GW,* 1:211; *SE,* 2:147.

39. Freud, *GW,* 1:200; *SE,* 2:138.

40. Freud, *GW,* 1:99; *SE,* 2:48.

41. Freud, *GW,* 1:108; *SE,* 2:56.

42. Freud, *GW,* 1:157; *SE,* 2:101.

43. Freud, *GW,* 1:115, n.; *SE,* 2:62.

44. Freud, *GW,* 1:116; *SE,* 2:63.

45. Freud, *GW,* 1:165-70; *SE,* 2:107-12.

46. Freud, *GW,* 1:165; *SE,* 2:108.

47. Freud, *GW,* 1:165; *SE,* 2:108.

48. Freud, *GW,* 1:166; *SE,* 2:109.

49. Freud, *GW,* 1:168; *SE,* 2:110.

50. Freud, *GW,* 1:208; *SE,* 2:145.

51. Freud, *GW,* 1:218; *SE,* 2:153.

52. Freud, *GW,* 1:201; *SE,* 2:139.

53. Freud, *GW,* 1:116; *SE,* 2:63.

54. Forrester, *Language and the Origins of Psychoanalysis,* 39.

55. Freud, *GW,* 1:176; *SE,* 2:118.

56. Freud, *GW,* 1:178-79; *SE,* 2:120-21.

57. Freud, *GW,* 1:188; *SE,* 2:128.

58. Freud, *GW,* 1:189; *SE,* 2:129.

59. Freud, *GW,* 1:192; *SE,* 2:131.

60. See Ellenberger, *Discovery of the Unconscious,* 627, for a table of differences between Freud and Adler.

61. Freud, *GW,* 1:227; *SE,* 2:161.

62. For further details of his neurological work, see Ellenberger, *Discovery of the Unconscious,* 433-35.

63. Ibid., 477.

64. For the persistence of the same prejudice against psychiatry in favor of neurology, see D.M. Thomas, *Pictures at an Exhibition,* 78-79: "You know how Dad felt about my becoming a shrink, . . . I didn't go through the castle gate into neurology, but turned left, as it were, into a career he considers second-rate and vulgar."

65. Freud, *Briefe,* 63; *Letters,* 19.

66. Freud, *Briefe,* 63; *Letters,* 18.

67. Significantly, the *Studies on Hysteria* actually reveal a telling instance of Freud's deliberate suppression in the 1895 version of what would then have been regarded as a particularly obnoxious fact. In 1924 Freud added a closing footnote to the third case, that of Katharina in which he admits that after so many years, he is willing to risk a break from the discretion he had earlier maintained ("getraue ich mich die damals beobachtete Diskretion aufzuheben") by disclosing that her assailant had been not her uncle but her father. Obviously, in the interest of "discretion," he had toned down a circumstance that made the

case even more shocking, although he admits, in an almost ironic understatement, that the shift is by no means without importance for an understanding of the case (Freud, *GW,* 1:195; *SE,* 2:134).

68. Vrettos, *Somatic Fictions,* 56.

69. Freud, *SE,* 9:289. Note that the patient is described as "eine Dame" (a lady), a term that denotes upper middle class status, in contrast to the normative "Frau" (woman).

70. Pontalis, "Le Séjour de Freud à Paris," 239.

71. Dinnage, *One to One,* 9.

72. Freud, *GW,* 1:227; *SE,* 2:160.

73. Sacks, *Awakenings,* 206.

74. Oppenheim, *"Shattered Nerves,"* 311.

75. Freud, *GW,* 1:233; *SE,* 2:165.

76. Reik, *Listening with the Third Ear,* 453.

77. Certeau, "Freudian Novel," 128.

78. Freud, *GW,* 1:133; *SE,* 2:79.

79. Freud, *GW,* 1:209; *SE,* 2:145.

3. "Digesting" Psychoanalysis

1. Anna Freud, foreword to *The Wolf-Man,* ed. Muriel Gardiner, ix.

2. Freud, *Three Cases,* 195.

3. Anna Freud, foreword to *The Wolf-Man,* ed. Muriel Gardiner, ix.

4. Because of this version's departures from the French, all translations are mine.

5. See Cohn, "Freud's Cases," 27.

6. M. Yalom, *Maternity, Mortality, and the Literature of Madness,* 117, n. 2, reveals that Cardinal's analyst was Michel de M'Uzan, a member of the Paris Psychoanalytic Society and author of *De l'art à la mort* (Paris: Gallimard, 1972).

7. Reik, *Listening with the Third Ear,* 110.

8. M. Yalom, *Maternity, Mortality, and the Literature of Madness,* 65.

9. Morrison, *Playing in the Dark,* vi. My thanks to Gunilla T. Kester for giving me this passage.

10. M. Yalom, *Maternity, Mortality, and the Literature of Madness,* 52.

4. "Ritualized Bellyaching"

1. Berman, *Talking Cure,* 245.

2. Berman, *Talking Cure,* 243.

3. Freud, *Briefe,* 63; *Letters,* 18.

4. Grebstein, "The Comic Anatomy of *Portnoy's Complaint,*" 160.

5. Resisting Psychoanalysis

1. See Svevo's letter to Valerio Javier, 10 December 1927, *Opere omnia,* 1:857. See also Fusco, "Italo Svevo e la Psicanalisi."

2. Furbank, *Italo Svevo,* 174.

3. Freud, *Selbstdarstellung, GW,* 14:37; *Autobiographical Study, SE,* 20:15.

4. See Veitch, "Four Thousand Years of Hysteria" and *Hysteria: the History of a Disease.*

7. Amateurish "Heart-to-Hearts"

1. "A boundary to a garden, pleasure-ground, or park, of such a kind as not to interrupt the view from within, and not to be seen until closely approached; consisting of a trench, the inner side of which is perpendicular and faced with stone, the outer sloping and turfed; a sunk fence," *Oxford English Dictionary* (1989).

2. Dawson herself graduated from Oxford in 1954; before returning to graduate study in philosophy in 1959, she worked at the Clarendon Press, on *The Oxford English Dictionary,* and as a social worker in a mental hospital.

3. Fromm-Reichmann's work with schizophrenics bears out their potential openness to psychotherapy, given a suitable approach with a sensitive therapist. See "Basic Problems in the Psychotherapy of Schizophrenia," "Psychotherapy of Schizophrenia," and "Transference Problems in Schizophrenia" in *Psycho-analysis and Psychotherapy.*

8. Ritualized Roles

1. Mortimer's first novel appeared in 1947 under the name Penelope Dimont. After her second marriage to John Mortimer in 1949 she published a long series of novels as well as *About Time: An Aspect of Autobiography* (1979) and *Queen Elizabeth: A Life of the Queen Mother* (1986). She had six children. See *An Encyclopedia of British Women Writers,* ed. Paul and June Schlueter, 336-38.

2. The useful German term for this psychological tactic is *vorbeireden,* literally, talking past (the issue).

3. Wolberg, *Technique of Psychotherapy,* 631.

4. Labov and Fanshel, *Therapeutic Discourse,* 334-35.

9. The Ogre and the Fairy Godmother

1. The obvious coincidence of time, place, and circumstances between Plath's life and Esther's has fostered the common autobiographical readings of *The Bell Jar* (e.g., Berman, *Talking Cure,* 121-38), Wagner-Martin, 103, 105-8, 155). My purpose is to focus on the novel's portrayal of psychotherapy.

2. See Wolberg, *Technique of Psychotherapy,* 484-86.

3. Ibid., 573-74.

4. Crichton, *Travels*, 11.

5. Dr. Gordon bears out Wolberg's laconic comment: "One cannot hatch an egg in a refrigerator" (*Technique of Psychotherapy*, 52).

6. Cited by Wolberg, *Technique of Psychotherapy*, 139, from *Psychiatric News* 7 (22): 1972.

7. Shorter, *History of Psychiatry*, 280.

8. See Wolberg, *Technique of Psychotherapy*, 154.

PART III. DUETS

1. The situation is echoed in fictionalized form in Judith Rossner's novel *August* (1983), which traces in tandem the vicissitudes in the lives of the patient, Dawn Henley, and her therapist, Dr. Lulu Shinefeld, through the course of a therapy extending over several years. However, this is a pretended duet since both figures emanate from a single authorial imagination, and neither produces a written account.

2. A somewhat parallel instance is *Tea with Demons* (1985) by Carol Allen and Herbert S. Lustig, although the therapist's input is limited to a concluding "Note" so that it can hardly be considered a duet.

11. MORE THAN JUST TALK

1. The title, *Every Day Gets a Little Closer*, derives from a song cited by the patient: "Every day seems a little longer / Every way love's a little stronger" (240). In a private conversation (15 June 1997) Dr. Yalom told me that this title was her choice for she had always dreamed of getting married to this song. He would have preferred the present subtitle to be the main title.

2. Anna Freud's term.

3. Subsequently Yalom became a best-selling writer with *Love's Executioner* (1989) and a successful novelist with *When Nietzsche Wept* (1992) and *Lying on the Couch* (1996).

12. CONTAINING THE BREAK

1. "Contain" is a word that several of Dinnage's subjects in *One to One* use to denote a valuable aspect of their psychotherapy.

13. THE ELUSIVE PATIENT

1. Rogers, "Ellen West—and Loneliness"; Burstow, "A Critique of Binswanger's Existentialist Analysis."

2. Studer, "Ellen West," in *Wahnsinnsfrauen;* Seinfeld, "The Tragic Case of Ellen West," in *The Empty Core;* and Chernin, *The Obsession.*

3. See, for instance, Appignanesi and Forrester, *Freud's Women;* Gardiner and Obholzer on the Wolf-Man.

4. Studer, "Ellen West," 231, cites Dr. Dieter Binswanger's negative reply to her request to see the papers in 1990.

5. Studer, "Ellen West," 237 and 245.

6. Binswanger, "The Existential Analysis of Thought," 191.

7. Ibid., 200.

8. Ibid., 193.

9. May, "The Origins and Significance of the Existentialist Movement," 11.

10. The translators of "The Case of Ellen West" opted to retain the German terms, referring readers in note 24 (269) to May's elucidations of them in *Existence*, 61-65.

11. Binswanger, "The Existential Analysis School of Thought," 202.

12. Ibid., 202.

13. Ibid., 200.

14. Ibid., 201.

15. Ibid., 201.

16. Binswanger, "Der Fall Ellen West," 53: 259; May, *Existence,* 243.

17. Binswanger, "Der Fall Ellen West," 53: 258; May, *Existence,* 241.

18. Binswanger, "Der Fall Ellen West," 53: 259; May, *Existence,* 241.

19. Binswanger, "Der Fall Ellen West," 53: 261; May, *Existence,* 247.

20. Binswanger, "Der Fall Ellen West," 53: 260; May, *Existence,* 245.

21. Binswanger, "Der Fall Ellen West," 53: 270 and 269; May, *Existence,* 258 and 256.

22. Binswanger, "Der Fall Ellen West," 53: 265; May, *Existence,* 252.

23. Binswanger, "Der Fall Ellen West," 53: 266; May, *Existence,* 253.

24. Binswanger, "Der Fall Ellen West," 53: 264; May, *Existence,* 249.

25. Binswanger, "Der Fall Ellen West," 55: 36; May, *Existence,* 361.

26. See Brumberg, *Fasting Girls,* and Werne, *Treating Eating Disorders.*

27. Binswanger, "Der Fall Ellen West," 55: 23; May, *Existence,* 349.

28. Binswanger, "Der Fall Ellen West," 55: 24; May, *Existence,* 350.

29. Binswanger, "Der Fall Ellen West," 55: 24; May, *Existence,* 350. It seems appropriate to cite here the translators' caveat to readers in their note 17 (*Existence,* 267): "The reader should be forewarned that some sections which follow may seem difficult to understand in English. Binswanger's style, in line with much German scientific and philosophical writing, uses built-up concepts, especially by hyphenating verb forms with other words, which mean something more than do the separate words in English. In translating, we had to decide whether to paraphrase or to render Binswanger more accurately. We chose to do the latter. We are of course aware that this does not make for writing that, as Kierkegaard put it, can be perused during the afternoon nap. But such was scarcely our intention."

30. Binswanger, "Der Fall Ellen West," 54: 71; May, *Existence,* 270.

31. Binswanger, "Der Fall Ellen West," 53: 272; May, *Existence*, 260.

32. Binswanger, "Der Fall Ellen West," 54: 345; May, *Existence*, 328.

33. Binswanger, "Der Fall Ellen West," 55: 348; May, *Existence*, 330.

34. Binswanger, "Der Fall Ellen West," 55: 18-29; May, *Existence*, 340-54.

35. Seinfeld, *The Empty Core*, 131-34.

36. Mendel, *Treating Schizophrenia*, 87.

37. Binswanger, "Der Fall Ellen West," 53: 256; May *Existence*, 238.

38. Binswanger, "Der Fall Ellen West," 53: 272; May, *Existence*, 260-61.

39. Binswanger, "Der Fall Ellen West," 53: 275; May, *Existence*, 264.

40. Binswanger, "Der Fall Ellen West," 53: 274; May, *Existence*, 263.

41. Binswanger, "Der Fall Ellen West," 53: 269; May, *Existence*, 257.

42. Binswanger, "Der Fall Ellen West," 53: 270; May, *Existence*, 271.

43. Binswanger, "Der Fall Ellen West," 53: 271; May, *Existence*, 259.

44. See Furst, "Anxious Patients/Anxious Doctor."

45. Burstow, "A Critique of Binswanger's Existential Analysis," 247.

46. May, *Existence*, 4; cited from Binswanger, "Daseinsanalyse und Psychotherapie," 303; "Existential Analysis and Psychotherapy," 144.

47. Burstow, "A Critique of Binswanger's Existential Analysis," 247.

14. Collecting and Disposing of Garbage

1. *Psychoanalysis and Psychotherapy*, 207; hereafter cited as *P&P. I Never Promised You a Rose Garden* is hereafter cited as *INPY*.

2. Rubin, "Conversations with the Author of *I Never Promised You*," 206.

3. Berman, *Talking Cure*, 162, 163-64, 165-66, lists parallel incidents.

4. Ibid., 161.

5. See *P&P*, 208, for the attributes necessary for a therapist working with schizophrenics.

6. Fromm-Reichmann, *P&P*, 190, 197, 204, 206, 213.

7. Berman, *Talking Cure*, 156.

8. Ibid., 170.

9. Although Fromm-Reichmann did subscribe to the then current theory of the schizophrenogenic mother, this aspect is not emphasized in *I Never Promised You*; on the contrary, as Dr. Fried gets to know Deborah's mother better, she finds "what is behind the façade is not so bad" (167).

Bibliography

PRIMARY SOURCES

Allen, Carol, with Herbert S. Lustig, M.D. *Tea with Demons.* New York: Morrow, 1984.

Bidart, Frank. "Ellen West." *In the Western Night: Collected Poems 1965-90,* 109-21. New York: Farrar Straus Giroux, 1990.

Binswanger, Ludwig. "Daseinsanalyse und Psychotherapie." *Ausgewählte Vorträge und Aufsätze,* 2:303-8. Bern: Francke, 1955. Trans. as "Existential Analysis and Psychotherapy." In *Progress in Psychotherapy,* ed. Frieda Fromm-Reichmann and J.L. Moreno, 144-48. New York: Grune & Stratton, 1956.

———. "Der Fall Ellen West: Eine anthropologisch-klinische Studie." *Schweizer Archiv für Neurologie und Psychiatrie* 53 (1944): 255-77; 54 (1944): 69-117, and 330-60; 55 (1945): 16-40. "The Case of Ellen West: An Anthropological-Clinical Study," trans. Werner M. Mendel and Joseph Lyons. In *Existence,* ed. Rollo May, Ernest Angel, and Henri F. Ellenberger, 237-364. New York: Simon and Schuster, 1958.

———. "Uber die daseinsanalytische Forschungsrichtung in der Psychiatrie." *Schweizer Archiv für Neurologie und Psychiatrie* 57 (1946): 209-25. Rpt. in *Ausgewählte Vorträge und Aufsätze.* Bern: Francke, 1947, 1:190-217. "The Existential Analysis School of Thought," trans. Ernest Angel. In *Existence,* ed. Rollo May, Ernest Angel, and Henri F. Ellenberger, 191-213. New York: Simon & Schuster, 1958.

Breuer, Josef, and Sigmund Freud. *Studien über Hysterie.* In Sigmund Freud, *Gesammelte Werke (GW),* 1:83-311. Frankfurt: Fischer, 1952. *Standard Edition (SE),* trans. and ed. James Strachey, 2:1-305. London: Hogarth Press, 1957.

Briquet, Paul. *Traité clinique et thérapeutique de l'hystérie.* Paris: 1859.

Britt, Lisa. *Ellen West: Portrait of an Obsession.* Marina Del Ray, Calif.: American Video Factory, 1983.

Cardinal, Marie. *Les Mots pour le dire.* Paris: Grasset, 1975. *The Words to Say It,* trans. Pat Goodheart. Cambridge, Mass.: Van Vactor and Goodheart, 1983.

Charcot, Jean-Martin. *L'Hystérie.* Textes choisis et présentés par E. Trillat. Toulouse: Privat, 1971.

———— and Paul Richer. *Les Démoniaques dans l'art.* Paris: Delahaye et Lecrosnier, 1887.

————. *Les Difformes et les malades dans l'art.* Paris: Lecrosnier et Babé, 1889.

Davies, Robertson. 1970. New York:Viking/Penguin, 1977.

————. *The Manticore.* 1972. New York: Viking/Penguin, 1987.

————. *World of Wonders.* 1976. New York: Viking/Penguin, 1977.

Dawson, Jennifer. *The Ha-Ha.* 1961. Harmondsworth: Penguin, 1962.

Drabble, Margaret. *A Natural Curiosity.* 1989. Harmondsworth: Penguin, 1990.

Eliot, T.S. *The Cocktail Party.* New York: Harcourt Brace Jovanovich, 1950.

Falret, Jean-Pierre. *Etudes cliniques sur les maladies mentales et nerveuses.* Paris: Baillère, 1890.

Freud, Sigmund. "Aus der Geschichte einer infantilen Neurose." In *Gesammelte Werke (GW),* 12:27-157. "From the History of an Infantile Neurosis," trans. and ed. James Strachey. *Standard Edition (SE),* 17:7-122.

————. *Briefe an Wilhelm Fliess, Abhandlungen und Notizen aus den Jahren 1887-1902.* London: Imago, 1950. *Complete Letters of Sigmund Freud to Wilhelm Fliess 1887-1904,* trans. and ed. Jeffrey M. Masson. Cambridge, Mass.: Harvard Univ. Press, 1985.

————. "Charcot." In *GW,* 1:21-35. London: Imago and Frankfurt: Fischer, 1952. *SE,* 3:11-23.

————. *Die Traumdeutung.* London: Imago, 1942. *The Interpretation of Dreams.* In *SE,* 4/5:1-627.

————. "Erinnern, Wiederholen und Durcharbeiten." In *GW,* 10:126-36. "Remembering, Repeating and Working-Through." In *SE,* 12:147-56.

————. *Selbstdarstellung.* In *GW,* 14:31-96. Frankfurt: Fischer, 1948. *Autobiographical Study.* In *SE,* 20:7-74.

————. *Studien über Hysterie. Gesammette Werke.* London: Imago, 1952. 75-251. *Studies on Hysteria,* standard edition, trans. and ed. James Strachey: London: The Hogarth Press, 1955, 2.

————. "Uber den Urpsrung des Nervus accusticus." *Monatsschrift für Ohrenheilkunde* 20, Neue Folge (1886): 245-51, and 277-82.

————. *Uber Psychoanalyse.* In *GW,* 8:1-60. London: Imago, 1948. *Psycho-Analysis.* In *SE,* 20:263-70.

————. "Zur Atiologie der Hysterie." In *GW,* 1:426-59.

Fromm-Reichmann, Frieda. *Psychoanalysis and Psychotherapy.* Ed. Dexter M. Bullard. Chicago: Univ. of Chicago Press, 1959.

————. "Academic Lecture Read to the Hundred and Tenth Annual Meeting of the American Psychiatric Association, 1954." In *Psychoanalysis and Psychotherapy,* 194-209.

————. "Basic Problems in the Psychotherapy of Schizophrenia." In *Psychoanalysis and Psychotherapy,* 210-17.

————. "Psychotherapy of Schizophrenia." In *Psychoanalysis and Psychotherapy,* 194-209.

————. "Transference Problems in Schizophrenia." In *Psychoanalysis and Psychotherapy,* 117-28.

Gardiner, Muriel, trans. and ed. *The Wolf-Man by the Wolf-Man.* New York: Basic Books, 1971.

Gilman, Charlotte Perkins. *The Yellow Wallpaper.* 1892; rpt. New York: Oxford Univ. Press, 1995.

Greenberg, Joanne. *I Never Promised You a Rose Garden.* New York: Penguin Books, 1964.

Jamison, Kay Redfield. *An Unquiet Mind.* New York: Knopf, 1995.

Janet, Pierre. *The Major Symptoms of Hysteria: Fifteen Lectures Given in the Medical School of Harvard University.* 1907. 2d ed. New York: Macmillan, 1924.

————. "Les Actes inconscients et le dédoublement de la personnalité pendant le somnambulisme provoqué," *Revue philosophique* 22 (1886): 577-92.

————. "Etude sur un cas d'amnésie antérograde dans la maladie de la désagrégation psychologique." In *International Congress of Experimental Psychology,* 26-30. London: Williams & Norgate, 1892.

————. "Kyste parasitaire du cerveau." *Archives générales de médecine,* 7th series, 28, no. 2 (1891): 464-72.

Kaysen, Susanna. *Girl Interrupted.* New York: Viking/Random, 1993.

Kramer, Peter. *Moments of Engagement: Intimate Psychotherapy in a Technological Age.* New York: Penguin, 1989.

————. *Listening to Prozac.* New York: Penguin, 1993.

Lodge, David. *Therapy.* New York: Penguin, 1995.

Manning, Martha. *Undercurrents: A Life Beneath the Surface.* San Francisco: Harper Collins, 1995.

May, Rollo. "The Origins and Significance of the Existential Movement in Psychology." In *Existence,* ed. Rollo May, Ernest Angel, and Henri F. Ellenberger, 3-36. New York: Simon & Schuster, 1958.

Minuchin, Salvador. "The Triumph of Ellen West: An Ecological Perspective." In *Family Kaleidoscope,* 195-246. Cambridge, Mass.: Harvard UP, 1984.

Mitchell, Silas Weir. *Lectures on Diseases of the Nervous System.* Philadelphia: Lea & Co., 1885.

Mortimer, Penelope. *The Pumpkin Eater.* Harmondsworth: Penguin, 1964.

Moser, Tilmann. *Years of Apprenticeship on the Couch: Fragments of My Psychoanalysis.* Trans. Anselm Hollo. New York: Urizen Books, 1977.

Nakhla, Fayek, M.D., and Jackson, Grace. *Picking Up the Pieces: Two Accounts of a Psychoanalytic Journey.* New Haven and London: Yale Univ. Press, 1993.

Obholzer, Karin. *The Wolf-Man: Conversations with Freud's Patient—Sixty Years Later.* Trans. Michael Shaw. New York: Continuum Books, 1982. *Gespräche mit dem Wolfsmann.* Reinbeck bei Hamburg: Rowohlt, 1980.

Plath, Sylvia. *The Bell Jar*. New York: Harper & Row, 1971.

Reik, Theodor. *Listening with the Third Ear*. New York: Farrar, Straus and Co., 1949.

Rich, Adrienne. "For Ellen West: Mental Patient and Suicide." In Kim Chernin, *The Obsession: Reflections on the Tyranny of Slenderness*, 177. 1981; rpt. New York: Harper/Perennial, 1994.

Rossner, Judith. *August*. 1983. New York: Warner Books, 1984.

Roth, Philip. *Portnoy's Complaint*. 1969. New York: Bantam, 1970.

Sacks, Oliver. *Awakenings*. 1973. New York: Dutton, 1983.

Shaffer, Peter. *Equus*. New York: Bard/Avon, 1975.

Siegel, Stanley, and Ed Lowe, Jr. *The Patient Who Cured His Therapist*. New York: Penguin, 1992.

Styron, William. *Darkness Visible: A Memoir of Madness*. New York: Vintage/Random, 1990.

Sutherland, Stuart. *Breakdown: A Personal Crisis and a Medical Dilemma*. 1976. Rev. ed. London: Weidenfeld and Nicolson, 1987.

Svevo, Italo. *La Coscienza di Zeno*. Bologna: L. Capelli, 1923. *The Confessions of Zeno* (1930), trans. Beryl de Zoete. Harmondsworth: Penguin, 1964.

———. *Opere omnia*. Ed. Bruno Maier. Milan: d'Oglio, 1968.

Taylor, E.W. "The Attitude of the Medical Profession toward the Psychotherapeutic Movement." *Journal of Nervous and Mental Disorders* 35, no. 6 (1908): 401-15.

Throwing Muses. "Ellen West." In *The Real Ramona*. New York: Sire, 1991.

Van Eeden, Frederik. *Happy Humanity*. New York: Doubleday, Page & Co., 1912.

Yalom, Irvin D. *Love's Executioner and Other Tales of Psychotherapy*. New York: Basic Books, 1989.

——— and Ginny Elkin. *Every Day Gets a Little Closer: A Twice-Told Therapy*. New York: Basic Books, 1974.

SECONDARY SOURCES

Abse, D. Wilfred. *Hysteria and Related Mental Disorders*. Bristol: Wright, 1987.

Akerknecht, Erwin H. *A Short History of Medicine*. 1955. Rev. ed. Baltimore and London: The Johns Hopkins Univ. Press, 1982.

———. *Medicine at the Paris Hospital*. Baltimore: The Johns Hopkins Univ. Press, 1967.

Almond, Barbara, and Richard Almond. *The Therapeutic Narrative: Fictional Relationships and the Process of Psychological Change*. Westport, Conn.: Praeger, 1996.

Altschule, Mark D. *Roots of Modern Psychiatry*. New York and London: Grune & Stratton, 1957.

————. *The Development of Traditional Psychopathology.* New York: John Wiley & Sons, 1987.

Appignanesi, Lisa, and John Forrester. *Freud's Women.* London: Weidenfeld & Nicolson, 1992.

Bailin, Miriam. *The Sickroom in Victorian Fiction: The Art of Being Ill.* New York: Cambridge Univ. Press, 1994.

Balint, Michael. *The Doctor, the Patient, and His Illness.* New York: International Press, 1957.

Beizer, Janet. *Ventriloquized Bodies: Narratives of Hysteria in Nineteenth-Century France.* Ithaca and London: Cornell Univ. Press, 1994.

Berman, Jeffrey. *The Talking Cure: Literary Representations of Psychoanalysis.* New York: New York Univ. Press, 1985.

Berrios, German E., and Roy Porter, eds. *A History of Clinical Psychiatry: The Origin and History of Psychiatric Disorders.* New York: New York Univ. Press, 1995.

Blacker, Kay H., and Joe P. Tupin. "Hysteria and Hysterical Structures: Developmental and Social Theories," In *Hysterical Personality,* ed. Mardi J. Horwitz, 95-141. New York: Jason Aronson, 1977.

Blum, Harold P., M.D. "The Borderline Childhood of the Wolf Man." In *Freud and His Patients,* ed. Mark Kanzer, M.D., and Jules Glenn, M.D., 341-58. N.Y.: Jason Aronson, 1980.

Borch-Jacobsen, Mikkel. *Remembering Anna O: A Century of Mystification.* New York and London: Routledge, 1996.

Boxer, Sarah. "Flogging Freud." *New York Times,* Book Review section, 10 August 1997, 12-13.

Branca, Patricia. "Image and Reality: The Myth of the Idle Victorian Woman." In *Clio's Consciousness Raised,* ed. Mary Hartman and Lois W. Banner, 179-91. New York: Harper, 1974.

Brumberg, Joan Jacobs. *Fasting Girls: The Emergence of Anorexia Nervosa as a Modern Disease.* Cambridge, Mass.: Harvard Univ. Press, 1988.

Burstow, Bonnie. "A Critique of Binswanger's Existentialist Analysis." *Review of Existentialist Psychology and Psychiatry* 17, nos. 2-3 (1980-81): 245-52.

Bynum, W.F., Roy Porter, and Michael Shepherd, eds. *The Anatomy of Madness: Essays in the History of Psychiatry.* 3 vols. London and New York: Routledge, 1985.

Byrd, Max. *Visits to Bedlam: Madness and Literature in the Eighteenth Century.* Columbia: Univ. of South Carolina Press, 1974.

Castel, Françoise, Robert Castel, and Anne Lovell. *La Société psychiatrique avancée: Le modèle américain.* Paris: Grasset, 1979. *The Psychiatric Society,* trans. Arthur Goldhammer. New York: Columbia Univ. Press, 1982.

Certeau, Michel de. "The Freudian Novel: History and Literature." *Humanities in Society* 4, nos. 2-3 (Spring and Summer 1981): 121-41.

Chernin, Kim. "The Mysterious Case of Ellen West." In *The Obsession. Reflections on the Tyranny of Slenderness,* 162-77. 1981; rpt. New York: Harper/Perennial, 1994.

Chodorow, Nancy J. "Freud on Women." In *The Cambridge Companion to Freud,* ed. Jerome Neu, 224-48. Cambridge and New York: Cambridge Univ. Press, 1991.

Clare, Anthony. "Freud's Cases: The Clinical Basis of Psychoanalysis." In *Anatomy of Madness: Essays in the History of Psychiatry,* ed. W.F. Bynum, Roy Porter, and Michael Shepherd, 1:271-88. 3 vols. London and New York: Routledge, 1985.

Clark, Michael. "The Rejection of Psychological Approaches to Mental Disorders in Late Nineteenth-Century British Psychiatry." In *Madhouses, Mad-Doctors, and Madmen: The Social History of Psychiatry in the Victorian Era,* ed. Andrew Scull, 271-312. Philadelphia: Univ. of Pennsylvania Press, 1981.

Cohn, Dorrit. "Freud's Case Histories and the Question of Fictionality." In *Telling Facts: History and Narration in Psychoanalysis,* ed. John H. Smith, M.D., and Humphrey Morris, M.D., 21-47. Baltimore and London: The Johns Hopkins Univ. Press, 1992.

Crabtree, Adam. *From Mesmer to Freud. Magnetic Sleep and the Roots of Psychological Healing.* New Haven: Yale Univ. Press, 1993.

Diagnostic and Statistical Manual of Mental Disorders—IV. Ed. Allen Francis. Washington, D.C.: American Psychiatric Association, 1994. Usually abbreviated as *DSM.*

Diamond, Hugh W. *The Faces of Madness and the Origin of Psychiatric Photography.* Ed. Sander L. Gilman. New York: Brunner/Mazel, 1976.

Didi-Huberman, Georges. *Invention de l'hystérie: Charcot et l'iconographie photographique de la Salpêtrière.* Paris: Macula, 1982.

Dinnage, Rosemary. *One to One: The Experience of Psychotherapy.* New York: Viking/Penguin, 1988.

Drinka, George Frederick, M.D. *The Birth of Neurosis: Myth, Malady and the Victorians.* New York: Simon & Schuster, 1984.

Ehrenwald, Jay. *The History of Psychotherapy.* New York: Jason Aronson, 1980.

Ellenberger, Henri. *The Discovery of the Unconscious: The History and Evolution of Dynamic Psychotherapy.* New York: Basic Books, 1980.

———. "Charcot and the Salpêtrière School." In *Beyond the Unconscious: Essays of Henri Ellenberger in the History of Psychiatry,* ed. Mark S. Micale, 139-54. Princeton: Princeton Univ. Press, 1993.

Ey, Henri. "History and Analysis of the Concept of Hysteria." *La Revue du practicien* 14 (1964): 1417-34. Rpt. in *Hysteria,* ed. Alec Roy, 1-16. New York: John Wiley & Sons, 1982.

Eysenck, H.J. *Fact and Fiction in Psychology.* Harmondsworth: Penguin, 1965.

Felman, Shoshana. *Writing and Madness.* Ithaca, N.Y.: Cornell Univ. Press, 1985.

Forrester, John. *Language and the Origins of Psychoanalysis.* New York: Columbia Univ. Press, 1980.

Foucault, Michel. *Madness and Civilization.* Trans. Richard Howard. New York: Random House, 1965; Vintage Books, 1988. *Histoire de la folie.* Paris: Plon, 1961.

———. *Mental Illness and Psychology.* Trans. Alan Sheridan. New York: Harper Colophon Books, 1976. *Maladie mentale et psychologie.* Paris: Presses universitaires de France, 1954.

Frank, Jerome D., and Julia B. Frank. *Persuasion and Healing: A Comparative Study of Psychotherapy.* 1961. 3d ed. Baltimore and London: The Johns Hopkins Univ. Press, 1991.

Furbank, P.N. *Italo Svevo: The Man and the Writer.* Berkeley and Los Angeles: Univ. of California Press, 1966.

Furst, Lilian R. "Anxious Patients/Anxious Doctor: Story-Telling in Freud's *Studies on Hysteria.*" *LIT* 8 (1998): 259-77.

Fusco, Mario. "Italo Svevo e la Psicanalisi." In *Il Caso Svevo,* ed. Giuseppi Petronio. Palermo: Palumbo: 1988, 57-79.

Gamwell, Lynn, and Nancy Tooms. *Madness in America: Cultural and Medical Perceptions of Mental Illness Before 1914.* Ithaca, N.Y.: Cornell Univ. Press, 1995.

Gatt-Rutter, John. *Italo Svevo: A Double Life.* Oxford: Clarendon Press, 1988.

Gilbert, Sandra M., and Susan Gubar. *The Madwoman in the Attic: The Woman Writer and the Nineteenth-Century Literary Imagination.* New Haven: Yale Univ. Press, 1979.

Gilman, Sander L. *Seeing the Insane.* New York: John Wiley & Sons, 1982.

———, ed. *The Face of Madness.* New York: Brunner/Mazel, 1976.

Gilman, Sander L., et al. *Hysteria Beyond Freud.* Berkeley, Los Angeles, and London: Univ. of California Press, 1993.

Goldstein, Jan. *Console and Classify: The French Psychiatric Profession in the Nineteenth Century.* Cambridge and New York: Cambridge Univ. Press, 1987.

Gosling, F.G. *Before Freud: Neurasthenia and the American Medical Community, 1870-1910.* Urbana: Univ. of Illinois Press, 1987.

Grebstein, Sheldon. "The Comic Anatomy of *Portnoy's Complaint.*" In *Comic Relief: Humor in Contemporary American Literature,* ed. Sarah Blacher Cohen, 1-16. Urbana: Univ. of Illinois Press, 1978.

Guillain, Georges. *J.-M. Charcot, 1825-1893: His Life and His Work.* Ed. and trans. Pearce Bailey. New York: Paul B. Hoeber, Inc. (Medical Book Department of Harper & Bros.), 1959.

Harms, Ernest. *Origins of Modern Psychiatry.* Springfield, Ill.: Charles C. Thomas, 1967.

Harrington, Anne. *Medicine, Mind and the Double Brain: A Study of Nineteenth-*

Century Thought. Princeton: Princeton Univ. Press, 1987.

Harris, Ruth. "Murder under Hypnosis in the Case of Gabrielle Bompard: Psychiatry in the Courtroom in Belle Epoque Paris." In *The Anatomy of Madness,* ed. W.F. Bynum, Roy Porter, and Michael Shepherd, 2:197-241. 3 vols. London and New York: Routledge, 1985.

Havens, Lester. *Safe Place: Laying the Groundwork of Psychotherapy.* Cambridge, Mass.: Harvard Univ. Press, 1989.

————. *Coming to Life: Reflections on the Art of Psychotherapy.* Cambridge, Mass.: Harvard Univ. Press, 1993.

Hawkins, Anne Hunsaker. *Reconstructing Illness: Studies in Pathography.* West Lafayette, Ind.: Purdue Univ. Press, 1993.

Herman, Nini. *Why Psychotherapy?* London: Free Association Books, 1987.

Hooker, Worthington. *Physician and Patient; or, A Partial View of the Mutual Duties, Relations and Interests of the Medical Profession and the Community.* 1849; rpt. New York: Arno Press and the New York Times, 1972.

Horwitz, Mardi J., ed. *Hysterical Personality.* New York: Jason Aronson, 1977.

Hunter, Richard, and Ida Macalpine. *Three Hundred Years of Psychiatry, 1535-1860.* London: Oxford Univ. Press, 1963.

Kahane, Claire. *Passions of the Voice: Hysteria, Narrative, and the Figure of the Speaking Woman, 1850-1915.* Baltimore and London: The Johns Hopkins Univ. Press, 1995.

Kanzer, Mark, M.D., and Jules Glenn, M.D., eds. *Freud and His Patients.* New York: Jason Aronson, 1980.

Kriegman, George, Robert D. Gardner, and Wilfred D. Abse, eds. *American Psychiatry Past, Present, and Future.* Charlottesville: Univ. Press of Virginia, 1975.

Krohn, Alan. *Hysteria: The Elusive Neurosis.* Psychological Issues 12, nos. 1-2, Monograph 45/6. New York: International Universities Press, 1978.

Labov, W., and D. Fanshel. *Therapeutic Discourse: Psychotherapy as Conversation.* New York: Academic Press, 1977.

Langs, Robert J., M.D. "The Misalliance Dimension on the Case of the Wolf Man." In *Freud and His Patients,* ed. Mark Kanzer, M.D., and Jules Glenn, Jules, M.D., 373-85. N.Y.: Jason Aronson, 1980.

Laplanche, J., and J.-B. Pontalis. *The Language of Psycho-Analysis.* New York: W.W. Norton, 1973. *Vocabulaire de la psychanalyse.* Paris: Presses universitaires de France, 1967.

Lebowitz, Naomi. *Italo Svevo.* New Brunswick, N.J.: Rutgers Univ. Press, 1978.

Lunbeck, Elizabeth. *The Psychiatric Persuasion: Knowledge, Gender, and Power in Modern America.* Princeton: Princeton Univ. Press, 1994.

Marcus, Steven. "Freud and Dora: Story, History, Case History." In *In Dora's Case: Freud-Hysteria-Feminism,* ed. Charles Bernheimer and Claire Kahane, 56-91. New York: Columbia Univ. Press, 1985.

Mendel, Werner M. "The Case of Ellen West." In *Treating Schizophrenia*, 89-114. San Francisco: Jossey-Bass, 1989.

Micale, Mark S., ed. *Beyond the Unconscious: Essays of Henri Ellenberger in the History of Psychiatry.* Princeton: Princeton Univ. Press, 1993.

Miller, Jonathan. "Going Unconscious." *New York Review of Books,* 20 April 1995, 59-65.

Morantz, Regina. "The Lady and Her Physician." In *Clio's Consciousness Raised,* ed. Mary Hartman and Lois W. Banner, 38-53. New York: Harper, 1974.

Morrison, Toni. *Playing in the Dark.* 1992. New York: Vintage, 1993.

Oppenheim, Janet. *"Shattered Nerves": Doctors, Patients, and Depression in Victorian England.* New York: Oxford Univ. Press, 1991.

Osler, William. *Counsels and Ideals.* Boston: Houghton Mifflin, 1905.

Pontalis, J.-B. "Le Séjour de Freud à Paris." *Nouvelle revue de psychanalyse* 8 (1973): 235-40.

Porter, Roy, and Mark S. Micale, eds. *Discovering the History of Psychiatry.* New York: Oxford Univ. Press, 1993.

Rogers, Carl. "Ellen West—and Loneliness." *Review of Existential Psychology and Psychiatry* 20 (1983-84): 209-18.

Rosenberg, Charles E. "The Crisis in Psychiatric Legitimacy: Reflections on Psychiatry, Medicine, and Public Policy." In *American Psychiatry Past, Present, and Future,* ed. George Kriegman, Robert D. Gardner, and Wilfred D. Abse, 135-48. Charlottesville: Univ. Press of Virginia, 1975.

———. "The Therapeutic Revolution: Medicine, Meaning, and Social Change in Nineteenth-Century America." In *The Therapeutic Revolution,* ed. Morris J. Vogel and Charles E. Rosenberg, 3-25. Philadelphia: Univ. of Pennsylvania Press, 1979.

———. "Body and Mind in Nineteenth-Century Medicine: Some Clinical Origins of the Neurosis Construct." In *Explaining Epidemics and Other Studies in the History of Medicine,* 74-89. Cambridge and New York: Cambridge Univ. Press, 1992.

Roth, Sheldon. *Psychotherapy: The Art of Wooing Nature.* Northvale, N.J., and London: Jason Aronson, 1987.

Rothfield, Lawrence. *Vital Signs: Medical Realism in Nineteenth-Century Fiction.* Princeton: Princeton Univ. Press, 1992.

Roy, Alec, ed. *Hysteria.* New York: John Wiley & Sons, 1982.

Rubin, Stephen E. "Conversations with the Author of *I Never Promised You a Rose Garden.*" *The Psychoanalytic Review* 59, no. 2 (1972): 201-15.

Schafer, Roy. "Reading Freud's Legacies." In *Telling Facts: History and Narration in Psychoanalysis,* ed. John H. Smith and Humphrey Morris, 1-20. Baltimore and London: The Johns Hopkins Univ. Press, 1992.

Schlueter, Paul, and June Schlueter, eds. *An Encyclopedia of British Women Writers.* New York: Garland, 1988.

Seinfeld, Jeffrey. "The Tragic Case of Ellen West." In *The Empty Core: An Object Relations Approach to Psychotherapy of the Schizoid Personality*, 113-39. Northvale, N.J.: Jason Aronson, 1991.

Shorter, Edward. *A History of Psychiarty: From the Era of the Asylum to the Age of Prozac*. New York: Wiley and Sons, 1997.

———. *From Paralysis to Fatigue: A History of Psychosomatic Illness in the Modern Era*. New York: The Free Press, 1992.

Showalter, Elaine. *The Female Malady: Women, Madness, and English Culture 1830-1980*. New York: Penguin, 1985.

Shryock, Richard Harrison. *The Development of Modern Medicine: An Interpretation of the Social and Scientific Factors Involved*. Madison: Univ. of Wisconsin Press, (1936) 1979.

Slavney, Phillip R. *Perspectives on "Hysteria."* Baltimore and London: Johns Hopkins Univ. Press, 1990.

Stone, Evelyn M., ed. *American Psychiatric Glossary*. Washington, D.C.: American Psychiatric Press, 1988.

Storr, Anthony. *The Art of Psychotherapy*. 2d rev. ed. New York: Routledge, 1990.

Studer, Lilliane. "Ellen West (ca. 1890-ca. 1924)." In *Wahnsinnsfrauen*, ed. Sibylle Duda and Luise F. Pusch, 226-54. Frankfurt: Suhrkamp, 1992.

Tatar, Maria M. *Spellbound: Studies in Mesmerism and Literature*. Princeton: Princeton Univ. Press, 1978.

Thompson, C., ed. *The Origins of Modern Psychiatry*. Chichester and New York: Wiley & Sons, 1987.

Trillat, Etienne. *Histoire de l'hystérie*. Paris: Seghers, 1986.

Vaughan, Susan C. *The Talking Cure: The Science behind Psychotherapy*. New York: Putnam's, 1997.

Veith, Ilza. "Four Thousand Years of Hysteria." In *Hysterical Personality*, ed. Mardi J. Horwitz, 7-93. New York: Jason Aronson, 1977.

———. *Hysteria: the History of a Disease*. 1965. Chicago: Univ. of Chicago Press, 1970.

Vrettos, Athena. *Somatic Fictions: Imagining Illness in Victorian Culture*. Stanford: Stanford Univ. Press, 1995.

Wagner-Martin, Linda. *Sylvia Plath*. New York: Simon & Schuster, 1987.

Warner, John Harley. *The Therapeutic Perspective: Medical Practice, Knowledge, and Identity in America*. Cambridge, Mass.: Harvard Univ. Press, 1986.

Weckowicz, Thaddeus E., and Helen P. Liebel-Weckowicz. *A History of Great Ideas in Abnormal Psychology*. Amsterdam and New York: North-Holland, 1987.

Weintraub, Michael I. *Hysterical Conversion and Reactions: A Clinical Guide to Diagnosis and Treatment*. New York: SP Medical and Scientific Books, 1983.

Werne, Joellen, ed. *Treating Eating Disorders.* San Francisco: Jossey-Bass Pub-
    lishers, 1995.
Wolberg, Lewis R. *The Technique of Psychotherapy.* 4th ed. New York and Lon-
    don: Grune & Stratton, 1988.
Yalom, Marilyn. *Maternity, Mortality, and the Literature of Madness.* University
    Park: Pennsylvania State Univ. Press, 1985.
Zilboorg, Gregory. *A History of Medical Psychology.* New York: Norton, 1941.

Index